Quest

Second Edition

1

 **Listening and Speaking**

Laurie Blass

Pamela Hartmann

McGraw-Hill

Quest 1 Listening and Speaking, 2nd Edition

ISBN 13: 978-0-07-353392-6 (Student Book)
ISBN 10: 0-07-353392-0
1 2 3 4 5 6 7 8 9 VNH/VNH 12 11 10 09 08 07 06

ISBN 13: 978-0-07-326960-3 (Student Book with Audio Highlights)
ISBN 10: 0-07-326960-3
1 2 3 4 5 6 7 8 9 VNH/VNH 12 11 10 09 08 07 06

ISE ISBN 13: 978-0-07-110439-5 (International Student Edition)
ISE ISBN 10: 0-07-110439-9
1 2 3 4 5 6 7 8 9 VNH/VNH 12 11 10 09 08 07 06

Editorial director: Erik Gundersen
Series editor: Linda O'Roke
Development editor: Jennifer Monaghan
Production manager: Juanita Thompson
Production coordinator: James D. Gwyn
Cover designer: David Averbach, Anthology
Interior designer: Martini Graphic Services, Inc.
Photo researcher: PoYee Oster

McGraw-Hill

www.esl-elt.mcgraw-hill.com

The McGraw·Hill Companies

● ● ● ● ● ACKNOWLEDGEMENTS

The publisher and author would like to thank the following education professionals whose comments, reviews, and assistance were instrumental in the development of the Quest series.

- **Roberta Alexander,** San Diego Community College District

- **David Dahnke,** North Harris College (Houston, TX)

- **Mary Díaz,** Broward Community College (Davie, FL)

- **Judith García,** Miami-Dade College

- **Elizabeth Giles,** The School District of Hillsborough County, Florida

- **Patricia Heiser,** University of Washington, Seattle

- **Yoshiko Matsubayashi,** Kokusai Junior College, Tokyo

- **Ahmed Motala,** University of Sharjah, United Arab Emirates

- **Dee Parker and Andy Harris,** AUA, Bangkok

- **Alison Rice,** Hunter College, City University of New York

- **Alice Savage,** North Harris College (Houston, TX)

- **Katharine Sherak,** San Francisco State University

- **Leslie Eloise Somers,** Miami-Dade County Public Schools

- **Karen Stanley,** Central Piedmont Community College (Charlotte, NC)

- **Diane Urairat,** Mahidol Language Services, Bangkok

- **Pamela Vittorio,** The New School (New York, NY)

- **Anne Marie Walters,** California State University, Long Beach

- **Lynne Wilkins,** Mills College (Oakland, CA)

- **Sean Wray, Elizabeth Watson, and Mariko Yokota,** Waseda International University, Tokyo

Many, many thanks go to Marguerite Ann Snow, who provided the initial inspiration for the entire series. Heartfelt thanks also to Erik Gundersen and Linda O'Roke for their help in the development of the second edition. We would also like to thank Jennifer Monaghan, Dylan Bryan-Dolman, Susannah MacKay, Kristin Sherman, and Kristin Thalheimer, whose opinions were invaluable.

TABLE OF CONTENTS

TO THE TEACHER

Quest: The Series

Quest Second Edition prepares students for academic success. The series features two complementary strands—*Listening and Speaking* and *Reading and Writing*—each with four levels. The integrated *Quest* program provides robust scaffolding to support and accelerate each student's journey from exploring general interest topics to mastering academic content.

Quest parallels and accelerates the process native-speaking students go through when they prepare for success in a variety of academic subjects. By previewing typical college course material, *Quest* helps students get "up to speed" in terms of both academic content and language skills.

In addition, *Quest* prepares students for the daunting amount and level of listening, speaking, reading, and writing required for college success. The four *Listening and Speaking* books in the *Quest* series contain listening and speaking strategies and practice activities centered on authentic recordings from "person on the street" interviews, social conversations, radio programs, and university lectures. Listening passages increase in length and difficulty across the four levels.

The *Reading and Writing* books combine high-interest material from newspapers and magazines with traditional academic source materials such as textbooks. Like the *Listening and Speaking* books, the four *Reading and Writing* books increase in difficulty with each level.

Quest Second Edition Features

- New *Intro* level providing on-ramp to Books 1-3
- Redesigned, larger format with captivating photos
- Expanded focus on critical thinking and test-taking skills
- Expanded video program (VHS and DVD) with new lecture and updated social language footage
- Test-taking strategy boxes that highlight skills needed for success on the new TOEFL® iBT
- New unit-ending *Vocabulary Workshops*
- Teacher's Editions with activity-by-activity procedural notes, expansion activities, and tests
- Addition of research paper to *Reading and Writing* titles
- EZ Test® CD-ROM-based test generator for all *Reading and Writing* titles

Quest Listening and Speaking

Quest Listening and Speaking includes three or four distinct units, each focusing on a different area of university study— anthropology, art, biology, business, ecology, economics, history, literature, psychology, or sociology. Each unit contains two chapters.

TOEFL is a registered trademark of Educational Testing Service (ETS). This publication is not endorsed or approved by ETS.

Chapter Structure

Each chapter of *Quest 1 Listening and Speaking* contains five parts that blend listening and speaking skills within the context of a particular academic area of study. Listening passages and skill-development activities build upon one another and increase in difficulty as students work through the five sections of each chapter.

Part 1: Introduction
- Thinking Ahead – discussion activities on photos introduce the chapter topic.
- Reading – a high-interest reading captures students' attention and motivates them to want to find out even more about the chapter topic.
- Discussion – speaking activities check students' understanding and allow for further discussion.

Part 2: Social Language
- Before Listening – prediction activities and vocabulary preparation prepare students for the listening. Strategy boxes provide students with practical strategies they can use immediately as they listen to conversations.
- Listening – a high-interest conversation (available in video or audio) between students on or around an urban university campus allows students to explore the chapter topic in more depth.
- After Listening – comprehension, discussion, and vocabulary activities not only check students' understanding of the conversation but also continue to prepare them for the academic listening activities in Parts 4 and 5.

Part 3: The Mechanics of Listening and Speaking
- Chapter-specific pronunciation, intonation, language function, and collocation boxes equip students to express their ideas.
- Content-driven language function boxes are followed by contextualized practice activities that prepare students for social and academic listening.

Part 4: Broadcast English
- Before Listening – prediction activities and vocabulary preparation prepare students for listening to a short passage from an authentic radio program.
- Listening – a high-interest authentic radio interview allows students to practice their listening skills and explore the chapter topic in more depth.
- After Listening – Comprehension, discussion, and vocabulary activities not only check students' understanding of the interview but also continue to prepare them for the academic listening in Part 5.

Part 5: Academic English
- Before Listening – prediction activities and vocabulary activities prepare students for listening to an authentic academic lecture.
- Listening – an academic lecture written by university professors allows students to practice their listening and note-taking skills. One lecture in each unit is delivered via video.
- After Listening – comprehension activities allow students to use their lecture notes to answer discussion questions.
- Put It All Together – a longer speaking activity provides students with the opportunity to connect all three listening passages and give a short presentation on the chapter topic.

Teacher's Editions

The *Quest Teacher's Editions* provide instructors with activity-by-activity teaching suggestions, cultural and background notes, Internet links to more information on the unit themes, expansion black-line master activities, chapter tests, and a complete answer key.

The *Quest Teacher's Editions* also provide test-taking boxes that highlight skills found in *Quest* that are needed for success on the new TOEFL® iBT test.

Video Program

For the *Quest Listening and Speaking* books, a newly expanded video program on DVD or VHS incorporates authentic classroom lectures with social language vignettes.

Lectures

The lecture portion of each video features college and university professors delivering high-interest mini-lectures on topics as diverse as animal communication, personal finance, and Greek art. The mini-lectures run from two minutes at the *Intro* level to six minutes by Book 3. As students listen to the lectures they complete structured outlines to model accurate note taking. Well-organized post-listening activities teach students how to use and refer to their notes in order to answer questions about the lecture and to review for a test.

Social Language

The social language portion of the videos gives students the chance to hear authentic conversations on topics relevant to the chapter topic and academic life. A series of scenes shot on or around an urban college campus features nine engaging students participating in a host of curricular and extracurricular activities. The social language portion of the video is designed to help English-language students join study groups, interact with professors, and make friends.

Audio Program

Each reading selection on the audio CD or audiocassette program allows students to hear new vocabulary words, listen for intonation cues, and increase their reading speed. Each reading is recorded at an appropriate rate while remaining authentic.

SCOPE AND SEQUENCE

Chapter	Listening Strategies	Speaking Strategies
UNIT 1 BUSINESS		
Chapter 1: Career Planning • Social Language: Advice about Starting College • Broadcast English: Radio Program about College Today and College 50 Years Ago, and Advice for New Students • Academic English: Lecture by a Career Counselor to English-Language Students	• Understanding the Medial *T* • Taking Notes: Using a Graphic Organizer • Listening for Details • Taking Notes: Using an Outline • Understanding New Words • Organizing Your Notes: Paying Attention to Signposts	• Asking and Answering Comparison Questions • Giving Advice • Planning Ahead • Asking for Clarification
Chapter 2: The Global Economy • Social Language: Conversation about Products in the Global Economy • Broadcast English: Radio Program about Successful Textile Companies in China • Academic English: Lecture about a U.S. Company	• Listening for Supporting Information • Identifying a Causal Chain • Listening for an Anecdote • Asking Questions	• Outlining • Making Eye Contact
UNIT 2 BIOLOGY		
Chapter 3: Animal Behavior • Social Language: Conversation about Animals' Emotions and Intelligence • Broadcast English: Radio Program about Research on Language Learning in Animals • Academic English: Lecture about Humans and Animals	• Understanding Emotion from Tone of Voice • Previewing: Thinking Before Listening • Knowing When to Take Notes • Including Details in Your Notes	• Using Nonverbal Communication • Expressions of Disbelief and Skepticism

The Mechanics of Listening and Speaking	Critical Thinking Strategies	Test-Taking Strategies
UNIT 1 BUSINESS		
• Asking for Directions • Understanding Interjections • /θ/ vs. /s/ • Expressions for Giving Directions	• Interpreting Information on Tables • Recognizing Literal and Figurative Meanings	• Guessing the Meaning from Context
• *Wh-* Questions • Greeting People You Know • Responding to Greetings: General and Specific • Returning Greetings • Reduced Forms of Words • Expressions with *Look, Seem,* and *Sound* + Adjective	• Previewing: Brainstorming • Making Connections	• Making Predictions
UNIT 2 BIOLOGY		
• Changing Statements into Questions • Agreeing with Negative Questions • Disagreeing with Negative Questions • Reduced Forms of Words • Expressions of Disbelief and Skepticism	• Making Inferences • Understanding a Speaker's Point of View	• Listening for Stressed Words

Chapter	Listening Strategies	Speaking Strategies
Chapter 4: Nutrition • Social Language: Conversation about Food and Nutrition • Broadcast English: Radio Program about the Diet of the People in the Mediterranean Region • Academic English: Lecture about Nutrition	• Listening for Numerical Information • Guessing the Meaning from Context: *Such As* • Previewing: Asking Questions Before You Listen • Getting the Main Ideas from the Introduction • Listening for Categories and Definitions	• Taking Turns • Giving More Information: Reasons or Examples
UNIT 3 U.S. HISTORY		
Chapter 5: The Days of Slavery • Social Language: Conversation Between a Student and a Professor about an Assignment • Broadcast English: Radio Program about the Underground Railroad • Academic English: Lecture about the Underground Railroad	• Being Prepared for an Important Explanation • Listening for Examples in Groups • Listening for Dates	• Working Cooperatively • Giving and Getting Feedback
Chapter 6: U.S. History Through Film • Social Language: Conversation about a Movie • Broadcast English: Radio Program about Westerns • Academic English: Lecture about U.S. History as Seen Through Film	• Review: Taking Lecture Notes	• Talking about Symbols • Taking a Survey

The Mechanics of Listening and Speaking	Critical Thinking Strategies	Test-Taking Strategies
• Asking for More Information: Reasons • Asking for More Information: Examples • Giving More Information: Reasons or Examples • Reduced Forms of Words: Questions with *Do* and *Did* • Noun Phrases for Types of Food	• Comparing Sources of Information	• Listening for Reasons

UNIT 3 U.S. HISTORY

• Introducing Yourself to Someone Who Doesn't Remember You • Responding to an Introduction • Identifying Yourself on the Phone • /I/ vs. /i/ • Verb Phrases for Meeting People	• Using a Timeline	• Previewing: Brainstorming Possible Vocabulary
• Verbs Ending in *-ed* • Giving an Opinion • Agreeing and Disagreeing • Showing Disagreement with Intonation	• Synthesizing	• Review: Taking Lecture Notes

Welcome

Quest Second Edition prepares students for academic success. The series features two complementary strands—*Reading and Writing* and *Listening and Speaking*—each with four levels. The integrated Quest program provides robust scaffolding to support and accelerate each student's journey from exploring general interest topics to mastering academic content.

New second edition features

- New *Intro* level providing on-ramp to Books 1-3

- Redesigned, larger format with captivating photos

- Expanded focus on critical thinking skills

- Addition of research paper to *Reading and Writing* strand

- New unit-ending *Vocabulary Workshops*

- New end-of-book Academic Word List (AWL) in *Reading and Writing* strand

- Expanded video program (VHS/DVD) with new lecture and updated social language footage

- EZ Test® CD-ROM test generator for all *Reading and Writing* titles

- Test-Taking strategy boxes that highlight skills needed for success on the new TOEFL® iBT

- Teacher's Editions with activity-by-activity procedural notes, expansion activities, and tests

Captivating photos and graphics capture students' attention while introducing them to each academic topic.

INTRODUCTION

Getting Started

Discuss these questions:
- Where is the woman? What is she doing?
- What kinds of listening do students do in college?
- What kinds of speaking do students do in college?

Speaking Strategy

Using Nonverbal Communication

When we communicate, we don't always use words. We sometimes "speak" without words. We often express meaning through **nonverbal communication**–communication with our hands, face, and body. (*Nonverbal* means "without words.") Types of nonverbal communication are:

Body language = the way that people move (for communication)
Hand gestures = specific body language that uses the hands for communication
Facial expressions = specific body language that uses the face for communication

B. USING NONVERBAL COMMUNICATION Work with a partner. *Without words*, communicate at least six of the emotions or ideas in the box below to your partner. Use only body language, hand gestures, and facial expressions. Do not use words. Your partner will guess your emotion or idea. Then exchange roles.

Yes.	No.
I don't know.	I'm confused.
I'm bored.	Please, sit down.
Stop!	I'm angry.
Really??!!?!!!	That's crazy.
I'm surprised.	I absolutely refuse to do that.
I'm very interested in what you're saying.	I don't like this exercise.
Would you like to go and have something to eat?	I'm hungry.

Listening Strategy

Knowing When to Take Notes

It's important to take good notes during a lecture because exam questions will come from both the reading *and* the lectures. Some students just sit and listen, but this is a bad idea. Try following these suggestions.

- Write down everything that the professor puts on the board. Copy spelling correctly.
- Take notes whenever the professor says something more than one time, emphasizes a word or sentence, and seems to get excited about something (even if you don't understand why).

C. KNOWING WHEN TO TAKE NOTES There are different ways to take notes. In Chapters 1 and 2, you took notes on a T chart and in outline form. For the lecture in this chapter, you will take notes on a different kind of graphic organizer: a chart.

Look over the chart on page 105. What kinds of information will you write down? What words do you expect the speaker to explain?

Listening and Speaking Strategies guide students to develop effective academic listening and note-taking skills.

Three high-interest listening selections in each chapter introduce students to the general education course content most frequently required by universities.

B. VOCABULARY PREPARATION Read the sentences below. The words and phrases in red are from the conversation. Match the definitions in the box with the words and phrases in red. Write the correct letters on the lines.

> a. to be honest
> b. in the end
> c. ingredients and cooking style
> d. plants for flavoring food or making medicine
> e. a spicy dish made from cabbage
> f. starchy foods (like bread, potatoes, cereals, rice, and pasta) that give the body energy

_____ **1.** Italian **cuisine** is supposed to be very healthy because it uses olive oil.

_____ **2.** Italian food is also good for you because it has a lot of **complex carbohydrates**, such as pasta.

_____ **3.** I use **herbs** to stay healthy, but do you really think they work?

_____ **4.** **To tell you the truth**, I really don't think herbs keep you healthy.

_____ **5.** Well, I never get sick, so maybe herbs do some good **after all**!

_____ **6.** Katy's mother was born in Korea, so Katy often ate Korean dishes such as *kimchi*.

LISTENING

A. LISTENING FOR THE MAIN IDEA Listen to the conversation. As you listen, try to answer these questions:
• Does Rachel worry about eating healthy food? Why or why not?

3. Quaker Oats is a **consumer goods** company. It makes products that people buy and use quickly such as food and beverages.

Guess: _____

4. The displays in the store had a lot of **customer traffic**: a lot of people came up to look at them all day long.

Guess: _____

5. Unfortunately, there wasn't much **demand** for that product. Nobody wanted to buy it.

Guess: _____

6. One way to advertise something is by **point-of-purchase-displays**—advertisements that appear right in the store.

Guess: _____

7. The product had an **image problem**. It didn't *look* like a good product, so people didn't buy it.

Guess: _____

Now compare your guesses with a partner's guesses.

LISTENING

A. TAKING NOTES: USING AN OUTLINE Listen to the lecture. It's in four sections. You will listen to each section twice. Fill in as much of the outline on pages 74–75 as you can. Don't worry if you can't fill in everything. (You'll listen to the whole lecture again later.)

Gradual curve in each chapter from social language, to broadcast English, and then academic listening supports students as they engage in increasingly more difficult material.

Discussion, pair-work, and group-work activities **scaffold the students' learning process** as they move from general interest to academic content.

- Describe your diet. Explain what is (or isn't) healthy about it.
- Is it a good idea to take supplements? Explain your answer.
- Write about your favorite **ethnic food** (food from another culture, for example, Mexican, Chinese, Italian, or American food). What are some typical dishes? In your opinion, is it healthy?

Write about the topic for five minutes. Don't worry about grammar and don't use a dictionary. Just put as many ideas as you can on paper.

PART 2 SOCIAL LANGUAGE Rachel's Health Plan

BEFORE LISTENING

A. THINKING AHEAD You are going to listen to Ashley, Rachel, and Mike talk about food and nutrition. Before you listen, work with a partner to fill in the chart. Answer these questions:
- What do students in your school usually eat and drink? What kinds of food can you find on or near campus?
- Next to each item, write your opinion: Is it healthy?
- What nutrients are in it? For example, *protein, fat, carbohydrates, vitamins,* and *minerals.* If you're not sure, guess.

Food or Drink	Is it healthy?	Nutrients
orange juice	yes	vitamin C
hamburgers	not really	protein, fat

Unit-ending *Vocabulary Workshops* **reinforce key unit vocabulary** that also appears on high frequency word lists.

UNIT 1 VOCABULARY WORKSHOP

Review vocabulary items that you learned in Getting Started and Chapters 1 and 2.

A. MATCHING Match the definitions to the words and phrases. Write the correct letters on the lines.

Words and Phrases	Definitions
___b___ **1.** bucks	**a.** private teacher
_____ **2.** career	**b.** dollars
_____ **3.** flourish	**c.** great happiness
_____ **4.** higher education	**d.** grow; increase
_____ **5.** joy	**e.** approximately; more or less
_____ **6.** market	**f.** do in the best possible way
_____ **7.** perfect (v.)	**g.** group of people that buys a product
_____ **8.** process	**h.** college; university
_____ **9.** roughly	**i.** profession; work
_____ **10.** tutor	**j.** steps

B. TRUE OR FALSE? Which sentences are true? Which sentences are false? Fill in T for *True* or F for *False.*

1. If the **majority** of college students are women, that means that they are more than half of the student population.   Ⓣ   Ⓕ
2. **Quarters** are 10¢ coins in the U.S.   Ⓣ   Ⓕ
3. If something **appeals to** you, you don't like it very much.   Ⓣ   Ⓕ
4. A **cheap** car is one that costs a lot of money.   Ⓣ   Ⓕ
5. If you are **experimenting,** you are trying new things.   Ⓣ   Ⓕ
6. A college **workshop** is a special class.   Ⓣ   Ⓕ
7. Juice drinks with **fruit pulp** are completely clear.   Ⓣ   Ⓕ
8. A **nutritious** drink is bad for your health.   Ⓣ   Ⓕ

COMPREHENSIVE ANCILLARY PROGRAM

Expanded video program for the *Listening and Speaking* titles now includes mini-lectures to build comprehension and note-taking skills, and updated social language scenes to develop conversation skills.

Audio program selections are indicated with this icon 🎧 and include recordings of all lectures, conversations, pronunciation and intonation activities, and reading selections.

Teacher's Edition provides activity-by-activity teaching suggestions, expansion activities, tests, and special TOEFL® iBT preparation notes.

EZ Test® CD-ROM test generator for the *Reading and Writing* titles allows teachers to create customized tests in a matter of minutes.

INTRODUCTION

Getting Started

Discuss these questions:
- Where is the woman? What is she doing?
- What kinds of listening do students do in college?
- What kinds of speaking do students do in college?

INTRODUCTION TO ACADEMIC LIFE

Are you planning to go to school in the United States or Canada? Are you already attending a school in the United States or Canada? Then you need to know something about the system of higher education in those countries. What can you expect? What do you need to do?

A. LISTENING TO A LECTURE: SECTION 1

Read along as you listen to Section 1 of a lecture about some of the basics of higher education in the United States and Canada. Then listen again. This time don't read along while you listen.

A college in a small town

College in the United States and Canada

Section 1

Many students begin their higher education at a four-year college or university. Many others begin their first year (the **freshman** year) at a two-year **community college**. After their second year (the **sophomore** year), students get a certificate or an A.A. (Associate Degree) from the community college. Many students
5 transfer to a four-year school for their third (**junior**) and fourth (**senior**) years.

In the first four years of college, students are **undergraduates**. When they graduate, they receive a **degree**—probably a B.A. (Bachelor of Arts) or a B.S. (Bachelor of Science), depending on their **major** (what they choose to study).

Students who continue their studies after graduation are in **graduate school**.
10 For short, we call this grad school. They are grad students. They are in a master's program or a doctoral program. After two more years, they may receive a **master's degree**—perhaps an M.A. (Master of Arts), M.S. (Master of Science), M.B.A. (Master of Business Administration), or M.F.A. (Master of Fine Art). Some students attend for three or more years and get a **doctor of**
15 **philosophy** degree (Ph.D.). This is the highest university degree.

Most colleges are two-year community colleges. Some are four-year schools. It's important to note the difference between **college** and **university**. Both are kinds of higher education. Both are after high school. But a university is never a two-year school (such as a community college). Also, a university has a graduate
20 school, but most colleges do not. In Canada, students say, "I'm in college" or "I'm in university." But in the United States, undergraduate students usually just say, "I'm in college." This might really mean college, or it might mean university. Graduate students usually say, "I'm in grad school."

A university in a big city

Listening Strategy

Taking Lecture Notes

It's important for students to take good notes during a **lecture** (a professor's speech or talk). Often a lot of the material on an exam comes from the lectures in a class. Information in class lectures is often different from information in the textbook for a class. You'll practice taking lecture notes in every chapter of this book. Here are some suggestions.

• Take notes. Don't "just listen." You won't remember the information later.
• Don't try to write *everything*. Note taking is not dictation. If you try to write every word, you might not catch important points in the lecture.
• Write all important information. How do you know that it's important? Your professor might do the following:

    Tell you that it's important
    Emphasize it (say it loudly and clearly)
    Say it more than one time
    Write it on the board
    Give a **definition**

Definitions of new words are usually important. A definition is the meaning of a word. Sometimes your professor will say "X means Y." But more often the professor will say "X is Y" or "Xs are Ys." Very often the professor gives a **synonym** (a word with the same meaning) or a definition right after the new word.

Examples: *University* means **a college that includes a grad school.**
                 A university is **a college that includes a grad school.**
                 A university, **a college that includes a grad school,** is one form of higher education.

 B. TAKING LECTURE NOTES Look at the example of one student's lecture notes on page 4. Then look back at "College in the United States and Canada" on page 2. With a partner, compare the lecture and the notes. What information is in the notes? What information *isn't* in the notes?

College in the United States and Canada

I. Undergraduate Students

  A. Years

    1. Freshman (1st year)   2-year community college or 4-year school

    2. Sophomore (2nd)

    3. Junior (3rd)

    4. Senior (4th)

  B. Graduate/receive a degree

    1. A.A.

    2. B.A.

    3. B.S.

II. Graduate School (= grad school)

  A. Grad students—in a master's program or Ph.D. program

  B. Receive a master's degree (after 2 years)

    1. M.A.

    2. M.S.

    3. M.B.A.

    4. M.F.A.

  C. Receive a Ph.D.

III. Definitions: <u>College</u> and <u>University</u>

  A. Both after high school

  B. University

    1. Never just 2 years

    2. Has a grad school

  C. Canada: "I'm in college."/"I'm in university."

  D. U.S.: "I'm in college" = <u>college</u> or <u>university</u>

C. LISTENING TO A LECTURE: SECTION 2 Listen to Section 2 of the lecture. This time, take notes: fill in the blanks on the outline below with important information. Pay special attention to definitions. If necessary, listen to the lecture more than once.

College in the United States and Canada

Section 2

I. General Education Requirements (U.S. only)

   A. Definition: _____

   _____

   B. Examples: _____

   _____

II. Electives

   A. Definition: _____

   _____

   B. Good idea to: _____

   _____

III. Major

   A. Definition: _____

   _____

   B. Freshman and sophomore years: _____

   _____

   C. Junior and senior years: _____

   _____

WORDS IN PHRASES

Talking about Your Major

Phrases are words that go together. They are often combinations of verbs, prepositions, and nouns. It's important to learn these words *together*. There are several phrases that you can use to talk about your major.

The word *major* can be a noun.

Examples:

This is Evan. His **major** is broadcast journalism.

Her name is Chrissy. Her **major** is going to be psychology.

Major is also a verb. You can **major in*** a subject.

Examples:

His name is Brandon. He**'s majoring in** computer science.

This is Tanya. She**'s going to major in** business.

To ask about majors, you can say:

What's your major?
What are you going to major in?
What are you majoring in?
What do you think you'll major in?

To answer, you can say:

My major is . . .	I'm going to major in . . .
I think I'll major in . . .	I'm planning to major in . . .
I might major in . . .	I'm not sure yet.
I haven't decided yet.	I'm undecided.

*Notice the preposition *in.*

D. WORDS IN PHRASES Ask classmates about their majors and write their answers in the charts below.

Note: This is a good time to learn your classmates' names. Ask about spelling if you're not sure.

Example:
A: Hi. What's your name?
B: Klarissa.
A: How do you spell that?
B: K-L-A-R-I-S-S-A.
A: Klarissa. O.K., thanks. What are you majoring in?
B: My major is business.
A: Business. Great. Thank you.

Classmates	Majors
Klarissa	business

Classmates	Majors

INTRODUCTION TO LISTENING AND SPEAKING

You are going to hear three types of English in each chapter of this book:

• Conversations
• Radio broadcasts
• College (or university) lectures

You'll also practice speaking in different situations:

• Talking with a partner
• Interviewing classmates or discussing ideas in small groups
• Giving presentations

In this book, you will practice listening and speaking a lot, but it isn't enough. To learn English fast—and well—you need to practice outside of class, too.

Listening Strategy

Finding Practice Opportunities

Where can you practice *listening* to English? Here are just a few suggestions.

• Every day, listen to five minutes of the news (in English) on the radio or Internet. If possible, listen to it over and over.
• Choose a few TV programs in English. Watch these same programs every week.
• Record your favorite English-language TV program once a week. Watch it over and over.
• Rent movies in English.
• Visit a website with listening activities. Listen regularly. Examples are Dave's ESL Cafe and Randall's ESL Cyber Listening Lab. You can also listen to the radio and watch TV programs on the Internet. Examples are National Public Radio, BBC Radio, and CNN. (Use a search engine to find these websites.)

Speaking Strategy

Finding Practice Opportunities

Where can you practice *speaking* English? Here are just a few suggestions.

• Make social plans with a classmate who doesn't speak your language.
• Find an English-speaking student who is studying your language. Meet once a week. Practice 30 minutes in your language and 30 minutes in English.
• Volunteer at a hospital or a homeless shelter.
• Make small talk with workers in banks, shops, or at your school.

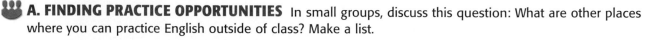 **A. FINDING PRACTICE OPPORTUNITIES** In small groups, discuss this question: What are other places where you can practice English outside of class? Make a list.

Now share at least one place with the class.

Speaking Strategy

Making Small Talk

Small talk is a conversation about things that are not very important. Often two strangers make small talk. They have short conversations; often just two sentences. In the first sentence, one person usually talks about the immediate situation (what's happening around him or her). This sentence often ends with a **tag question**—a question with a tag at the end that makes a statement into a question. In the second sentence, the other person gives a **reply**—an answer.

Example: **A:** It's cold today, isn't it?
                                  Tag Question
                B: Yes, it is.

Notice the reply. Because small talk usually isn't about important topics, the reply is short. Also, in the reply the person often agrees. This is a way to be polite.

Small talk is never about very important topics. It can be about the weather, sports, the time, and so on. It is a way to be friendly. (And it is one way to practice a new language!)

Here are some situations for small talk: at a bus stop, waiting in line, at a party, in a supermarket, in the school cafeteria, before a class starts, and at a music festival. Small talk seems to be less common in large cities and more common in small towns. Some people say that small talk is less common in England than in other English-speaking countries, including the United States, Canada, and Australia. In all of these countries (including England), there is usually a lot of small talk in a difficult situation. A "difficult situation" might be a very late bus or a train that breaks down.

Of course, it's necessary to be a little careful when making small talk. Choose "safe" people to speak to. For example, it's not a good idea to make small talk late at night with strangers on a dark street.

B. MAKING SMALL TALK In small groups, discuss the answers to these questions.

1. Do people sometimes make small talk with strangers where you live? If people do make small talk with strangers, what do they talk about? If people do not make small talk with strangers, why not?

2. What are seven good situations for making small talk? What are seven bad situations for making small talk?

3. What do you think about making small talk with strangers?

Now share your group's answers with the class.

Speaking Strategy

Using Tag Questions

In a tag question, a "tag" at the end of a statement makes the statement into a question. People often use tag questions in small talk. Tag questions help to keep the conversation going.

Affirmative Statement	Negative Tag
It's cold today,	isn't it?
Joy's the foreign student advisor,	isn't she?
These are expensive,	aren't they?
We had Chapter 3 for homework,	didn't we?
The oranges look good,	don't they?
The professor speaks fast,	doesn't she?

Negative Statement	Affirmative Tag
This isn't ready,	is it?
Ray hasn't done it yet,	has he?
You don't have one,	do you?
You didn't take Business 101,	did you?
There aren't any lab fees,	are there?
The students weren't in the lab,	were they?

Note: For an affirmative statement, the tag is *negative*. For a negative statement, the tag is *affirmative*.

C. USING TAG QUESTIONS Write the correct tag question to complete each sentence.

1. They're busy, _aren't they?_ _____

2. This bus goes to Brand Street, _____

3. It was a great movie, _____

4. This bus doesn't go to Riverside, _____

5. The biology books are over there, _____

6. The food at this party is fabulous, _____

7. The test wasn't very hard, _____

8. The homework was interesting, _____

9. We didn't have to do Chapter 5, _____

10. The history department isn't offering History 207 this semester, _____

Listening Strategy

🎧 Understanding the Intonation of Tag Questions

If you really need information and you really aren't sure about the answer, your voice goes *up* on a tag question. Your voice going up lets people know it's a real question.

Example: They're busy, **aren't they?** ↗ (= I'm not sure. Are they busy?)

If you know the answer and are just making small talk, your voice goes *down* on the tag.

Example: They're busy, **aren't they?** ↘ (= I know that they are busy.)

🎧 **D. UNDERSTANDING THE INTONATION OF TAG QUESTIONS** Listen to 10 questions. Are they "real" questions? (Does the speaker really need information?) Circle *Yes* or *No*.

1. Yes   No   6. Yes   No

2. Yes   No   7. Yes   No

3. Yes   No   8. Yes   No

4. Yes   No   9. Yes   No

5. Yes   No   10. Yes   No

Ashley, Mike, and Rachel

Now listen again. Repeat each sentence after the speaker.

E. UNDERSTANDING THE INTONATION OF TAG QUESTIONS
Listen to the conversations. Is the first person really asking for information? Or is this just small talk? Circle *Real Question* or *Small Talk.* If necessary, listen several times.

1. Real Question   Small Talk

2. Real Question   Small Talk

3. Real Question   Small Talk

4. Real Question   Small Talk

5. Real Question   Small Talk

F. USING TAG QUESTIONS IN CONVERSATIONS
Work with a partner. Have conversations about situations. Take turns being Student A and Student B. Follow the directions in the boxes on page 13. Listen carefully. Sometimes Student A needs real information. Sometimes Student A is just making small talk.

Examples: **Situation for Student A:** You're choosing classes for the new semester. You think that English 101 is a required class, but you aren't sure. (You have a real question.)

  Situation for Student B: You're choosing classes for the new term. English 101 is a required class.

  Conversation: **A:** We have to take English 101, don't we?

  B: Yeah, we do.

  Situation for Student A: You're leaving your English class. You just took a test. You think it was hard. (You are making small talk.)

  Situation for Student B: You're leaving your English class.

  Conversation: **A:** That test was hard, wasn't it?
  B: Yes, it was.

Student A

Start a conversation with Student B. Use a tag question in each situation. (If you need information, make sure that your voice goes up. If you know the answer, make sure that your voice goes down.)

Situation 1: You're taking a tour of Valley College. It's a nice **campus** (the place where buildings of a college or university are located).

Situation 2: You're in the school cafeteria. The soup looks good.

Situation 3: You're in history class. The homework last night was really hard.

Situation 4: You're in the school bookstore. You need to buy a book for your math class, but there aren't any.

Situation 5: You're at a new coffee shop. You're trying something called Iced Mocha. It's delicious.

Situation 6: You're leaving a movie theater. The movie was sad.

Situation 7: You're leaving your English class. You don't think that the teacher gave you any homework, but you aren't sure.

Situation 8: You're in a computer store. You see a computer game, but it's expensive.

Situation 9: You want to study at the library. You think it's closed on Sunday, but you aren't sure.

Situation 10: It's a very, very hot summer day. You walk into a cool building.

Student B

Make small talk with Student A. If your partner asks a "real" question, you can use the information below, or you can make up an answer.

Situation 1: You're taking a tour of Valley College.

Situation 2: You're in the school cafeteria.

Situation 3: You're in history class.

Situation 4: You're in the school bookstore. There aren't any more books for the math class.

Situation 5: You're at a new coffee shop. You're trying something called Iced Mocha.

Situation 6: You're leaving a movie theater.

Situation 7: You're leaving your English class. The teacher didn't give any homework.

Situation 8: You're in a computer store. You see a computer game. It's very expensive.

Situation 9: You're on campus. It's a Sunday. The library isn't open on Sunday.

Situation 10: It's a very, very hot summer day. You're inside a cool building.

Listening Strategy

Listening for the Main Idea

You don't always understand everything when people speak. Sometimes 90 percent (%) of their words are impossible to understand! But if the main idea is in the other 10 percent, then you understand the important information. That's good! The main idea *is* the important information. The other words are not as necessary.

How can you find the main idea? Here are some suggestions.

- Sometimes a speaker basically tells you, "This is the main idea." The speaker might say the following:
  My point is . . .
  What I mean is . . .
  The idea is that . . .
- Sometimes the person speaks more slowly, loudly, and carefully for the main idea.
- The main idea is *not* a detail (a small idea). It's not an example. (Examples usually come *after* the main idea.)
- The main idea is often at the beginning or end of a group of sentences.
- The main idea is sometimes the answer to an important question.

G. LISTENING FOR THE MAIN IDEA Listen to part of a radio program. (On this program, people call in to a radio station and give their opinions.) This program is about college. The caller answers the question: What advice can you give new college students? Listen for his answer. The answer is the main idea. Fill in the correct bubble. If necessary, listen several times.

Daniel says that it's good for students to _____.

- Ⓐ enter college
- Ⓑ listen to their parents
- Ⓒ study what they like
- Ⓓ be excited about leaving home

Listening Strategy

Understanding Fast or Difficult English

Many people speak fast or use difficult vocabulary. You can't understand everything. What can you do? Here are some suggestions.

- Don't be shy. Ask the person to repeat. Say one of the following:
  Excuse me?
  Could you repeat that?
  What was that again?
- Practice with the radio. Record a small part of a radio program or find a podcast of a radio program on the Internet. Listen over and over. Soon it will seem slower.
- Don't worry about every word.
- Listen for the main idea and *important* details.
- Have questions in mind as you listen.

H. UNDERSTANDING FAST OR DIFFICULT ENGLISH Listen to the next speaker, a guest on the same radio program. He speaks fast. How much can you understand? First, read the seven sentences below. Then listen to the speaker. Fill in T for *True* or F for *False*. If necessary, listen several times.

1. The speaker agrees with the first caller.   (T)   (F)

2. The young woman in the story was majoring in business.   (T)   (F)

3. She enjoyed her major.   (T)   (F)

4. She wanted to major in dance.   (T)   (F)

5. She could make a lot of money as a dancer.   (T)   (F)

6. She gave up her dreams.   (T)   (F)

7. The speaker thinks that the woman's story is sad.   (T)   (F)

I. DISCUSSION In small groups, discuss these questions.

1. Which is better?
    *   To major in something that you love
    *   To major in something that will get you a good job

2. Is there a "perfect" major?

Now share your group's answers with the class.

CHAPTER 1

Career Planning

Discuss these questions:
- What is happening in the picture? Why might the woman look happy?
- What might happen next in her life?
- How are you planning for your career?

A college class 50 years ago

A college class today

A. THINKING AHEAD Think of a country you know well (the country where you live or come from). Then with a partner, discuss these questions about the country.

1. How many students study at a college or at a university after high school: 5 percent? 10 percent? 50 percent? 80 percent?

2. Does a college education help a person to be successful in life?

3. What are some popular college majors right now? Why do you think they are popular?

4. What does *success* mean to you? (Does it mean money? Love? Happiness?)

B. READING TABLES Read the tables on pages 21–22 from the U.S. Department of Labor. As you read, try to answer these questions:
• How does education influence a person's **income** (salary, pay)?
• Which jobs will probably be easy to find in the near future? Which jobs will probably be hard to find?

Table A: Earnings by Educational Level in the U.S.

Educational Level	Average Weekly Salary
Doctorate (Ph.D.)	$1,349
Professional*	$1,307
Master's degree	$1,064
Bachelor's degree	$900
Community college	$672
Some college, no degree	$622
High school diploma	$554
Some high school, no diploma	$396

Source: U.S. Department of Labor (2004)

* For example, a lawyer or a doctor

Table B: Fastest Growing Occupations in the U.S., 2002–2012

Occupation	Percent of Growth
Medical assistants[1]	+ 59%
Network systems and data[2] communications analysts	+ 57%
Physician[3] assistants	+ 49%
Social and human service assistants	+ 49%
Home health aides[4]	+ 48%
Medical records and health information technicians	+ 47%
Physical therapist aides	+ 46%
Computer software engineers, applications	+ 46%
Computer software engineers, systems software	+ 45%
Physical therapist assistants	+ 45%

Source: U.S. Department of Labor (2004)

[1] **assistants** = helpers
[2] **data** = information
[3] **physician** = medical doctor
[4] **aides** = helpers

Table C: Occupations with the Largest Job Decline in the U.S., 2000–2012

Occupation	Percent of Decline
Telephone operators	- 56%
Word processors and typists	- 39%
Textile[1] knitting and weaving machine operators	- 39%
Sewing machine operators	- 31%
Textile winding, twisting, and drawing out machine operators	- 30%
Textile bleaching and dyeing machine operators	- 29%
Fishers and related fishing workers	- 27%
Textile cutting machine setters and operators	- 23%
Farmers and ranchers	- 21%
Sewers, by hand	- 21%

Source: U.S. Department of Labor (2004)

[1] **textile** = cloth; material

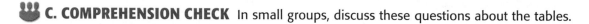 **C. COMPREHENSION CHECK** In small groups, discuss these questions about the tables.

1. Which educational level allows a person to have the highest salary?

2. For which educational level does a person receive the lowest salary?

3. What is the one fastest growing occupation—the one with the most new jobs?

4. What is the one occupation that is losing the most jobs?

Critical Thinking Strategy

Interpreting Information on Tables

Tables (such as the three on pages 21–22) give **statistics**–facts in the form of numbers–but they do not interpret or explain the statistics. As the reader, you need to interpret tables yourself. To interpret information in tables, follow these suggestions with examples from Table C above:

• Look first at the extremes–the highest and lowest figures (**-56% and -21%**).
• Look for similarities–things that are similar–and differences (**textile winding and textile bleaching machine operators; telephone operators and farmers**).
• As you read the tables, keep asking yourself, "Why?"

D. INTERPRETING INFORMATION ON TABLES In small groups, discuss these questions about the tables on pages 21–22.

1. According to Table A, if a person wants to make a high salary in the future, what is necessary?

2. In what area are seven of the occupations on Table B? In what area are the other three occupations on Table B?

3. In what area are six of the occupations on Table C?

4. What is similar about the occupations on Table C?

5. Which age group (young, middle-aged, or elderly) usually needs the most medical care? Which age group in the United States is probably growing fast? (Make an **inference**—a guess—based on Table B.)

6. What might be happening in the United States to cause the job losses on Table C? (What is happening to these jobs?)

7. Extension: How might statistics such as these be different in other countries?

E. RANKING VALUES In choosing a major in college or a career after college, you need to consider your **values**—what is most important to you. Look at the list below. What is important to *your* happiness? Rank the list from 1–12 (1 = the most important; 12 = the least important).

_____ family life   _____ income (money)   _____ work

_____ friends   _____ leisure (free time) activities   _____ your children's education

_____ health   _____ love life   _____ your education

_____ helping others   _____ religion   _____ other: _____

Speaking Strategy

Asking and Answering Comparison Questions

Sometimes in a conversation with friends or classmates, you talk about your values. Often in this type of conversation, you compare different values. That is, you tell which values are more important than other ones. To do this, you need to know how to ask and answer comparison questions.

Examples: **Questions:**   What's **most** important to you?
                              Is love **more** important to you than income?

                Answers: To me, **the most** important thing in life is friends.
                              Love is **much more** important to me than income.
                              To me, love and money are **equally** important.

F. ASKING AND ANSWERING COMPARISON QUESTIONS Compare your answers to Activity E with a partner. Use phrases from the box above.

G. JOURNAL WRITING In this book, you are going to keep a journal. In your journal, you are going to do freewriting activities. In freewriting, you write quickly about what you are thinking or feeling. Grammar, punctuation, and spelling are not very important in freewriting. Your ideas and thoughts are important. You will have a time limit of five minutes for your journal writing in this book. You can buy a special notebook for your journal, or you can write your ideas on separate pieces of paper and keep them in a binder or folder.

Choose *one* of these topics.

• What is important to your happiness? Why?
• Can having an education make you happier?
• Is a college education necessary for your work or your career choice?

Write about the topic for five minutes. Don't worry about grammar and don't use a dictionary. Just put as many ideas as you can on paper.

PART ② SOCIAL LANGUAGE College for Beginners

BEFORE LISTENING

Speaking Strategy

Giving Advice

Sometimes friends tell you about problems. At other times, friends are planning to have an experience that you have already had. In both cases, you can help by giving **advice**—making suggestions about what to do. Some advice is affirmative. That is, it suggests what the person should do. Some advice is negative. It suggests what the person should *not* do.

Examples:

Strong suggestion
Study hard. (**Affirmative**)
Don't go out with your friends tonight. (**Negative**)

Should
You should take the bus. (**Affirmative**)
You shouldn't drive your car. (**Negative**)

Be sure to
Be sure to bring extra pens. (**Affirmative**)
Be sure not to drink too much coffee. (**Negative**)

Note: A strong suggestion is a less polite way to give advice. *Should* and *be sure to* are more polite ways to give advice.

A. GIVING ADVICE What advice can you give to students who are starting high school? Write a list of "dos" (affirmative advice) and "don'ts" (negative advice) in the chart below.

Dos	Don'ts
Be sure to do your homework every day.	You shouldn't write in library books.

B. COMPARING IDEAS In small groups, share your charts. Was there any piece of advice on everyone's list? Share one piece of advice with the class.

C. THINKING AHEAD You're going to listen to interviews. Eleven people are going to give advice to students who are starting college in the United States. What will they say? With a partner, make six predictions about their advice. Write your predictions on the lines.

1. _____

2. _____

3. _____

4. _____

5. _____

6. _____

LISTENING

 **A. LISTENING FOR THE MAIN IDEA** Listen to the speakers' advice. Don't worry about new words or fast English. After you listen, write the answer to this question on the line.

What advice do most of the speakers give—to work hard (especially to study hard) or do something else (some other thing)?

_____

B. LISTENING FOR DETAILS Listen again. What advice does each speaker give? Check (✓) the correct boxes.

Speaker	Work/Study Hard	Enjoy Yourself/Have Fun	Something Else
1			✓
2			
3			
4			
5			
6			
7			
8			
9			
10			
11			

Test-Taking Strategy

Guessing the Meaning from Context

On a standardized test, such as the TOEFL® iBT, when you listen to test items, you usually won't understand everything. For example, you may hear words that you don't know. Of course, you can't stop the test to use a dictionary. But you can often **guess the meaning from context**. This means that the context (other words *around* the new word) can often help you to guess the meaning of a new word. How can you use the context? Listen for words that mean the same as the new word. People often repeat the same thing in different ways.

Examples: My brother **dropped out** of business school. Our parents weren't happy that he quit, but he never really liked business. (Here you see that *dropped out* means "quit.")

The **majority** of college students are now women. They are more than half of the student population. (Here you see that *majority* means "more than half.")

Note: It's also important to focus on (think about) things that you *do* understand. Don't focus on things that you *don't* understand.

C. GUESSING THE MEANING FROM CONTEXT Listen to three of the speakers again. They use the words and phrases below. Guess the meanings of the words and phrases from the context. Write your guesses on the lines.

1. **silly:** _____

2. **apply yourself:** _____

3. **don't get sucked in by social pressures:** _____

_____

D. LISTENING FOR SPECIFIC IDEAS Listen to some of the speakers again. Listen for the answers to these questions. Write your answers on the lines.

1. **Speaker 1:** Why should students ask questions?

_____

2. **Speaker 2:** How much time should students spend on homework?

_____

3. **Speaker 5:** How can students be more open-minded, in her opinion?

_____

4. **Speaker 9:** What shouldn't students worry about? Why?

_____

AFTER LISTENING

A. DISCUSSION In small groups, discuss these questions.

1. Were you surprised by any advice that you heard? If so, what surprised you?

2. How was the advice similar to your predictions on page 25? How was it different?

3. What advice do you think was the best?

Speaking Strategy

Planning Ahead

In the interviews, one speaker advised students ". . . not to be afraid to ask questions." But sometimes it's difficult to ask questions in a new language. Planning ahead makes asking questions easier. Doing the two steps below will help you feel more relaxed and confident the next time you have to ask questions.

Step 1: Imagine situations where you will need help (finding a new classroom, or finding out when the library is open, for example).

Step 2: Plan and practice questions in these situations *before you need to ask*.

Also, remember this: Most people like to help, so don't be shy.

B. PLANNING AHEAD What are good questions for the answers below? (Don't use any of the words in red in your questions.)

1. **Question:** _How are you?_
   Answer: I'm **fine**, thanks.

2. **Question:** _____
   Answer: His name is **Dr. Levi**.

3. **Question:** _____
   Answer: The library is open **from 8:00 A.M. to 9:00 P.M.**

4. **Question:** _____
   Answer: We have to read **Chapter 5**.

5. **Question:** _____
   Answer: The class meets **on Tuesdays and Thursdays**.

6. **Question:** _____
   Answer: **Yes**, the test was **really** hard.

7. **Question:** _____
   Answer: *T.A.* means "**teaching assistant**."

8. Question: _____

   Answer: No, it isn't far.

9. Question: _____

   Answer: The counseling center is **in Edison Hall, next to the admissions office**.

10. Question: _____

   Answer: Go down one block and turn left. The copy center is right there.

Now practice your 10 questions with a partner. Take turns asking and answering the questions.

C. ASKING THE RIGHT QUESTIONS What questions can you ask in the situations below? Write questions on the lines.

1. You meet the office assistant in the English Department. He tells you his name, but you don't hear him clearly. What can you ask him?

   Question: _____

2. You're in the college library. You don't know how to use the online catalog to find a book. What can you ask the librarian?

   Question: _____

3. You want a job on campus (at the college). You go to the Career Planning and Placement Office, but you don't know how to apply for a job. How can you ask for advice?

   Question: _____

4. You're confused about your major. You want to study something that you really like. You also want a good job when you graduate. You need an appointment with a career counselor. What can you ask at the Career Planning and Placement Office?

   Question: _____

5. It's the first day of your history class. It meets on Mondays, Wednesdays, and Fridays. The professor tells the class, "Your discussion section will meet on Thursdays at 10:00." You don't understand _discussion section_. What can you ask a classmate?

   Question: _____

6. On the first day of class, a classmate next to you says, "I've heard that if you apply yourself, you can get a good grade in this class." You don't understand _apply yourself_. What can you ask the classmate?

   Question: _____

7. You're in class. You were absent yesterday. You want to know what happened in class. What can you ask the classmate next to you?

   Question: _____

8. You're in the cafeteria. You want to get the soup, but you don't eat meat. You worry that there is meat in the soup. What can you ask a cafeteria worker?

Question: _____

9. It's your first week of classes, and you're a little lost. You also need some money. You want to find an ATM (automatic teller machine). What can you ask a student?

Question: _____

10. You're near campus. You need to find a copy store because you need to copy a classmate's notes. You don't know this neighborhood well. What can you ask a stranger on the street?

Question: _____

Now compare your questions with a partner's questions.

D. GETTING INFORMATION What confuses you about your class, school, neighborhood, or city? On a separate piece of paper, write five questions. Then in small groups, discuss your questions.

Examples: Where do I go to get information on part-time jobs?
What are some good cheap places to eat near school?

PART ③ THE MECHANICS OF LISTENING AND SPEAKING

LANGUAGE FUNCTION

Asking for Directions

When you are lost or need to go somewhere unfamiliar, there are several ways to ask for directions. When you ask strangers for directions, it's polite to say *Excuse me* before you ask.

Examples: Excuse me. **Could/Can you tell me where to find** an ATM?
Excuse me. **Could/Can you tell me where** an ATM **is**?
Excuse me. **Could/Can you tell me how to get to** an ATM?

Note: Use either *can* or *could* in the questions.

A. FOLLOWING DIRECTIONS Listen to people giving directions. As you listen, look at the map below. Follow the directions. Write the letter of each place on the line. If necessary, listen to each conversation several times.

_____C_____ **1.** college library   _____ **3.** bookstore   _____ **5.** career planning

_____ **2.** drugstore   _____ **4.** bank

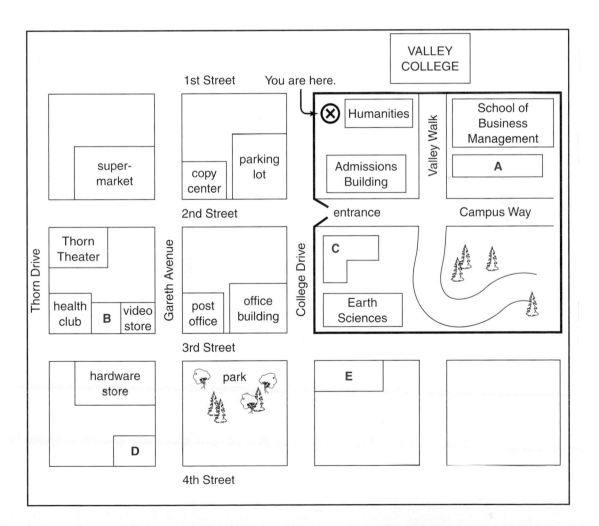

INTONATION

 Understanding Interjections

Interjections are short words that are spoken suddenly, sometimes to express emotions. Interjections in English are common in conversation. They are informal but very important. In a conversation, if you do not use interjections, people may think that you do not understand what they said. Notice the intonation in the following examples.

Interjections	Meanings
Uh-huh.	Yes./You're welcome.
Uh-huh!	Oh, *now* I understand.
Huh?	What?/Pardon?
Uh-uh.	No.
Uh . . . /Um . . .	I'm thinking./I'm not sure what to say.
Hmm!	That's interesting.
Uh-oh.	I made a mistake./There is a problem.

B. UNDERSTANDING INTERJECTIONS Listen to the conversations. What does the second person mean? Check (✓) the correct boxes in the chart below.

Conversation	Yes	No	You're welcome.	What?/Pardon?	There's a problem!
1				✓	
2					
3					
4					
5					
6					

C. USING INTERJECTIONS Work with a partner. Follow the directions in the boxes below and on page 33.

Example: **A:** Are you busy?
　　　　　　　B: Uh-uh.

Student A

Say each question or statement to your partner. Wait for a response.

1. Could I borrow your pencil?
2. Thanks a lot.
3. Are you hungry?
4. I think the teacher might surprise us with a big test tomorrow.
5. Have you been to Algeria?

Now respond to your partner's questions and statements. Use one of the interjections from the Intonation box above in your response.

PRONUNCIATION

/θ/ vs. /s/

The letters *th* can stand for several different sounds. One of these is in *thanks*. To pronounce the /θ/ sound, put the tip of your tongue *between* your teeth *just a little* and blow. *Do not stick your tongue between your lips!* The /θ/ sound is different from the /s/ sound. Can you hear the difference?

Examples:

/θ/	/s/
thank	sank
thick	sick
thaw	saw
path	pass
tenth	tense

Many ordinal numbers contain the /θ/ sound at the end.

Examples:

fourth (4th)	seventh (7th)	tenth (10th)
fifth (5th)	eighth (8th)	eleventh (11th)
sixth (6th)	ninth (9th)	twelfth (12th)

D. REPEATING WORDS WITH /θ/ AND /s/ Look again at the box above. Repeat the words after the speaker.

E. HEARING THE DIFFERENCE BETWEEN /θ/ AND /s/ Circle the words that you hear.

1. thank	(sank)		5. path	pass		9. theme	seem
2. things	sings		6. worth	worse		10. tenth	tense
3. thaw	saw		7. fourth	force		11. eighth	eights
4. thick	sick		8. thigh	sigh		12. thumb	some

F. PRONOUNCING /θ/ AND /s/ IN CONVERSATIONS Read along as you listen to the conversation below. Then listen again and repeat the sentences. Pay special attention to words with *th*.

A: Excuse me. I **th**ink I'm lost. I'm looking for **Th**orn **Th**eater.

B: Oh, it's not far. It's on **Th**orn Drive, between Nin**th** and Ten**th** Streets. It's the four**th** building from the corner.

A: **Th**anks a lot.

WORDS IN PHRASES

Expressions for Giving Directions

To give directions or explain where something is, you need to use certain common phrases. Here are some.

Go down (or up) one/two/three blocks.*   Go straight for one/two/three blocks.
Turn left/right.   Make a left/right.
Go past the _____.   It's right there.
It's right there on your left/right.   It's across from the _____.
It's on Thorn Drive/Third Street.**   Make a left/right at the light.
It's next to the _____.   Make a left/right at the stop sign.
It's on the corner of _____   It's the first/second/third street on your left/right.
   and _____.
It's in the middle of the block.

* In English, people usually count *blocks*, not streets.
** Notice that in English, street names don't have *the* before them.

Note: If someone asks you for directions and you can't give them, you can say "I'm sorry, I don't know."

G. INFORMATION GAP: WORDS IN PHRASES Work with a partner. Student A looks at the map on page 201. Student B looks at the map on page 205. Don't look at your partner's map. Take turns asking and answering questions about the location of buildings on your map. Put the correct letters on your map.

Example: **A:** Where's Sam's Store?
           B: It's on Gareth Avenue. It's the second building from the corner.

PUT IT TOGETHER

A. ASKING FOR AND GIVING DIRECTIONS Use the map on page 31 to ask for and give directions with a partner. Use the expressions in the box above to give directions.

B. TALKING ABOUT YOUR NEIGHBORHOOD Work with a partner. Think of two or three places near your school. Then ask your partner for directions to these places. Now draw a map of the neighborhood around your house, but don't include names of places. Give directions to three places while your partner finds them on the map.

PART ④ BROADCAST ENGLISH College Today

BEFORE LISTENING

A. THINKING AHEAD You are going to hear more of the radio program you listened to in the *Getting Started* chapter (pages 14–15). The speakers talk about two topics: (1) differences between college today and college 50 years ago and (2) advice to new students. To prepare to listen to the program, discuss these questions in small groups.

1. How are colleges today different from colleges 50 years ago? Think about libraries, technology, possible majors, activities, and students. Write your ideas in the chart below.

50 Years Ago	Today
most students were rich	students are middle class and poor, too

2. In Part 2 of this chapter, you listened to advice for new college students. Now you'll listen to more advice—this time from *experts* (people who know a lot about a subject). Discuss three pieces of advice that you expect to hear.

B. VOCABULARY PREPARATION The words and phrases in the box below are from the radio program. Before you listen, read the words and phrases and their definitions. Then write the correct words and phrases on the lines.

Words/Phrases	Definitions
higher education	college; university
roughly	approximately; more or less
~~majority~~	most; more than half
quarters	25¢ coins in the U.S.
appeals to you	you like or enjoy it
joy	great happiness
experimenting	trying new things
dropping out	stopping, leaving school before you finish
percent	a part that is one one-hundredth; %
seek out	go and find

1. At my college, the _majority_ of students are Canadian. If fact, more than 75 percent of my classmates come from Canada.

2. Do you like biology? If so, you should take that class in botany if it _____. It's not a general education requirement, but don't worry about that.

3. The system of _____ in the United States is different from the university system in France.

4. I know you are worried about your grade. You should _____ someone in your class to help you.

5. This machine doesn't take dollar bills. It takes only _____.

6. _____ half of the students in my economics class are majoring in business.

7. Julia thought about _____ for a year, but her family wants her to graduate soon.

8. I'm thinking of majoring in dance. I always feel such _____ in dance classes! Right now I'm studying Thai dance, and I just love it.

9. Almost 30 _____ of the students in my history class can speak more than one language.

10. Mike is _____ with many subjects. He's taking classes in biology, acting, Japanese, economics, and history. He'll decide on a major later.

LISTENING

Listening Strategy

Understanding the Medial *T*

In English, the letter *t* is not always pronounced as the /t/ sound that you expect. This is true of a "medial *t*" (a *t* that is not the first or last sound in a word). Sometimes a medial *t* sounds like a /d/. For example, numbers that end in *-teen* can sound similar to numbers that end in *-ty*. Listen to these numbers and pay attention to the stress (the accent) and the pronunciation of the *t*.

Examples:

13	30	15	50	17	70	19	90
14	40	16	60	18	80		

As you hear, in numbers that end in *-teen*, the *t* really sounds like a /t/. However, for numbers that end in *-ty*, the *t* sounds more like a /d/.

Sometimes a medial *t* is followed by an /n/ sound. Notice the pronunciation of the *t*.

Examples: bitten   certain   cotton   fountain   gotten   mountain   written

A. HEARING THE MEDIAL *T* Circle the numbers that you hear.

1. 13 (30)	**6.** 18 80	**11.** 16 60
2. 14 40	**7.** 19 90	**12.** 17 70
3. 15 50	**8.** 13 30	**13.** 18 80
4. 16 60	**9.** 14 40	**14.** 19 90
5. 17 70	**10.** 15 50	

B. HEARING THE MEDIAL *T* IN SENTENCES Write the numbers that you hear on the lines.

1. Almost _____50_____ percent of the class can speak another language.

2. William started college when he was _____.

3. Roughly _____ percent of all high school graduates went to college.

4. Zach's family moved to Kenya when he was _____.

5. The average age is _____.

6. Many students lived in dormitories _____ years ago.

7. Becky graduated _____ years ago.

8. Ethan got married when he was _____.

9. A person who is _____ or _____ can enjoy college more that someone who is _____ or _____.

C. HEARING THE MEDIAL *T* FOLLOWED BY /N/ Write the words that you hear on the lines.

1. I was _____ by some insect yesterday.

2. Do you know where I can find a drinking _____?

3. I bought a blue _____ shirt.

4. Are you _____ of that?

5. I have a _____ of homework tonight.

D. LISTENING FOR THE MAIN IDEA: SECTION 1 Listen to Section 1 of the radio program. Listen for the answer to this question. Fill in the correct bubble.

How different is college these days from college 50 years ago (in the United States)?

Ⓐ Very different

Ⓑ A little different

Listening Strategy

Taking Notes: Using a Graphic Organizer

If you take notes as you listen to an interview, presentation, or lecture, you will be able to focus better and will probably understand more. One good way to take notes is with a **graphic organizer**. A graphic organizer visually shows the relationships between ideas.

One type of graphic organizer is a T-chart (shaped like the letter *T*). This is a good organizer to show **advantages** or **disadvantages** or to show **contrast** between two different things.

E. TAKING NOTES: USING A GRAPHIC ORGANIZER Listen to part of Section 1 again. As you listen, fill in the T-chart.

	50 Years Ago	Today
High school graduates going to college	15%	
Men/Women		
Average age		
Ethnicity (groups of people)		
Full-time/Part-time		

🎧 **F. LISTENING FOR THE MAIN IDEA: SECTION 2** Listen to Section 2. Listen for the answer to this question. Fill in the correct bubble.

> *In general,* what advice do you hear?
> (A) Try everything and enjoy college.
> (B) Study extra hard and try to graduate early.

🎧 **G. LISTENING FOR NUMBERS** Listen to part of Section 2 again. As you listen, write the numbers that you hear. If necessary, listen several times.

And my last piece of advice to a student on the younger end of the range, the

_____17_____ or _____ year-old, would be: think about
    1   2

dropping out—because very often those years of _____,
                                            3

_____, and 20, uh, campuses are forced to do a lot more babysitting than they
    4

probably should. It's people who are 20, _____,
                                      5

_____ that really enjoy and get a great deal out of the undergraduate investment.
    6

Listening Strategy ⬤⬤⬤

Listening for Details

Details are small points. They aren't as general as the main idea. They are important because they **support** ("hold up" or explain) the main idea. Details are often examples or numbers. When you listen, try to focus on the details the speaker gives, such as numbers, dates, or lists of examples. Listening for details will help you to understand the main idea better.

🎧 **H. LISTENING FOR DETAILS** On the lines below, write the examples that you hear.

I would say try everything, you know, _____Thai dance_____,

_____, South American _____—'cause no one cares

if you turn out to be not any good at it. You know, you're in college, and you're supposed to be

experimenting.

🎧 **I. LISTENING FOR THE MAIN IDEA: SECTION 3** Now listen to Section 3—the last, short, section of the program. As you listen, try to answer this question:
• Who is Jeff (the caller)?

J. LISTENING FOR DETAILS Read these questions. Then listen to Section 3 again. Write your answers on the lines.

1. Who should the students seek out?

   _____

2. Who should students talk to?

   _____

3. What shouldn't students worry about?

   _____

4. What should students do for the first couple of years?

   _____

AFTER LISTENING

A. DISCUSSION In small groups, discuss these questions.

1. Did any advice in the radio program surprise you? If so, what?

2. Is any advice in the radio program different from advice in your culture? If so, what?

3. One speaker says: "Think about dropping out" for a while. What is her reason for this? What might be a good reason *not* to drop out?

Critical Thinking Strategy

Recognizing Literal and Figurative Meanings

Many words can have both a **literal** meaning (the actual meaning) and a **figurative** meaning (not the true meaning). A figurative meaning creates a "picture" in the mind of the listener. You can usually understand most figurative expressions if you visualize the literal meaning first.

Examples: I climbed a **mountain** on my vacation. **(Literal)**
I have a **mountain** of homework. **(Figurative: here** *mountain* **means "a lot.")**

B. RECOGNIZING LITERAL AND FIGURATIVE MEANINGS Anne Matthews gave this advice in the radio program. In small groups, discuss the questions below.

1. **"Take enough quarters for laundry."**
   She means this literally. Why do you think she gives this advice to high school students who are going to start college soon?

2. **"I would say talk to professors, go to office hours. If you find a class that appeals to you, even ask them for extra reading. They'll kiss your feet in amazement and joy."**
   She means this figuratively. What do you think she really means?

C. TAKING A SURVEY Talk to English speakers: friends, classmates, teachers, neighbors, or workers at your school. Ask each person this question and write their answers in the chart.
• What advice can you give to students who are just beginning college?

Names	Advice

D. DISCUSSING SURVEY RESULTS Tell the class about your survey. Did any advice surprise you? Was any advice similar to advice in this chapter?

BEFORE LISTENING

A. THINKING AHEAD In Parts 2 and 4 of this chapter, you heard advice for students beginning college. In Part 5, you are going to hear a lecture by a career counselor to English-language students. What do you think he will say? Will his advice be different from the other advice you heard in this chapter? Work with a partner. On a separate piece of paper, write the advice that you think the college counselor will give.

B. VOCABULARY PREPARATION Read the sentences. The words and phrases in red are from the lecture. Guess their meanings from the context. Fill in the correct bubbles.

1. The **key** to success is education. Without a good education, it's very difficult to be successful.

   Ⓐ a thing that locks a door   Ⓑ a thing that helps you reach a goal   Ⓒ a thing that makes a person rich

2. The **process of** choosing a good college isn't fast or easy. You probably need about a year. In this process, you need to get catalogs from different schools, read them, visit campuses, and talk with many people.

   Ⓐ choice of a school   Ⓑ need to   Ⓒ steps in

3. I want to choose my major carefully. It's important for my future **career**.

   Ⓐ studies   Ⓑ profession; work   Ⓒ most important area of study; major

4. First, you need to **set** your goals. Then you need a plan: How are you going to reach your goals?

   Ⓐ decide on   Ⓑ reach   Ⓒ put

5. The college offers a two-hour **workshop** on how to prepare for a job interview.

   Ⓐ place to work   Ⓑ special class   Ⓒ place to buy things

6. To make a little extra money, I work five hours a week as a **tutor** for a high school student who needs help with his math.

   Ⓐ volunteer   Ⓑ mathematician   Ⓒ private teacher

Taking Lecture Notes: Using an Outline

When you take lecture notes, you should organize them on a graphic organizer, if possible. You already know one type of graphic organizer, a T-chart. Another type is an outline.

An informal outline has general ("larger") ideas or points on the left. Specific ("smaller") points are indented to the right.

Example:

Social Sciences
    Psychology
    Sociology
    Anthropology
        Cultural Anthropology
            Symbolism
            Religion
        Physical Anthropology
    Political Science
Natural Sciences
    Biology
        Microbiology
        Botany
    Chemistry
    Physics

A formal outline has general points on the left and specific points on the right. The difference between this and an informal outline is that each point on a formal outline has a number or letter.

Example:

I. Social Sciences
    A. Psychology
    B. Sociology
    C. Anthropology
        1. Cultural Anthropology
            a. Symbolism
            b. Religion
        2. Physical Anthropology
    D. Political Science
II. Natural Sciences
    A. Biology
        1. Microbiology
        2. Botany
    B. Chemistry
    C. Physics

 Look at the formal outline above. How many *kinds* of numbers are there? How many *kinds* of letters are there? What are the two most general groups of points? What kind of number indicates the most general points? What kind of letter indicates the most specific points?

C. TAKING NOTES: USING AN OUTLINE Below is a list of some libraries, services, and activities for students at one university in the United States. With a partner, use the list and follow these steps.

1. Write *L* next to libraries, *S* next to services, and *A* next to activities.

2. Put the items in order on the outline below and on page 45.

3. There is no order to the list. Which items are more general? Write *gen* next to these items.

~~Tennis~~	Undergraduate Library	Karate Club
~~Services~~ *S, gen*	Soccer	Swimming
~~Chess Club~~	~~Language Lab~~	Writing Lab
Research Library	Engineering Library	~~University Library System~~
Student Health Clinic	Ski Club	~~Activities~~
Labs	Art Library	Lecture Note Service
Career Planning Office	Football	~~Sports~~
International Student Club	Medical Library	ATMs
Clubs	Mathematics Lab	~~Child Care Center~~
Basketball		

Outline

I. University Library System _____

    A. _____

    B. _____

    C. _____

    D. _____

    E. _____

II. Services _____

    A. Child Care Center _____

    B. _____

    C. _____

        1. Language Lab _____

        2. _____

        3. _____

    D. _____

    E. _____

    F. _____

III. Activities _____

  A. Sports _____

    1. Tennis _____

    2. _____

    3. _____

    4. _____

    5. _____

  B. _____

    1. Chess Club _____

    2. _____

    3. _____

    4. _____

LISTENING

Listening Strategy

Understanding New Words

Professors often give definitions of new words in their lectures. Listen for a definition immediately after a new word.

Examples: A **goal** is **a carefully planned purpose**.
You need to highlight important points with a **highlighter—a thick yellow, orange, or green pen**.

Professors often use certain expressions before they give a definition. If you don't understand a word, listen for these expressions.

Examples: **I mean . . .**
This means . . .
This is . . .
In other words, . . .

A. UNDERSTANDING NEW WORDS Listen to these sentences from the lecture. You will hear each sentence twice. Write the definitions for the words on the lines.

1. **academic:** _____

2. **self-assessment:** _____

3. **skills:** _____

4. **values:** _____

5. **transition:** _____

Organizing Your Notes: Paying Attention to Signposts

Professors often use **signposts** (guides) in lectures. These are special words that help you to organize your notes. Some common signposts are *first, second, third* (etc.), *next, one, another, then, finally,* and *last.*

When you hear these words, move down to the next line in your notes or on your outline.

Example: **The professor says:** "The second key to academic success is setting a goal."
You write on a new line: II. Setting a Goal

B. TAKING NOTES: USING AN OUTLINE Listen to the lecture. It is in four sections. You will listen to each section twice. Fill in as much of the outline as you can. Don't worry if you can't fill in everything. (You'll listen to the whole lecture again later.)

Keys to Academic Success

Section 1
Introduction

I. Self-assessment = _____

    A. You can understand your:

        1. _____

        2. _____

        3. _____

        4. _____

    B. Places to take a self-assessment test

        1. _____

        2. _____

        3. _____

II. Setting a Goal

    A. Goals for different time periods

    B. Plan of action for your goal

Section 2

III. Knowing the College Culture and Environment

    A. How to learn about this

        1. Study _____

        2. Find out _____

        3. Study _____

        4. Read _____

        5. _____

    B. Important to know about your college because

        1. _____

        2. _____

Section 3

IV. Developing Academic Skills

    A. _____

    B. _____

    C. _____

    D _____

    E. _____

    F. _____

        1. Student Services: _____

        2. Math Lab: *tutor* _____

        3. Writing Center: _____

Section 4

V. Transition to the World of Work

    A. Part-time job

    B. _____

        1. *learn to write a résumé* _____

        2. _____

        3. _____

        4. _____

Source: Adapted from a lecture by Patrick Delices, Ph.D.

C. CHECKING YOUR NOTES Listen to the lecture again. Fill in any missing information. As you listen, try to answer this question:
• There are five keys to academic success. Which one is most important, in the speaker's opinion?

To answer this question, pay attention when the speaker tells you that it's important, emphasizes it, or says something more than one time. Put a star (*) next to this part of the outline.

AFTER LISTENING

A. USING YOUR NOTES In small groups, use your notes to discuss these questions about the lecture.

1. What is important to know about yourself?

2. Where can you take a self-assessment test?

3. How can you learn about your college?

4. In the speaker's opinion, what's the most important key to academic success? How do you know that he thinks this is the most important key?

B. GETTING TO KNOW A COLLEGE CAMPUS Here is a list of 10 places at Valley College. Read the sentences about things that you might need to do. Where can you go for each one? Work with a partner. Write the correct letters in the blanks.

a. Admissions Office	f. Counseling Center
b. Career Planning Office	g. Research Library
c. Child Care Center	h. Snack Shack
~~d.~~ College Dental Clinic	i. Writing Center
e. Copy Center	j. XKVC Campus Radio

_____d_____ **1.** You need to go to a dentist, but you don't have a lot of money.

_____ **2.** You were absent yesterday. You want to make a photocopy of your friend's lecture notes.

_____ **3.** You're very unhappy. You can't sleep at night. You worry all the time.

_____ **4.** You want to take a class, but you have a child. You don't have a babysitter.

_____ **5.** You are wondering (asking yourself) this: What are possible jobs for people with my major?

_____ **6.** Your friend wants to come to Valley College. Your friend needs an application form.

_____ **7.** You want lunch.

_____ **8.** You need to find an article from *Business Week* magazine from last year.

_____ **9.** It's difficult for you to write compositions in English. You need help.

_____ **10.** You think, "It would be fun to work for a radio station."

C. MAKING CONNECTIONS In Parts 2, 4, and 5, you heard advice for students who are beginning college. On a separate piece of paper, make a list of all the advice that you remember.

Now in small groups, share your lists. Answer these questions.

1. Is there any advice that you heard in all three parts?

2. Is there any advice that you think is especially helpful?

3. Is there any advice that you disagree with?

PUT IT ALL TOGETHER

You are going to give a short presentation.

Step 1

Choose two colleges or universities. They can be:
• the college that you go to now and one other
• the colleges that you are thinking of going to
• colleges near your home
• colleges or universities in two different countries

Step 2

Write five questions about the two schools that you chose. What are you curious about?

1. _____

2. _____

3. _____

4. _____

5. _____

 ## Step 3

Go to the websites for the two schools. Explore the websites and take the virtual (online) tours if they have them.
• Look for the answers to your questions.
• Look for something special or different about these colleges or universities. (For example, are there any unusual majors? Are there interesting activities, services, or clubs? Are there any programs for international students?)

Step 4

Take notes on this T-chart. Compare the two schools.

School #1	School #2
Name: _____	Name: _____

Speaking Strategy

Asking for Clarification

To be a good listener, you also need to be a good *speaker* in one way: you need to be able to ask for **clarification**. In other words, you need to ask specific questions when you don't understand something. Use phrases such as the following to ask for clarification.

Examples: Excuse me. How do you spell that?
Sorry. I didn't get that.
Could you repeat that?
Sorry. What do you mean?
Can you give an example of that?
I don't think I understand. What does that mean?

Step 5

In small groups, share some of the most interesting things that you learned about the two schools that you chose. Then as your classmates are speaking, take notes on a separate piece of paper. Ask for clarification when necessary.

CHAPTER 2

The Global Economy

Discuss these questions:

- Look at the picture. Where is the man? What might he be doing?
- What country might he be in? Explain your answer.
- Do you buy things made in other countries? What do you buy?

Some global products

👥 **A. THINKING AHEAD** You are going to look at and discuss a magazine **advertisement** (or **ad**)—a notice to sell a product. Before you look at it, in small groups do the following.

1. Describe an ad that you like. It can be from a magazine, TV, radio, or any other place. Say why you like it.

   Example: In the iPod ad, a woman is listening to her iPod. She's walking normally down the street but her shadow is dancing. I like this ad because it's creative and funny.

2. Describe an ad that you *don't* like. Say why you don't like it.

   Example: In the bank ad, they play an old rock song. I don't like the ad because I don't like the song.

3. Describe an ad that is in your native language.

B. STUDYING AN AD Look at the ad. In small groups, discuss these questions:
- What product is the company advertising?
- Where do you think the product comes from?
- Where can you buy the product?

C. DISCUSSION With a partner, discuss these questions.

1. Who is the **target audience** for the ad? In other words, who is the ad hoping to sell to, in your opinion? Is it for someone like you? For someone older? Someone younger? Someone in the United States? Someone in another country?

2. Is this an **effective** ad? In other words, does it make you want to buy the product?

3. Would this ad be effective in any country in the world? Why or why not?

D. JOURNAL WRITING Choose *one* of these topics.
- Describe an ad that you like. What is the product? Who is the target audience?
- Describe an ad that you don't like. What is the product? Who is the target audience?
- What kind of advertising—radio, TV, or print (newspapers and magazines)—do you think is most effective for selling cell phones? Why?

Write about the topic for five minutes. Don't worry about grammar and don't use a dictionary. Just put as many ideas as you can on paper.

BEFORE LISTENING

Critical Thinking Strategy

Previewing: Brainstorming

Brainstorming is thinking about all the ideas that you have on a topic. It's a good idea to brainstorm before listening. You can brainstorm alone or in a group. When you brainstorm, you can think about your ideas and write them down, or you can talk about them. This prepares you for listening. Also, it helps you to understand what you are going to hear.

A. BRAINSTORMING You are going to listen to Brandon and Chrissy talking about products in the **global economy** (products from one country that people buy in other countries). Before you listen, fill in the chart below. Follow these directions.

Make a list of things that you use or wear every day, such as pens, cell phones, shoes, jackets, and backpacks.

Where was each item made? Look for the country. Look for **labels** or writing on the products themselves. Look for "Made in _____" or "Imported from _____." If there is no writing on the products, then guess where it came from. Write the information in the chart.

Products	Where They Are Made
pen	Japan

B. DISCUSSION Talk about the products in your chart. In small groups, discuss these questions.

1. Compare the products in your chart with those in your group members' charts. Are any products the same? What are they? Are any countries the same? What are they?

2. Describe each product. Is it good quality?

3. Is the item expensive or inexpensive?

4. Where did you buy this product? Where can people buy products like it?

5. Have you seen an ad for the product? If so, describe it. Is it an effective ad? Why or why not?

C. VOCABULARY PREPARATION Read the conversations below. The informal words in red are from the conversation between Brandon and Chrissy.

1. **A:** Do you like that Old Navy ad?
   B: Nope. I hate it.

2. **A:** Do you like the Gap ad?
   B: Yeah, it's nice.

3. **A:** What's all that **stuff** in your backpack?
   B: That's my lunch, my English book, my glasses, my new pen . . .

4. **A:** Do you think my new hat looks good on me?
   B: Yes! It looks very **cool!**

5. **A:** How much did your new hat cost?
   B: Five **bucks.**

6. **A:** How do you like my new shirt?
   B: Wow! It's **wild.** The colors are so bright, they hurt my eyes!

7. **A:** So the next day, I called Drew, and he said—
   B: Whoa, it's later than I thought! We have to get going now!

Now match the words and the definitions below. Write the correct letters on the lines.

____*a*____ **1.** bucks   ~~a.~~ U.S. dollars

_____ **2.** cool   **b.** extreme, unusual, or intense

_____ **3.** nope   **c.** things, objects, or activities

_____ **4.** stuff   **d.** no

_____ **5.** whoa   **e.** nice

_____ **6.** wild   **f.** yes

_____ **7.** yeah   **g.** stop; wait a minute

LISTENING

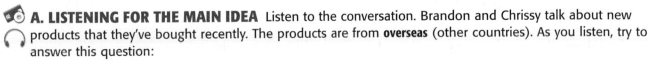

A. LISTENING FOR THE MAIN IDEA Listen to the conversation. Brandon and Chrissy talk about new products that they've bought recently. The products are from **overseas** (other countries). As you listen, try to answer this question:

• What products did Brandon and Chrissy buy?

B. LISTENING FOR DETAILS Listen again. As you listen, complete the chart below.

Products	Countries the Products Are From
	China
Chrissy's shoes	

C. LISTENING FOR DESCRIPTIVE LANGUAGE Listen again. This time, you are going to hear only part of the conversation. As you listen, listen for the descriptive adjectives in the box. Write them on the correct lines.

American	**curious**	**odd**
bad	**little**	**old**
British	**local (use two times)**	**wild (use two times)**
Note: Use a dictionary to find the meanings of any words that are new to you.		

Brandon: Hey, speaking of stuff made overseas, have you seen that new ad for Super Mints?

Chrissy: Um, I don't know.

Brandon: It's really _____ wild _____. There are all these _____
1   2

couples—an _____ lady and a _____ boy,
3   4

a woman and her dog, two guys—and one wants to kiss the other.

Chrissy: Oh, yeah, but the other refuses because the one that wants a kiss has

_____ breath!
　　　　5

Brandon: Yeah, it's done in _____ colors and settings, like a music video. I
　　　　　　　　　　　　　　6

was so _____, I bought some. I noticed they're from England. I was
　　　7

wondering if the commercial is _____, too. It just didn't look
　　　　　　　　　　　　　　　　8

_____.
　　　　9

Chrissy: I don't know. I think they remake commercials for the country they want to sell the product

in 'cause you have to appeal to the _____ market. You've got to
　　　　　　　　　　　　　　　　　　10

relate the product to _____ values.
　　　　　　　　　　　　11

Brandon: Yeah, and there's stuff you can do in commercials in other countries that you _sure_ can't do here.

Listening Strategy

Listening for Supporting Information

When people give ideas or opinions, they often also give support for the ideas or opinions. Sometimes you hear the word _because_ when supporting information is given. Other times, an example or an explanation follows without the word _because_.

Examples:　I don't buy clothes that are made overseas **because I want to support workers who live in my country.**

Your new shoes are really wild! **The high heels and that bright green color are cool!**

D. LISTENING FOR SUPPORTING INFORMATION Listen to the same part of the conversation again. This time listen for the information that supports or explains the statements below. Write the information on the lines.

1. That Super Mints commercial is really wild.

Supporting Information: _____

_____

2. I think they remake commercials for the country they want to sell the product in.

Supporting Information: _____

_____

AFTER LISTENING

A. INFORMATION GAP Work with a partner. Student A works on page 202. Student B works on page 206. Don't look at your partner's page. Take turns asking and answering questions about imported food products in a catalog. Write the answers on the lines on your catalog page. Ask these questions:

- Where is the product from?
- How much does it weigh? OR How much is there?
- How much does it cost? OR How much do they cost?

B. TAKING A SURVEY Talk to three classmates. Ask their opinions about products that come from different countries. First, think about your answers to the questions in the chart below. Write your own question in the bottom row. Then interview your classmates. Write their answers in the chart.

Example: **A:** Do you buy products from other countries?
B: Yes.
A: Which ones?
B: I buy makeup and shoes.
A: Why do you buy them?
B: The makeup is good quality, and the shoes are cheap.

	Classmate 1	Classmate 2	Classmate 3
1. Do you buy products from other countries?			
2. Which ones? Examples: food, clothing, electronics			
3. Why do you buy them?			
4. How do they compare with the same items from another country?			
Your question:			

C. DISCUSSING SURVEY RESULTS Form small groups. Try not to be in a group with someone that you interviewed. Discuss the results of your survey. Discuss these questions:

- What types of products from other countries do your classmates buy most? Why?

PART ③ THE MECHANICS OF SPEAKING AND LISTENING

INTONATION

🎧 *Wh-* Questions

When you ask a question with a *wh-* word (*who, what, when, where, why,* and *how*), your voice goes down at the end of the sentence.

Examples: What's up?   How's it going?

What have you been doing lately?   Where did you get those shoes?

How are you?   Where did you buy that?

🎧 **A. *Wh-* QUESTIONS** Listen to and repeat the *wh-* questions in the box. Make sure that your voice goes down at the end of each question.

👥 **B. ASKING AND ANSWERING *Wh-* QUESTIONS** Work with a partner. Ask your partner six questions about what he or she is wearing. Ask *wh-* questions. Make sure your intonation goes down for the *wh-* questions. Then answer your partner's questions.

Example: **A:** Where did you get those shoes?
               B: I bought them at Shoe Pavilion.

LANGUAGE FUNCTIONS

Greeting People You Know

There are several ways to greet (to say hello to) someone you already know. Here are some.

Examples: Hi. How are you?   Hi. What's new?
               Hi. How's it going?   Hi. What's up? (= What's new?)
               Hi. What have you been up to* lately? Hello. How have you been?

*up to = doing

You answer a *how* question with *fine, not bad, well,* or something similar. You answer a *what* question with *nothing, not much,* or something similar.

Examples: **A.** How are you?   **A.** What's new?
               B. Fine, thanks.   **B.** Not much.

 Which expressions sound informal? Which sound formal?

C. GREETING PEOPLE YOU KNOW Listen to the conversations. Write the words that you hear on the lines.

1. **A:** Hi. _What's up?_____

   B: Oh, nothing much.

2. **A:** Hi. How's it going?

   B: _____

3. **A:** Hi. _____

   B: Not bad.

4. **A:** Hi. How are you?

   B: _____

5. **A:** Hi. What have you

   _____ lately?

   B: _____

Responding to Greetings: General

When someone you already know greets you, there are several ways to answer. Usually, for *how* questions, you give short answers that explain your feelings *in general*. For *what* questions, you give short answers that explain your activities *in general*. Use these answers with friends–people you know well, and **acquaintances**–people you don't know as well as friends but who are not strangers.

Examples:

A: Hi. How are you?
B: Fine.
Fine, thanks.
Not bad.
I'm well, thanks.
Great!

A: Hi. How's it going?
B: Well.
It's going well, thanks.
Great.

A: What's new?
B: Nothing.
Nothing much.
Not much.

D. RESPONDING TO GREETINGS: GENERAL Listen to each greeting. Is it a *how* question or a *what* question? Circle the best answer to the greeting that you hear.

1. Fine.   Not much.

2. Not bad.   Nothing.

3. Great!   Nothing much.

4. I'm well, thanks.   Nothing.

5. Fine.   Nothing much.

6. Not bad.   Not much.

Returning Greetings

With both good friends and acquaintances, it's polite to return greetings. You return a greeting by asking the other person another greeting question. Sometimes you repeat the greeting question. Sometimes you give a different version of it. *How about you?* is a common way to repeat a greeting question.

Examples:
    A: Hi. How are you?
    B: Fine. **How about you?**

    A: What's new with you?
    B: Not much. **How about you?**

Look at this example of a longer greeting.

Example:
    A: Hi. **How are you?**
    B: Fine. **How about you?**
    A: Just great. **What's new with you?**
    B: Not much. **What's new with you?**
    A: Not much.

E. RETURNING GREETINGS Complete the conversation. Use expressions from the box above.

A: Hi, Bob.

B: Hi, Annie. How _____

A: I'm fine. _____

B: I'm fine, too. _____

A: Not much. What's _____

B: _____

Responding to Greetings: Specific

On page 60, you saw general ways to answer greetings. Friends often want to share real or honest information with each other. Therefore, with good friends, you can give specific answers about your feelings and your activities, if you want to. People sometimes give a general answer and then add real information.

Examples:
    A: Hi! How's it going?
    B: O.K., but I'm tired! I stayed up all night studying!
        Great! I just got an "A" on my English test!

    A: Hi. What's new with you?
    B: Hi. Not much, but I just got a cat.

Note: In general, you don't give answers such as these to acquaintances.

F. RESPONDING TO GREETINGS: SPECIFIC Work with a partner. One student is Student A, and the other is Student B. Follow the directions in the boxes on page 62. Exchange roles after you do the activity three times. Remember that your voice goes down when you ask *wh-* questions.

Example:
    A: Hi! How's it going?
    B: I'm tired! I stayed up all night studying!

Student A

You haven't seen your friend for a week. Greet him or her with one of the expressions from page 59.

Student B

You meet a friend. Your friend starts a conversation. Continue the conversation. Choose one of the options below. You can give a polite answer or a real answer.

Option 1: You stayed up all night studying for an exam. You're tired.
Option 2: What a day! You've just won $1,000 in the lottery.
Option 3: You are having a terrible week. Yesterday you were in a car accident. Today you lost your job. Also, you have a cold.
Option 4: You're late for class, but you're happy to see your friend.
Option 5: You have a very boring life. Nothing exciting has happened to you in a long time.
Option 6: You have a very exciting life. You saved a child who fell into a swimming pool. A TV news crew came and interviewed you. You were on the news last night!

PRONUNCIATION

∩ Reduced Forms of Words

When people speak quickly, two or three words often become reduced. They are pushed together so that they sound like one word. Here are some examples.

Examples:	**Long Forms**		**Reduced Forms**
	What's up?	→	**Whasup**?
	How is it going?	→	**Howzit** going?
	What have you been up to?	→	**Whatuv** you been up to?
	How **about you**?	→	How **'boutchu**?
	How **are you** doing?	→	How **ya** doing?
	I don't have **a lot of** money.	→	I don't have **a lotta** money.
	I don't know.	→	**I dunno.**

People usually *say* the reduced forms but *write* the long forms. (The reduced forms are not correct in formal writing.)

∩ **G. REDUCED FORMS OF WORDS** Listen to the conversation. You'll hear the reduced forms of some words. Write the *long* forms on the lines.

A: Hi. _____What's up_____?
                    1

B: Hi. Not much. _____ going with you?
                              2

A: I _____. I've been busy lately. _____ you
                3   4

been up to?

B: I've been busy, too. _____ doing in English?
5

A: Not bad, but it's a _____ work.
6

WORDS IN PHRASES

> ### Expressions with *Look, Seem,* and *Sound* + Adjective
>
> In conversations with friends, you often give comments on the other person's possessions or activities. One way to make these comments is with the verbs *look, seem,* or *sound* plus an adjective.
>
> **Examples:**   I like your sunglasses. They **look cool**.
> I like your new shoes. They **seem comfortable**.
> You went to the beach last weekend? That **sounds fun**!

H. WORDS IN PHRASES Work with a partner. Talk about what he or she is wearing or ask about what he or she did last weekend. Give your opinions using expressions with *look, seem,* and *sound* + adjective.

Examples: **A:** I like your shirt. It looks really cool.
B: Thanks.

A: What did you do last weekend?
B: I went to a basketball game.
A: That sounds great.

PUT IT TOGETHER

A. GREETING CLASSMATES You are going to greet and have conversations with your classmates.

Step 1
Make a list of your recent activities. Write eight things that you did this week.

Recent Activities

1. _____
2. _____
3. _____
4. _____
5. _____
6. _____
7. _____
8. _____

Step 2

Form two teams, Team A and Team B.

• Students on Team A will greet and talk to as many students on Team B as possible in five minutes. Team A students will **keep track of** (write down) how many people they talked to. Team A students will try to use the *look*, *seem*, and *sound* expressions.

• Students on Team B will use their Recent Activities lists from Step 1 on page 63 to give specific answers to greetings or they will just give general answers.

Then teams exchange roles. The team that greets and talks to the most classmates wins.

Example:
A: Hi. What have you been doing lately?
B: Well, yesterday I saw a movie.
A: That sounds nice.

A: Hi. What's up?
B: Hi! I just bought some new glasses.
A: They look very cool.

 B. TALKING ABOUT THE WEEK With a partner, discuss what you did last week.

Step 1
Write things that you did last week on the one-week agenda (calendar).

Week of _____ to _____

MONDAY

TUESDAY

WEDNESDAY

THURSDAY _____

_____
_____
_____
_____

FRIDAY _____

_____
_____
_____
_____

SATURDAY _____

_____
_____

SUNDAY _____

_____
_____
_____

Step 2
• Take turns greeting and talking to your partner.
• Answer with specific information.
• Ask one or two questions to continue the conversation. Remember to use correct question intonation. Also, try to use the _look_, _seem_, and _sound_ expressions.

Example: **A:** Hi. What have you been up to lately?
   B: Well, yesterday I played soccer.
   A: Really? That sounds cool. Do you play a lot of soccer?
   B: Yeah. I usually play on Sunday in the park with friends. And this week we played on Saturday, too.

PART 4 BROADCAST ENGLISH The Travels of a T-Shirt

BEFORE LISTENING

A man wearing a T-shirt

A. THINKING AHEAD You are going to hear a radio program about one place where T-shirts are made. In small groups, discuss these questions.

1. Do you own any T-shirts? If yes, how many do you have?

2. What material are T-shirts usually made of?

3. Think about your favorite T-shirt. What do you like about it? What makes it your favorite? If you don't wear T-shirts, think about what makes a T-shirt high quality.

4. Where do you think T-shirts are made?

5. Which country makes the best T-shirts, in your opinion?

B. VOCABULARY PREPARATION The words in the box below are from the radio program. Before you listen, read the words and their definitions. Then write the correct words on the lines on page 67.

Words	Definitions
cheap	inexpensive
diversify	do many different things
dominate	have control over
flourish	grow; increase
infrastructure	things (such as roads) that make transportation possible
manufacture (n.)*	creation; making
perfect (v.)**	do in the best possible way
postmodern	a modern architecture style
textile	cloth; material
workforce	people who work

*(n.) means *noun*
**(v.) means *verb*

1. Lisa thinks that her business can _____ if she makes high-quality items.

2. Adam took classes in order to _____ his sewing skills. Now he sews even better than before.

3. Alicia used to make dresses and shirts. Then she decided to _____. Now she makes coats and jackets, too.

4. Jorge wants to make more money than other clothing companies. He wants to _____ the clothing business.

5. There is an expensive way to make clothing and a _____ way to do it.

6. The older buildings are gone. Now, there are mainly _____ skyscrapers in the center of the city.

7. Many people work in T-shirt factories in Shanghai. The _____ of T-shirts is an important business.

8. The _____ factory makes clothing from cotton, wool, and silk.

9. The sewing factory has a large _____. Over 500 people work there.

10. The clothing factories are doing well; now the country can improve its _____. This will make trading with other countries easier.

Test-Taking Strategy

Making Predictions

When you make a prediction, you guess. Making predictions about what you are going to hear in the listening section on standardized tests *before* you hear it helps you to focus better and to understand more while you are listening. When you know the topic before you listen, try to predict what you might hear on the test.

Example: **You know:** The topic is the global economy.

You predict: The listening section might be about international business.

C. MAKING PREDICTIONS The radio program is about successful textile companies in Shanghai, China. In small groups, discuss this question to make predictions about the topic:
- Will the program say that the effects of the textile **industry** (type of business) in Shanghai are positive, negative, or both positive and negative?

LISTENING

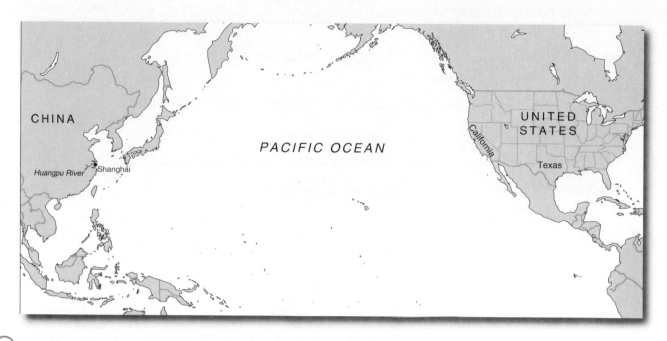

🎧 **A. LISTENING FOR THE MAIN IDEA** Listen to the radio program. As you listen, try to answer this question. Write your answer on the lines.

What made Shanghai a wealthy city? _____

_____

🎧 **B. LISTENING FOR DETAILS** Listen to part of the program again. As you listen, use your finger to follow on the map above the **route** (the way) that cotton follows to get to Shanghai. Then answer these questions.

1. From where does most of Shanghai's T-shirt cotton come? _____

2. From what state does it leave the U.S.? _____

Listening Strategy

Identifying a Causal Chain

When you listen to information about business, it's important to understand the causes (reasons for) and effects (results) of events. Some effects are the immediate result of a cause. Sometimes, there is a chain of causes that result in a certain effect. Words and expressions that introduce causes include: *because, because of,* and *due to.*

Examples: **Because of** the clothing manufacturers, the city has become richer.
Because the city has become richer, there is more money for infrastructure.
Due to better infrastructure, businesses can expand.

C. IDENTIFYING A CAUSAL CHAIN A flow chart, one type of graphic organizer, is one way to "see" a causal chain—all the causes that lead to an effect. Listen to part of the program. As you listen, write the causes from the box below in the correct order on the flow chart to answer this question.
• How did Shanghai become a rich, modern city?

~~British and Japanese build cotton factories in Shanghai~~
infrastructure can be built
trade flourishes
factories diversify
the workforce gains skills

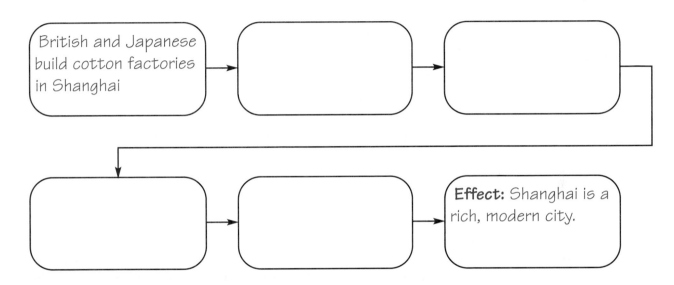

British and Japanese build cotton factories in Shanghai

Effect: Shanghai is a rich, modern city.

Listening Strategy

Listening for an Anecdote

An anecdote is a short story. It's one way to support an idea in a discussion. When you hear an anecdote, listen for how it explains or supports the speaker's ideas.

Example: Last week, I went to a department store to buy some new pants. I picked out five pairs and tried them on. They were the latest styles. They were well made and looked good on me. Then I noticed the labels. Not one pair of pants was made here. They were all made overseas. That's when I realized that our clothing industry probably isn't doing very well right now.

D. LISTENING FOR AN ANECDOTE Listen for the anecdote that Greg Burgess tells in the radio program. As you listen, answer the question below. Write your answer on the lines.

How did Greg Burgess know that he might have to find another job?

_____

_____

AFTER LISTENING

Making Connections

Connecting the topic of a radio program, lecture, or presentation to something that you already know increases your understanding of the topic. You can connect topics to:

• something that you read recently
• something that you did recently
• something that you discussed recently
• a class that you took
• a program that you saw on TV or heard on the radio

Example: In Part 2 of this chapter, you made a list of products that you use from other countries. In Part 4 of this chapter, you heard about T-shirts made in China. You can use the information in the radio program in Part 4 to think about the positive and negative things about the products that you use from other countries.

A. MAKING CONNECTIONS In small groups, discuss these questions:
• Look at the lists of products that you made in Part 2 on page 54. What are the positive effects of buying products like these that are made in one country and sold in another? What are the negative effects? Think about the price and the quality of the products. Also, think about the workers who made them. Who is it good for? Who isn't it good for?

B. EXTENSION Imagine that you run a successful T-shirt company. In small groups, design a T-shirt that you think will sell well overseas. What is it made of? What does it look like? Why will it be popular with your target audience?

PART ⑤ ACADEMIC ENGLISH Selling Snapple in Japan

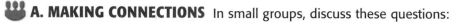

BEFORE LISTENING

A. THINKING AHEAD You are going to listen to a lecture about a U.S. **beverage** (drink) company. Before you listen, form small groups. Brainstorm ideas about cold beverages. Think about drink types, ingredients (what is in them), and words that describe the drinks. (For example: How do cold beverages make you feel? How do they taste? Why do you drink them?) Write your ideas in the chart below.

Types	Main Ingredients	Descriptions
soda	sugar	sweet, tastes good

B. VOCABULARY PREPARATION The words and phrases in the box are from the lecture. Complete the sentences below with the correct words and phrases from the box. Write the correct words and phrases on the lines.

fruit pulp	nutritious	thirst quenching
highly desirable trait	seed	

1. Many people like juice drinks that have _____—little pieces of fruit— floating in them.

2. Jane found an orange _____ in her juice—she's going to plant it and see if it will grow into a tree.

3. Juice is a wholesome and _____ drink because it contains vitamins. It's good for your health.

4. Juice is very _____, but soda always leaves me thirsty.

5. This drink is popular because it's made from natural ingredients, a _____, in my opinion.

C. VOCABULARY PREPARATION: THE WORD *MARKET*
You are going to hear many words and phrases for marketing. **Marketing** means getting products from the manufacturer to the customer. First, study these forms of the word *market*. Then write the correct forms of *market* in the box below. Use each form once.

Nouns
- a **market**/a **marketplace**: customers; a place, country, region, or group of people that buys a product
- a **marketer**: a person who works to sell a product
- **marketing**: the act of getting a product from manufacturer to customer

Verb
- to **market**: to get a product from manufacturer to customer

---

Marketing Overseas

A company with a successful product wants to sell its product overseas. The first step in this process is to gather information about the foreign _____*market*_____. The company

finds the answer to this question: Will the product be popular in the new

_____? A good _____ learns about the culture of

the new country. He or she does research. Sometimes a company decides to change a product for a

different country. Sometimes it may decide not to _____ the product at all

in the other country. When a company does decide to sell a product in a new country, it must also

find out the best way to advertise the product. Research also helps the company to design an

effective marketing campaign. Because of all this, the _____ of a product in

a new country is a complex process: This is true even for a product successful in another country.

D. GUESSING THE MEANING FROM CONTEXT
Read the sentences below. The words and phrases in red are from the lecture. Guess their meanings from the context. Write your guesses on the lines.

1. The purpose of advertising is **to generate a positive attitude toward** a product so that people will like it and want to buy it.

   Guess: _to make people like_

2. Jeans are popular in many different **segments** of the clothing market—for example, among both teenagers and middle-aged people.

   Guess: _____

3. Quaker Oats is a **consumer goods** company. It makes products that people buy and use quickly such as food and beverages.

   Guess: _____

4. The displays in the store had a lot of **customer traffic**: a lot of people came up to look at them all day long.

   Guess: _____

5. Unfortunately, there wasn't much **demand** for that product. Nobody wanted to buy it.

   Guess: _____

6. One way to advertise something is by **point-of-purchase-displays**—advertisements that appear right in the store.

   Guess: _____

7. The product had an **image problem**. It didn't *look* like a good product, so people didn't buy it.

   Guess: _____

Now compare your guesses with a partner's guesses.

LISTENING

A. TAKING NOTES: USING AN OUTLINE Listen to the lecture. It's in four sections. You will listen to each section twice. Fill in as much of the outline on pages 74–75 as you can. Don't worry if you can't fill in everything. (You'll listen to the whole lecture again later.)

Selling Snapple in Japan

Section 1

I. Background

    A. The Quaker Oats Company

        1. _Everyone knows it for its high-quality products_ _____

        _____

        2. It had a problem with _____

    B. Snapple in the U.S.

        1. Snapple beverages included _____

        _____

        2. Drinks contained _____

    C. Failure in Japan after only _____

Section 2

II. Quaker introduces Snapple in Japan

    A. Point-of-purchase displays

        1. Looks: _____

        2. Customer response: _____

    B. Product image problems

        1. In drinks, Japanese liked _____

        2. To the Japanese, Snapple _____

    C. Attitude of Quaker marketing department

        1. It didn't believe that _____

        2. Sales would improve when Japanese realize that pulp means _____

Section 3

III. Quaker's 1st Marketing Mistake: Market Research

    A. Purpose of market research: to discover _____

    _____

    B. Research would have shown that the Japanese _____

    _____

    C. Research is important in another country because _____

    _____

IV. Quaker's 2nd Marketing Mistake: Advertising

    A. Advertising could have _____

        _____

    B. With advertising, Japanese customers might have _____

        _____

Section 4

V. Quaker's 3rd Marketing Mistake: Financial

    A. Quaker used up marketing and financial resources because _____

        _____

    B. As a result, management could not _____

        _____

Source: Adapted from a lecture by Jeff Streiter, Ph.D.

 B. CHECKING YOUR NOTES Listen to the lecture again. Fill in any missing information on your outline.

Listening Strategy

Asking Questions

Some professors like students to ask questions during a lecture. Others want students to wait until the lecture is over. If you have a professor who wants you to wait, write down your questions as you take notes. Write them in the margin next to the point that you want to ask about. Write them in another ink color or circle them so that you won't forget to ask. You can ask:

• for a definition of a word you don't understand
• about something that is not clear or that you didn't understand
• for more information about something that interests you

C. ASKING QUESTIONS Listen to Section 4 again. As you listen, write three questions about selling Snapple in Japan. Try to write one of each kind: for a definition, about something that is not clear, and to get further information.

1. _____

2. _____

3. _____

 Now compare your questions with a partner's questions.

AFTER LISTENING

A. USING YOUR NOTES Work with a partner. Use your notes to discuss these questions about the lecture.

1. What did people in the U.S. like about Snapple drinks?

2. What were the Snapple displays in Japan like?

3. What didn't the Japanese like about the Snapple drinks?

4. What did the marketing people at Quaker Oats think when they heard about the problem in Japan?

5. What were Quaker Oats' three possible marketing mistakes?

B. TAKING A MARKET SURVEY Quaker Oats didn't do a market survey before it decided to sell Snapple in Japan. This was a mistake. In small groups, do a market survey to see which type of fruit drink your classmates like to buy.

Step 1

1. Read the survey below. Write a check (✓) for the drink type you prefer in the chart.

2. Ask the people in your group the question in the chart. Write a check for the drink type they prefer.

3. Write the total number of votes for each choice in the chart.

4. What's your group's favorite choice? What's your group's least favorite choice?

Market Survey		
Which fruit drink do you prefer?		
Type 1: One hundred percent real fruit juice, with pulp and seeds. No added sugar or vitamins. **Prefer:** _____ **Group Vote Total:** _____	**Type 2:** One hundred percent real fruit juice, clear without pulp and seeds. No added sugar or vitamins. **Prefer:** _____ **Group Vote Total:** _____	**Type 3:** Real fruit juice mixed with carbonated (soda) water and sugar. Vitamins and minerals minerals added. **Prefer:** _____ **Group Vote Total:** _____

Step 2
Compare your answers with those of another group. Do both groups like and dislike the same type of fruit drink?

PUT IT ALL TOGETHER

You are going to give a presentation on selling a new product.

A. INTERVIEWING Follow these steps to conduct your interview.

Step 1
Think of a product. Answer these questions about it:

• What's the product?
• Who is it for? What (or who) is the target market? Can you sell it in any other markets?
• What makes it special? How is it useful? How is it attractive? How is it different?

Step 2
Interview three people. They can be classmates, teachers, or other people at your school. Do the following.
1. Describe the product.
2. Ask these questions:
   • What do you think about the product?
   • Who do you think would buy it? (Children? Teenagers? Adults?)
   • Would you buy it as it is now?
   • What changes would make the product more attractive to you?
   • What are good ways to advertise the product?

Take notes as you conduct your interviews. You will need your notes later.

B. GIVING A PRESENTATION Now you are ready to prepare your presentation.

Step 1
Decide on an ad for the product. Draw a picture of it and/or write the **copy** (the words that appear in the ad). Remember to think about who you want to sell your product to.

Speaking Strategy

Outlining

Before you give a presentation, it's a good idea to make an outline of what you want to say. An outline helps you to decide what you want to say and helps you to stay on your subject while you are speaking. You can use the outline while you speak, but you need to look up from it frequently. An example of a presentation outline is on page 78.

Step 2
Use the outline on page 78 to prepare a presentation on your product and ad design.

Presentation Outline

I.   Description of the product:

_____

_____

_____

II.   Description of the target market (Who will buy the product?):

_____

III.   Changes in the product (Does the product need to be changed for different target markets? Why or why not?):

_____

_____

_____

_____

IV.   Advertising in this market (What kind of advertising works best for this kind of product?):

_____

_____

V.   Description of your ad:

_____

_____

_____

_____

_____

Speaking Strategy

Making Eye Contact

When you give a presentation, make eye contact with your audience. Look at the faces of the people that you are speaking to. Making eye contact helps to keep the audience's attention. If you are speaking to a big group, move your eyes around the room to look at everyone. Don't keep your eyes on just one member of the audience.

Step 3

Now give your presentation to the class or to a small group of students. Your presentation should last no more than three minutes. Remember to look up from your outline and make eye contact while you give your presentation.

UNIT 1 VOCABULARY WORKSHOP

Review vocabulary items that you learned in Getting Started and Chapters 1 and 2.

A. MATCHING Match the definitions to the words and phrases. Write the correct letters on the lines.

Words and Phrases	Definitions
_b_ **1.** bucks	**a.** private teacher
_____ **2.** career	~~b.~~ dollars
_____ **3.** flourish	**c.** great happiness
_____ **4.** higher education	**d.** grow; increase
_____ **5.** joy	**e.** approximately; more or less
_____ **6.** market	**f.** do in the best possible way
_____ **7.** perfect (v.)	**g.** group of people that buys a product
_____ **8.** process	**h.** college; university
_____ **9.** roughly	**i.** profession; work
_____ **10.** tutor	**j.** steps

B. TRUE OR FALSE? Which sentences are true? Which sentences are false? Fill in T for *True* or F for *False*.

1. If the **majority** of college students are women, that means that they are more than half of the student population.   (T)   (F)

2. **Quarters** are 10¢ coins in the U.S.   (T)   (F)

3. If something **appeals to** you, you don't like it very much.   (T)   (F)

4. A **cheap** car is one that costs a lot of money.   (T)   (F)

5. If you are **experimenting**, you are trying new things.   (T)   (F)

6. A college **workshop** is a special class.   (T)   (F)

7. Juice drinks with **fruit pulp** are completely clear.   (T)   (F)

8. A **nutritious** drink is bad for your health.   (T)   (F)

C. HIGH FREQUENCY WORDS

In the box below are some of the most common words in English. Fill in the blanks with words from the box. You will use some words twice. When you finish, check your answers in the reading on page 2.

college	degree	four	receive	students	~~university~~
continue	first	highest	second	studies	years

College in the United States and Canada

Many students begin their higher education at a four-year college or

_____ university _____. Many others begin their _____ year (the
                1   2

freshman year) at a two-year **community** _____. After their
                                                        3

_____ year (the **sophomore** year), _____ get a
        4   5

certificate or an A.A. (Associate Degree) from the community college. Many students transfer to a

_____-year school for their third (**junior**) and fourth (**senior**)
        6

_____.
        7

In the first _____ years of college, students are **undergraduates**. When
                        8

they graduate, they receive a _____—probably a B.A. (Bachelor of Arts) or a
                                              9

B.S. (Bachelor of Science), depending on their **major** (what they choose to study).

Students who continue their _____ after graduation are in **graduate**
                                            10

school. For short, we call this grad school. They are grad students. They are in a master's program or a

doctoral program. After two more _____, they may
                                                11

_____ a **master's degree**—perhaps an M.A. (Master of Arts), M.S. (Master of
        12

Science), M.B.A. (Master of Business Administration), or M.F.A. (Master of Fine Art). Some students

attend for three or more _____ and get a **doctor of philosophy**
                                    13

_____ (Ph.D.). This is the _____ university degree.
        14   15

BIOLOGY

Chapter 3
Animal Behavior

Chapter 4
Nutrition

CHAPTER 3

Animal Behavior

Discuss these questions:
- What kind of animal do you see in the picture?
- What are they doing?
- What do you know about this animal?

PART ① INTRODUCTION Strange but True

Bulls are often aggressive toward humans who come into their territory

A herd of oryx in Kenya, East Africa

A pride (family) of lions

A baby hippo and an old tortoise in Kenya

👥 **A. THINKING AHEAD** In small groups, discuss the animals in these pictures.

1. What kinds of food do these animals eat?

2. Which of these animals are **predators** (hunters and eaters of other animals)?
What kinds of animals are their **prey** (hunted by predators)?

3. Do you know something about any of these **species** (kinds) of animals? If so, tell your group.

• What is similar about all three stories?
• What is surprising about these stories?

Strange but True

On a farm in West Wales, in the United Kingdom, a huge, angry bull attacked a farmer named Donald Mottram. Mottram was in serious trouble. He lay unconscious on the ground for 90 minutes. When he woke up, he saw something that amazed him. A group of his female cows was standing around
5 him in a circle. They were protecting him from the bull until he could crawl to the other side of the fence, safely away from the aggressive bull.

* * * * *

In the early 2000s, something amazing happened in Kenya's Samburu National Reserve. A young female lion adopted a baby oryx (a kind of antelope) as her own. Normally, oryxes are *prey* for lions; lions eat them. However, this
10 lion protected the baby oryx from other predators. The oryx felt safe enough to rest curled up next to the lion. The lion did not hunt and went hungry for many days because she did not want to leave the oryx alone, unprotected. Finally, after 16 days, when the young lion was asleep, the oryx was killed by another lion. However, since that time, the same young lion has never hunted oryxes,
15 and she has adopted several other baby oryxes.

* * * * *

In early 2005, a baby hippo almost died in the terrible tsunami that hit South Asia and East Africa. He was swept down a river, into the Indian
20 Ocean, and then onto a beach. He survived, but his mother did not. Baby hippos are very close to their mothers, so this little hippo looked around for another mother. He found a 100-year-
25 old male tortoise. They established a close relationship. They ate, slept, and walked together. If a human came close to the tortoise, the hippo became very aggressive, apparently protecting his
30 new friend.

Kenya

C. VOCABULARY CHECK Read the definitions below. Use the line numbers to find the words and phrases in the reading on page 85. Write the correct words and phrases on the lines.

<u>**Definitions**</u>   <u>**Words and Phrases**</u>

1. not awake (Line 3)   _____

2. move along the ground, not standing up (Line 5)   _____

3. taking care of; keeping someone safe (Lines 5, 29)   _____

4. quick to become angry and attack (Lines 6, 29)   _____

5. took another's child as one's own (Line 8)   _____

6. moved by the force of water (Line 19)   _____

7. lived through a bad situation (Line 21)   _____

D. DISCUSSION In small groups, discuss these questions.

1. In what two ways are these three stories similar?

2. Did anything in the reading surprise you? If so, what?

3. Do you know any other strange-but-true animal stories? If so, tell one to your group.

E. JOURNAL WRITING Choose *one* of these topics.

• Write your opinion of one or more of the unusual situations in the reading.
• Describe an animal that you know about.
• Tell a story about any other surprising animal.

Write about the topic for five minutes. Don't worry about grammar and don't use a dictionary. Just put as many ideas as you can on paper.

PART ② SOCIAL LANGUAGE That Darn Cat

BEFORE LISTENING

A **domestic** (not wild) cat

A domestic parrot

A. THINKING AHEAD In small groups, talk about the animals in the pictures above. What do you know about their ability to communicate, their intelligence, and their emotions?

B. TAKING A SURVEY Talk to 10 classmates, teachers, and other people at your school. Ask them these questions:
• Do you have a pet (an animal such as a dog, cat, or bird)? OR Did you have a pet in the past?
• Do animals feel emotions?

Record their answers in the chart. Put a | for each answer (for example,  | = 6).

Do Animals Feel Emotions?			
Answers from people with pets		**Answers from people without pets**	
Yes	No	Yes	No

C. DISCUSSING SURVEY RESULTS In small groups, discuss the results of the survey. Answer these questions.

1. Do most people *with* pets think that animals feel emotions?

2. Do most people *without* pets think that animals feel emotions?

3. Are the two groups' ideas similar?

4. Do most people think that animals feel emotions?

D. BRAINSTORMING With a partner, brainstorm everything that you know about dolphins. Answer the questions below.

1. What kind of animal is a dolphin?

2. What do you know about the relationship between humans and dolphins? In other words, are dolphins friendly or not?

3. Do you think that dolphins are intelligent? Explain your answer.

Dolphins

LISTENING

A. LISTENING FOR THE MAIN IDEA Listen to the conversation. As you listen, try to answer this question:
• What does each student believe about animals' emotions and intelligence?

B. LISTENING FOR DETAILS Read the questions. Then listen to the conversation again. Write your answers on the lines.

1. Why does Jennifer have this cat? _____

_____

2. Why does Jennifer say, "Cats are very sensitive"? _____

_____

3. Why does Jennifer think that dolphins understand a lot? _____

_____

4. Why is Brandon sneezing? _____

_____

Test-Taking Strategy

🎧 Listening for Stressed Words

In English, people usually stress the important words in a sentence. The important words are higher, clearer, and louder than other words.

When you listen, pay close attention to the words that are higher, clearer, and louder than the others. If you understand only the stressed words in a sentence, you probably understand the important information.

Example: Is **he** going to live **here** with **us**?

C. LISTENING FOR STRESSED WORDS Listen to part of the conversation again. Fill in the blanks with the stressed words. Use the words in the box.

animals	do	embarrassed	humans	push	smart	trouble
beach	dolphins	hates	laughs	~~sensitive~~	stupid	zillion

Jennifer: Cats are very _____*sensitive*_____. You know, sometimes when a cat does
                                    1

something kind of _____—I don't know, falls off a table or
                          2

something   and everybody _____? You can just tell that the cat feels
                                  3

really _____. It _____ to be laughed at.
              4   5

Tanya: I don't buy that. Why do people always think that _____ have the
                                                                    6

same emotions that _____ have?
                          7

Jennifer: Because they _____. And maybe they understand a lot more than
                                 8

we realize.

Brandon: Yeah. There are a _____ stories about how
                                    9
_____ animals are.
          10

Jennifer: Like _____. You know, sometimes they save a swimmer in the
                              11

ocean who gets in _____ and can't swim back to the
                            12

_____. They come right up, get right under the swimmer, and
          13

_____ him up to the surface.
          14

Listening Strategy

⌒ Understanding Emotion from Tone of Voice

People express emotion with intonation (tone of voice). Intonation is the movement of the voice up and down. It often carries as much meaning as a word or phrase itself. The same word or phrase can have different meanings depending on the tone of voice. When you're listening, notice not only the words but also the speaker's intonation.

Examples: **Yeah!** (The person agrees and is excited.)
          Yeah. (The person agrees unhappily.)
          Yeah . . . (The person isn't sure and maybe even disagrees.)

⌒ **D. UNDERSTANDING EMOTION FROM TONE OF VOICE** Listen to these short conversations. The second person uses the word or words in **bold**. What does this person really mean? Fill in the correct bubbles.

1. O.K.

Ⓐ Yes, I agree, and I'm happy about this.

Ⓑ I agree, but I'm not happy about it. I'm a little angry with you.

2. O.K.

Ⓐ Yes, I agree, and I'm happy about this.

Ⓑ I agree, but I'm not happy about it. I'm a little angry with you.

3. You're kidding.

Ⓐ This surprises me, but I believe you.

Ⓑ I think you're making a joke and you're not telling me the truth.

4. You're kidding.

Ⓐ This surprises me, but I believe you.

Ⓑ I think you're making a joke and you're not telling me the truth.

AFTER LISTENING

A. CHECKING YOUR UNDERSTANDING With a partner, discuss this question:
• What do Jennifer, Brandon, and Tanya believe about animals?

B. VOCABULARY CHECK: WORDS FOR EMOTIONS Fill in the blanks with the noun or adjective form of each word in the chart below (the adjectives will describe how people feel). Use a dictionary if necessary.

Nouns	Adjectives
1. amazement	amazed
2. anger	
3. _____	confused
4. embarrassment	
5. fear	fearful/afraid
6. _____	happy
7. pride	
8. sadness	
9. _____	satisfied
10. _____	skeptical

Now work with a partner. Look at the pictures on page 92. Write the correct adjective from the chart under each picture.

A. _____

B. _____

C. _____

D. _____

E. _____

F. _____

G. _____

H. _____

I. _____

92 UNIT 2 Biology

C. INTERVIEWING Find three classmates who have (or had) a pet. Interview them about their pets. Do (did) the pets show emotions? If so, which ones? How do (did) the pets show these emotions? Complete the chart.

Classmates	Types of Pet	Emotions	How the Pets Show Emotions
Kenji	cat	sadness	just sat by the window for days after another cat who lived in the house died

PART THE MECHANICS OF LISTENING AND SPEAKING

INTONATION

Changing Statements into Questions

In a conversation, people often change a statement into a question simply by making their voice go up at the end. This intonation shows that the speaker thinks that the information in the statement is true. The speaker just wants to check or to make sure.

Examples: **Statement:**   Mr. Jensen isn't in town.

   Question: Mr. Jensen isn't in town?

A statement doesn't require (need) an answer. A question *does* require an answer.

A. CHANGING STATEMENTS INTO QUESTIONS Listen to each sentence. Is it a statement or a question? Circle *Statement* or *Question*.

1. Statement   Question   5. Statement   Question

2. Statement   Question   6. Statement   Question

3. Statement   Question   7. Statement   Question

4. Statement   Question   8. Statement   Question

LANGUAGE FUNCTIONS

Agreeing with Negative Questions

In many languages, when people agree with a negative question, they say "yes" because they're thinking: "Yes. That's correct." However, in English, the answer is "no."

Example: **A:** Mr. Jensen **isn't** in town?
B: No. (= Mr. Jensen isn't in town.)

After this "no," it's possible to add a short answer.

Examples: **A:** Mr. Jensen **isn't** in town?
B: No, he isn't.

A: You **don't have** a pet?
B: No, I don't.

It's also helpful to add more information.

Examples: **A:** Mr. Jensen **isn't** in town?
B: No, he's not. He's away on vacation.

A: You **don't have** a pet?
B: No. I'm allergic to dogs and cats.

A: You **don't like** cats?
B: No, I don't. They're too independent.

B. AGREEING WITH NEGATIVE QUESTIONS Work with a partner. One of you is Student A, and the other is Student B. Take turns asking the negative questions in the boxes below. Agree and use "no" in your responses.

Example: **A:** You don't know them?
                B: No, I don't.

Student A

Ask Student B these questions. Make sure that your voice goes up at the end.

• Today isn't Sunday?
• You're not from Alaska?
• Mark can't speak Swahili?
• Jessica and Bill aren't here yet?
• I shouldn't try it?
• Linda won't be able to do it?

Answer Student B's questions. Agree and use a short answer. You can add more information.

Student B

Answer Student A's questions. Agree and use a short answer. You can add more information.

Ask Student A these questions. Make sure that your voice goes up at the end.

• Jodi doesn't like dogs?
• You didn't find it?
• You haven't taken Biology 121?
• You haven't seen my book?
• You don't know Kevin?
• Barry doesn't have a cat?

🎧 Disagreeing with Negative Questions

Sometimes the person who asks a negative question is incorrect, so the other person disagrees. In this case, the answer is "yes." It's important to use emphasis in the voice. Notice the intonation in these questions and the emphasis in the answers.

Examples: **A:** You mean you **don't like** cats?
                B: Yes, I *do*. I *love* cats.

                A: Tom **isn't** in your biology class?
                B: Yes, he *is*. He sits next to me.

                A: You **didn't see** that movie?
                B: Yes, we *did*.

                A: Kelly **can't speak** English?
                B: Yes, she *can*.

                A: Jim and Ali **won't be** able to do it?
                B: Yes, they *will*.

The emphasis in the voice is important. Without it, the meaning is unclear.

C. DISAGREEING WITH NEGATIVE QUESTIONS With the same partner you worked with in Activity B, go back to page 95. Do Activity B again. This time, *dis*agree (and use a short answer).

Example: **A:** You don't know them?
B: Yes, I *do*. They live next door to me.

D. NEGATIVE QUESTIONS Think of five negative questions about the conversation you heard in Part 2. Then work with two other classmates. Ask them your questions. They will answer with the correct information.

Examples: **A:** Tanya isn't allergic to cats?
B: No, she isn't.

A: Brandon isn't allergic to cats?
C: Yes, he *is*.

PRONUNCIATION

🎧 Reduced Forms of Words

When people speak naturally, some words (and combinations of sounds) become reduced, or shortened. Here are some examples.

Examples:	Long Forms		Reduced Forms
	You'll like **him**.	→	You'll like **'im**.
	Don't call **her** tonight.	→	Don't call **'er** tonight.
	Is **he going to** live here?	→	Is **'e gonna** live here?
	I've **got to** get **out of** here.	→	I **gotta** get **outta** here.

🎧 **E. REDUCED FORMS OF WORDS** Listen to the conversation. You'll hear the reduced forms of some words. Write the *long* forms on the lines.

A: Are you _____ take Biology 121 next term?
1

B: I might. Is Dr. Hurst teaching it?

A: Yeah, I think so. You'll like _____ .
2

B: Well, Brandon says she's really hard.

A: Oh, don't listen to _____ . Besides, you know, you've
3

_____ take it before you take Biology 152. And it's a required class. You
4

can't get _____ taking it some time.
5

WORDS IN PHRASES

 Expressions of Disbelief and Skepticism

Speakers use certain expressions when they don't believe something or when they are skeptical (unsure) of something. Some of these expressions are:

Oh, come on.
You're kidding.
I don't believe that.

You're joking.
You've got to be kidding. (pronounced *gotta*)
I don't buy that at all.

Example: **A:** I'm not going to study for the test.
B: Oh, come on. Dr. Hendersen said it was 15 pages long!

Note: These expressions are informal. You probably should not use them with an employer or professor.

PUT IT TOGETHER

 Step 1

Work with a partner. Write seven short negative sentences that you *think* are true. These can be sentences about your partner, class, school, or city, or something in the news.

Examples: You aren't from Madagascar.
The food in the school cafeteria isn't very good.
You don't want to stay in this city.

Step 2

Read one of your negative sentences to your partner as a *question*. (Make sure that your voice goes up at the end.) Your partner will agree (or disagree) and add a short answer. Then your partner will read a negative sentence to you. Take turns asking and answering questions with your partner. If you don't believe your partner's answer, express skepticism with one of the phrases from the box above.

Examples: **A:** You aren't from Madagascar?
B: No, I'm not.

B: The food in the school cafeteria isn't very good?
A: No. It's terrible.

A: You don't want to stay in this city?
B: Yes, I *do*.
A: You're kidding.

BEFORE LISTENING

Rico, a dog

Kanzi, an **ape**

A. THINKING AHEAD You are going to hear a radio program about language learning. Specifically, you will hear about new research with two animals—Rico, a dog, and Kanzi, an ape. Before you listen, check (✓) your answers to the questions in the chart below.

Which animals can . . .	Humans	Dogs	Apes
• learn new words?			
• **fetch** (go and bring back) things **on command** (when someone tells them to)?			
• remember a new word one month later, after hearing it one time?			
• have the **capacity** (ability) or **potential** (possible ability in the future) to learn grammar?			
• learn **syntax** (meaning that comes from the order of words)?			
• understand **novel** sentences—in other words, new sentences that they have not heard before?			

👥 Now in small groups, compare your answers.

B. VOCABULARY PREPARATION The words in the box below are from the radio program. Before you listen, read the words and their definitions. Then write the correct words on the lines.

Words	Definitions
acquired	got; received; learned
border	line that indicates the limit of an area (literal or figurative)
colleagues	people who have the same career
familiar	not strange; something or someone that you recognize
linguistic (adj.)*	dealing with language
prodigies	unusually intelligent young people with special talents
prompt (v.)	help someone by reminding them
remarkable	amazing; special
skeptics	people who are skeptical
workaholic	a person who works all the time

*(adj.) means *adjective*

1. Albert knows all the irregular verbs, and I don't have to _____ him at all.

2. Emma has amazing _____ ability. She speaks English, Japanese, and Thai.

3. Each of these children has a _____ ability to play musical instruments. The children are all musical _____.

4. I lived in Xenrovia for several years, but unfortunately, I never really _____ much of the language.

5. When you cross the *actual* _____ into Xenrovia, you also cross a *figurative* one in the way of thinking and culture.

6. His name sounds _____ to me, but I can't remember where I met him.

7. Don't be such _____! This might be surprising, but it's the truth!

8. After the meeting, Dr. Garcia met with her _____ for lunch. All they did was discuss work.

9. We'll have to *make* Steve come with us for his birthday dinner. He's such a _____! He'll probably want to stay at the office late to finish his project.

LISTENING

A. LISTENING FOR THE MAIN IDEA: SECTION 1 Listen to Section 1 of the radio program. As you listen, try to answer these questions:
- What does new research show us?
- What can Rico do?

B. LISTENING FOR DETAILS Listen to Section 1 again. As you listen, answer these questions. Write your answers on the lines.

1. What does Rico know? _____

2. How many toys could Rico fetch on command? _____

3. How many words has Rico added to his vocabulary? _____

4. When scientists asked Rico to fetch a new toy by using a word for it that he had never heard before, what happened? _____

   _____

5. On the graphic organizer below, where would you put Rico, based on his linguistic ability—in box A, B, or C? Write his name in one of the boxes.

```
                              ┬
        ┌─────────────────────┼─────────────────────┐
┌───────────────┐  ┌───────┐  ┌───────┐  ┌───────┐  ┌───────────────┐
│ No ability to │  │   A   │  │   B   │  │   C   │  │ Very          │
│ learn         │  │       │  │       │  │       │  │ complex       │
│               │  │       │  │       │  │       │  │ language      │
└───────────────┘  └───────┘  └───────┘  └───────┘  └───────────────┘
```

C. LISTENING FOR THE MAIN IDEA: SECTION 2 Listen to Section 2 of the radio program. As you listen, try to answer this question:
• What can animals learn?

D. LISTENING FOR DETAILS Listen to Section 2 again. As you listen, answer these questions.

1. On the graphic organizer above, where would you put Kanzi, based on his linguistic ability? Write his name in one of the boxes.

2. What can Kanzi understand or do? Write four things on the lines. (Listen to Section 2 several times if necessary.)

   _____

   _____

   _____

   _____

Critical Thinking Strategy

Making Inferences

When you listen, it's important to be able **to make inferences**–to understand things that speakers don't say directly–because a lot of information is indirect.

Example: **You hear:** "If any dog could learn new words the way children do, it would be Rico."
You infer: People knew that Rico was very smart even before they began to teach him vocabulary.

Use both the information that you hear *and* your own logic to make inferences.

E. MAKING INFERENCES Listen to one short part of Section 2 again. As you listen, answer these questions.

1. What kind of animal is a bonobo? _____

2. Did Kanzi actually put the pine needles ("leaves" from a pine tree) in the refrigerator? How do you

know? _____

_____

AFTER LISTENING

A. DISCUSSION In small groups, discuss these questions.

1. Were you surprised by anything in the radio program? If so, what?

2. You heard that "A month later, Rico was able to remember a new toy's name about half the time even though he'd heard the word only once." Are you able to do this with new words in English?

3. Approximately how many words in English do you know?

4. What are ways in which you learn new vocabulary in English? Which ways work well for you? Which ways don't work well?

B. EXTENSION Do an Internet search. Follow these steps.

1. Choose one of the animals from the chart below. Each animal is learning some form of language from scientists.

2. Read about the animal that you chose. What scientist(s) are working with the animal? What can the animal do? What has the animal learned? Go to a search engine. Use key words to find this information about the animal. Write notes in the chart below.

3. In small groups, share what you've learned.

4. Listen to your group members and take notes in the chart about the animals they chose.

Animals	Species	Scientist(s)	What the Animals Can Do or Have Learned
Kanzi	bonobo		
Alex	parrot		
Washoe	chimpanzee		
Koko	gorilla		

BEFORE LISTENING

Listening Strategy

Previewing: Thinking Before Listening

Before you listen to a lecture, think about the topic for a few minutes. Do you have any ideas or opinions about this topic? Thinking about the topic before you listen will help you to focus more and to understand the lecture better. *While* you listen to the lecture, ask yourself: Are my ideas right or wrong?

Example: Before listening to the lecture in Chapter 1, you probably wondered, "What advice will the counselor give?" Then you listened to the lecture. You were probably surprised to hear that the counselor believes that the most important key to academic success is knowing the college culture and environment.

A. PREVIEWING: THINKING BEFORE LISTENING You're going to hear a lecture about humans and non-human animals. To prepare for the lecture, discuss the questions below with a partner.

1. In your opinion, are humans a kind of animal?

2. Do you feel **insulted** (bothered and a little angry) when scientists call humans "animals"? Explain your answer.

3. You know that humans can learn things. Can *other* animals learn to do things, or do they do them by instinct (naturally, without learning)?

4. In your opinion, can (non-human) animals do any of the following?
   - feel emotion (if so, which emotions?)
   - use tools
   - make tools
   - learn language

5. In your opinion, what makes humans different from other animals? In what ways are they similar?

6. The lecturer mentions the animals in the pictures below. What do you know about them?

A **sea otter**

A **monkey**

Speaking Strategy

Using Nonverbal Communication

When we communicate, we don't always use words. We sometimes "speak" without words. We often express meaning through **nonverbal communication**–communication with our hands, face, and body. (*Nonverbal* means "without words.") Types of nonverbal communication are:

Body language = the way that people move (for communication)
Hand gestures = specific body language that uses the hands for communication
Facial expressions = specific body language that uses the face for communication

B. USING NONVERBAL COMMUNICATION Work with a partner. *Without words*, communicate at least six of the emotions or ideas in the box below to your partner. Use only body language, hand gestures, and facial expressions. Do not use words. Your partner will guess your emotion or idea. Then exchange roles.

Yes.	No.
I don't know.	I'm confused.
I'm bored.	Please, sit down.
Stop!	I'm angry.
Really??!!!?!!!	That's crazy.
I'm surprised.	I absolutely refuse to do that.
I'm very interested in what you're saying.	I don't like this exercise.
Would you like to go and have something to eat?	I'm hungry.

Listening Strategy

Knowing When to Take Notes

It's important to take good notes during a lecture because exam questions will come from both the reading *and* the lectures. Some students just sit and listen, but this is a bad idea. Try following these suggestions.

• Write down everything that the professor puts on the board. Copy spelling correctly.
• Take notes whenever the professor says something more than one time, emphasizes a word or sentence, and seems to get excited about something (even if you don't understand why).

C. KNOWING WHEN TO TAKE NOTES There are different ways to take notes. In Chapters 1 and 2, you took notes on a T-chart and in outline form. For the lecture in this chapter, you will take notes on a different kind of graphic organizer: a chart.

Look over the chart on page 105. What kinds of information will you write down? What words do you expect the speaker to explain?

LISTENING

🎙️🎧 **A. TAKING NOTES** Listen to the lecture. It's in four sections. You will listen to each section twice and fill in as much of the chart as you can. Listen for the definitions of the vocabulary words. Write them at the bottom of the chart. Don't worry if you can't fill in everything. (You'll hear the whole lecture again later.)

As you listen, take notes to help you answer these questions:
• In what ways are humans and non-human animals similar?
• How are they different?

Areas	Humans	Non-humans
1.		
2.		
3.		
4.		

Vocabulary

wag:	galah:	branch:
slide:	grasp:	macaque:

Listening Strategy

Including Details in Your Notes

Many students take notes, but they don't write down enough **details**–small points. How can you know the amount of detail to include? Usually, you will have this answer when you take the first exam in a class. If you do well, you have probably taken good notes and studied them. If you do badly (although you studied), it's possible that you didn't put enough information in your notes.

One kind of detail is an **example**. Examples support the speaker's main points. Sometimes an example helps a listener to understand the main points. It makes them clear. Listen for the words *for example* and *such as*, and write down what comes after them.

 B. CHECKING YOUR NOTES FOR DETAILS Before you listen to the entire lecture again, turn to page 105. Use your notes to help you answer the questions in Activities A, B, and C in After Listening (below and page 107). For any question that you cannot answer, you will need to fill in your notes as you listen to the lecture.

AFTER LISTENING

A. USING YOUR NOTES: CHECKING MAIN IDEAS With a partner, use your notes to discuss these questions:

- In what ways are humans and other animals similar?
- How are they different?

B. USING YOUR NOTES: CHECKING DETAILS Use your notes to find the answers to these questions. Write your answers on the lines.

Section 1

1. What are three examples of animals that seem to express emotion?

_____

2. What are the emotions?

_____

3. How do they express these emotions?

_____

Section 2

4. What is one example of an animal using a tool?

_____

5. What does it do with this tool?

_____

6. Who is the researcher who discovered this?

_____

7. Where did the researcher discover this?

_____

Section 3

8. What are two examples of animals learning something?

_____

9. What do they learn?

_____

10. Where does this happen?

_____

Section 4

11. What are three examples of animals who are learning language? (Names? Species?)

_____

_____

12. What are examples of original words or sentences that they have created?

_____

_____

C. USING YOUR NOTES: CHECKING VOCABULARY The lecturer used these words in the lecture. Without using a dictionary, discuss their meanings with a partner.

1. The lecturer used words _and_ hand gestures to help with the meanings of the words. Using nonverbal communication, show what they mean. (If you are using the audio only, can you guess from the context?)

branch	grasp	slide	wag

2. Make inferences to complete the sentences below.

A galah is a kind of _____.

A macaque is a kind of _____.

Critical Thinking Strategy

Understanding a Speaker's Point of View

Sometimes speakers tell you their **point of view** (opinion; way of looking at something). The speakers may not say their opinion directly, but you can make an inference about it.

Example: Well, most of us who have been around domestic dogs, cats, horses, and even birds think that these animals *also* have emotions.

The speaker uses the pronoun *us*. The speaker includes himself in the group of people with this opinion about animals: animals have emotions. You can infer that it is the speaker's point of view that animals have emotions.

D. UNDERSTANDING A SPEAKER'S POINT OF VIEW Below are sentences from the lecture. Read them and answer the questions.

> Another very cute example of play behavior is from the Australian galahs. They slide down a wire.

1. Does the speaker think that animals can play? Explain your answer.

_____

2. Does the speaker enjoy watching animals? Explain your answer.

_____

E. MAKING CONNECTIONS Think about the research from the radio program in Part 4 and the lecture in Part 5. In small groups, discuss these questions.

• What general inference can you make about the animals in these studies?
• Are you surprised by anything that you learned, or do you think that science is now learning what most people have always believed?

PUT IT ALL TOGETHER

A. DOING RESEARCH In this activity, you'll study nonverbal communication. Collect information to discuss with your group.

Step 1
Choose *one* of the situations below for a homework project.

• Watch gorillas or chimpanzees. (You can go to a zoo or rent a nature video.)
• Watch humans. (Choose a place where you can see a lot of nonverbal communication—maybe a shopping center or public park.)
• Watch humans from a different culture. (You can watch people at an international school, at an international festival, or in a foreign film.)
• Watch a TV program with the sound on *mute* (silent).

Step 2
Watch your situation for 30 minutes. As you watch, pay attention to body language, hand gestures, and facial expressions. In Column 1 of the chart below, record everything that you notice.

Step 3
Try to interpret your notes. In your opinion, what is the meaning of this nonverbal communication? Put this in Column 2.

Example:

Column 1: Body Language, Hand Gestures, and Facial Expressions	Column 2: What Does It Mean?
One man hits another on the back. Both are smiling.	Congratulations? You did a good job?

Nonverbal Communication

Column 1: Body Language, Hand Gestures, and Facial Expressions	Column 2: What Does It Mean?

B. REPORTING RESULTS In small groups, discuss your project. What did you learn about the nonverbal communication in your situation? How much could you understand without words? Find classmates with the same situation as yours. How do your ideas compare?

CHAPTER 4

Nutrition

Discuss these questions:

- What is the man in the picture probably doing?
- Do you usually eat healthy food? Why or why not?
- How can eating healthy food improve your life? How can eating unhealthy food affect your life?

PART ❶ INTRODUCTION Nutrition Facts and Fiction

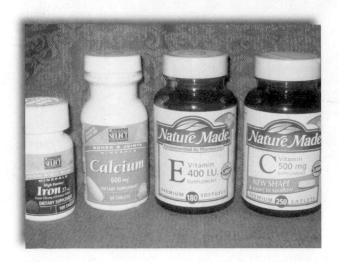

Vitamins and supplements

Foods with sugar

Foods with protein

Foods with fat

A. THINKING AHEAD You are going to read about **nutrition** (the study of food and health). Before you read, test your nutrition knowledge. Look at the photos above and read these statements. Fill in T for *True* or F for *False*.

1. Sugar causes disease.　　　　　　　　　　　　　　　 Ⓣ　　Ⓕ

2. Protein builds muscle.　　　　　　　　　　　　　　　 Ⓣ　　Ⓕ

3. You don't have to have a healthy **diet** (way of eating) if you take vitamins.　 Ⓣ　　Ⓕ

4. Eating fat makes you fat.　　　　　　　　　　　　　　 Ⓣ　　Ⓕ

1. Are your answers the same or different?

2. What are the reasons for your answers?

3. In your opinion, what are some **myths** (things that aren't true) about food and health?

C. READING Read about nutrition myths. As you read, think about this question:
• What are some myths about vitamins, sugar, protein, and fat?

Nutrition Myths

There are many myths about nutrition. Don't be confused. Become a critical consumer: read food labels and nutritional information carefully and learn about some common nutrition myths.

Myth 1: Vitamin supplements provide everything you need to
5 **stay healthy.**

The Facts: Vitamins alone can't keep you healthy. For example, they can't supply the disease-fighting **phytochemicals** (chemicals in plants that are good for the body) and fiber that fruits, vegetables, and whole grains have. The best way to stay healthy is to eat a well-balanced diet, enjoy regular physical activity,
10 get enough sleep, and try to reduce stress. It is not a bad idea to take a daily multivitamin and mineral pill to supplement your healthy diet. But keep in mind that more is not better. Large amounts of some vitamins and minerals can cause disease.

Myth 2: Sugar is bad for you.

15 **The Facts:** Many articles say that sugar causes everything from heart disease to diabetes. But this isn't true. Sugar can make some diseases worse, but it doesn't *cause* disease. Sugar is a simple carbohydrate—It provides energy. Many of the foods we eat contain sugar naturally, such as fruit, juice, and milk. Sugar is safe, but when it is added to foods like candy, soda, and other sweets,
20 it supplies "empty calories," calories that do not have nutrients. It also can cause tooth decay, so **moderation** (not using too much) is important.

Myth 3: High protein diets are necessary to build muscle.

The Facts: Heavy weight training (doing exercises with weights), not eating extra protein, builds muscle. Extra calories, especially from carbohydrates, help
25 with this type of training. This is because the body stores carbohydrates in the muscles for energy during exercise. Active people do need more protein than sedentary people, but they still only need 12–15% of their total calories from protein. Since active people—especially people who do weight training—eat more total calories per day, they will probably get more total protein per day.

30 Myth 4: Eating fat makes you fat.

   The Facts: The body **burns** (uses) fat for energy just like it burns carbohydrates and protein. You only store body fat when you eat more *calories* than you need. (It doesn't matter if the extra calories come from fat, carbohydrates, or protein.) Fat is a very **concentrated** source of calories; it has more than
35 twice as many calories per gram than either carbohydrate or protein. So a diet high in fat is more likely to be high in calories as well.

Source: Adapted from "Nutrition Myths 101" (The Regents of the University of California) "The data provided is researched and interpreted by health professionals at UCLA. Varying opinions may be held by others in the health-care field."

D. VOCABULARY CHECK Read the definitions below. Use the line numbers to find the words and phrases in the reading. Write the correct words and phrases on the lines.

<u>Definitions</u>   <u>Words and Phrases</u>

1. able to make judgments (Line 1)   _____

2. a diet that includes all types of foods
   that are good for you (Line 9)   _____

3. a compound in food that gives you energy (Line 17)   _____

4. compounds in food that help the body grow and
   stay healthy, for example, carbohydrates, protein,
   and vitamins (Line 20)   _____

5. keeps (Line 25)   _____

6. not active (Line 27)   _____

7. a type of measurement for small amounts of weight;
   0.035 ounces (Line 35)   _____

E. DISCUSSION In small groups, discuss these questions.

1. Look again at your answers in Activity A (page 112). Which were correct, according to the reading?

2. Did any information in the reading surprise you? What information? Do you agree with the information in the reading? Explain your answers.

3. What foods do you eat regularly? Do you think you have a healthy diet?

4. What ideas about healthy eating are common in your culture? What myths about healthy eating are common in your culture?

5. In your opinion, is it better to get vitamins and minerals from food or from **supplements** (vitamins and minerals in pills)? Do you take supplements? Which ones?

6. In addition to eating well, what other things can people do to stay healthy?

F. JOURNAL WRITING Choose *one* of these topics.

• Describe your diet. Explain what is (or isn't) healthy about it.
• Is it a good idea to take supplements? Explain your answer.
• Write about your favorite **ethnic food** (food from another culture, for example, Mexican, Chinese, Italian, or American food). What are some typical dishes? In your opinion, is it healthy?

Write about the topic for five minutes. Don't worry about grammar and don't use a dictionary. Just put as many ideas as you can on paper.

PART ② SOCIAL LANGUAGE Rachel's Health Plan

BEFORE LISTENING

 **A. THINKING AHEAD** You are going to listen to Ashley, Rachel, and Mike talk about food and nutrition. Before you listen, work with a partner to fill in the chart. Answer these questions:

• What do students in your school usually eat and drink? What kinds of food can you find on or near campus?
• Next to each item, write your opinion: Is it healthy?
• What nutrients are in it? For example, *protein*, *fat*, *carbohydrates*, *vitamins*, and *minerals*. If you're not sure, guess.

Food or Drink	Is it healthy?	Nutrients
orange juice	yes	vitamin C
hamburgers	not really	protein, fat

B. VOCABULARY PREPARATION Read the sentences below. The words and phrases in red are from the conversation. Match the definitions in the box with the words and phrases in red. Write the correct letters on the lines.

> a. to be honest
> b. in the end
> c. ingredients and cooking style
> d. plants for flavoring food or making medicine
> e. a spicy dish made from cabbage
> f. starchy foods (like bread, potatoes, cereals, rice, and pasta) that give the body energy

_____ **1.** Italian **cuisine** is supposed to be very healthy because it uses olive oil.

_____ **2.** Italian food is also good for you because it has a lot of **complex carbohydrates**, such as pasta.

_____ **3.** I use **herbs** to stay healthy, but do you really think they work?

_____ **4.** **To tell you the truth**, I really don't think herbs keep you healthy.

_____ **5.** Well, I never get sick, so maybe herbs do some good **after all**!

_____ **6.** Katy's mother was born in Korea, so Katy often ate Korean dishes such as *kimchi*.

LISTENING

A. LISTENING FOR THE MAIN IDEA Listen to the conversation. As you listen, try to answer these questions:
• Does Rachel worry about eating healthy food? Why or why not?

B. LISTENING FOR OPINIONS Listen again. Listen to Rachel, Ashley, and Mike's comments and opinions about some topics. Match the topic with comments or opinions. Write the correct letters on the lines.

_____ **1.** chili soup　　　　　　　　**a.** not too spicy

_____ **2.** chili pepper　　　　　　　**b.** give you energy

_____ **3.** fast-food tacos　　　　　　**c.** contains vitamin C

_____ **4.** gingko and ginseng　　　　**d.** healthy

_____ **5.** Mexican food　　　　　　　**e.** not spicy enough

C. LISTENING FOR DETAILS Listen to part of the conversation again. This time, listen for details about Rachel's health plan. Fill in each blank below with the word, letter, or number that you hear. Use the items in the box.

Words		Letters	Number
ginkgo	vitamins	C	1,000
energy	milligrams	B	
herbs			

Rachel: Well, I don't worry too much about eating foods that are healthy anyway 'cause I

take _____.
　　　　　　　　　　1

Ashley: Like what?

Rachel: Well . . . Uh, every day I take _____ milligrams of vitamin
　　　　　　　　　　　　　　　　　　　　　　　　　2

_____, and 1,000 _____ of E,
　　　　3　　　　　　　　　　　　　　　　　　　　　　4

_____ complex—
　　　5

Mike: That sounds like a lot!

Rachel: I take _____, too.
　　　　　　　　　　　　6

Ashley: Such as?

Rachel: _____, ginseng—
　　　　　　　7

Mike: What are those for?

Rachel: They give you _____ and help your brain, I think.
　　　　　　　　　　　　　　8

CHAPTER 4 Nutrition　　**117**

AFTER LISTENING

A. INFORMATION GAP Work with a partner. Student A works with the food label on page 203. Student B works with the label on page 207. Don't look at your partner's label. Ask and answer questions about the vitamins and minerals in the fruit drink. Write the information on your label.

B. DISCUSSION In small groups, discuss these questions.

1. What do you usually have for lunch?

2. Where do you usually eat lunch? Why do you eat there?

3. Do you ever eat at fast-food restaurants? Is the food good? Is it good *for* you?

4. What ethnic foods do you like? Can you get your favorite ethnic foods near your school? If not, where can you get them?

5. Is it a good idea to take supplements? Why or why not?

6. If you take supplements, how do you get information about which to take and how much to take? (From reading? From a doctor? From a friend?)

PART ③ THE MECHANICS OF LISTENING AND SPEAKING

LANGUAGE FUNCTIONS

Asking for More Information: Reasons

Sometimes in a conversation you need more information because you don't understand what someone says. One way to get more information is to ask for reasons.

Examples: **A:**   Real Mexican food is supposed to be very healthy.

           B: | **How come?**
               | **Why?**
               | **Why is** real Mexican food supposed to be very healthy?
               | **In what way?**
               | **In what way is** Mexican food very healthy?
               | **Why do you say that?**
               | **What do you mean?**
               | **What do you mean, exactly?**
               | **Excuse me. What do you mean?**
               | **Excuse me, but what do you mean by that?**

Which of the expressions above are informal? Which are formal?

🎧 **A. ASKING FOR MORE INFORMATION: REASONS** Listen to the conversations. On the lines, write the words and expressions that you hear.

1. **A:** Chili pepper is supposed to be good for you.

   B: _Why?_____

   A: It has a lot of vitamin C.

2. **A:** Eating too much sugar is supposed to be bad for you.

   B: Why _____

   A: It can cause tooth decay.

3. **A:** Weight training is more important than eating a lot of protein.

   B: _____

   A: It can help you build muscles.

4. **A:** I think gingko is good for you.

   B: What _____

   A: It can give you energy.

5. **A:** Eating fat can make you fat.

   B: Excuse me, but _____

   A: Fat has a lot of calories.

B. ASKING FOR MORE INFORMATION Listen to the conversations. Speaker A makes a statement. Speaker B asks for more information. Which questions are informal? Which questions are formal? Circle *Informal* or *Formal*.

1. Informal   Formal

2. Informal   Formal

3. Informal   Formal

4. Informal   Formal

5. Informal   Formal

Asking for More Information: Examples

Another way to get more information on a topic is to ask for examples. Here are some ways to ask for examples.

Examples: **A:** I take supplements.
             B: Like what?
                Such as . . . ?
                Give me an example.
                Give me some examples.
                Can you give me an example?
                Can you give me some examples?

You can also ask for examples by asking about the topic:

Examples: **A:** I take supplements.   **A:** I speak several languages.
             B: What do you take?   **B: What do you** speak?

 Which of the expressions above are informal? Which are formal?

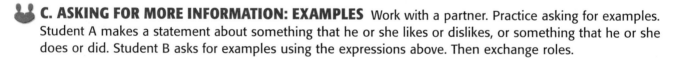

C. ASKING FOR MORE INFORMATION: EXAMPLES Work with a partner. Practice asking for examples. Student A makes a statement about something that he or she likes or dislikes, or something that he or she does or did. Student B asks for examples using the expressions above. Then exchange roles.

Example: **A:** I like to cook.
           B: What do you like to cook?
           A: I like to make Mexican food.
           B: Such as . . . ?

Giving More Information: Reasons or Examples

When someone asks you for reasons, you can use one of these expressions:

Because . . .
That's because . . .
The reason is (that) . . .

Example: **A:** I take a lot of vitamins.
   B: Why?
   A: Because I don't eat a well-balanced diet.

You can also give the reason without one of the expressions above. This is less formal than using an expression.

Example: **A:** I take a lot of vitamins.
   B: Why?
   A: I don't eat a well-balanced diet.

When someone asks you for examples, you can use one of these expressions:

Like . . .
Such as . . .
Well, for example, . . .

Example: **A:** I take vitamins.
   B: Like what?
   A: Like A and E.

 D. GIVING MORE INFORMATION: REASONS OR EXAMPLES Work with a partner. Student A makes statements about one of the topics below. Student B asks for more information, for reasons, or examples. Student A gives reasons or examples. Then exchange roles.

Examples: **A:** I like the food at the cafeteria.
   B: How come?
   A: Because they have a lot of ethnic food.

   A: I like spicy food.
   B: Such as . . . ?
   A: Such as *kimchi*.

Topics
• Food that's good for you
• Food that's bad for you
• Types of food that you like
• Types of food that you dislike
• Restaurants that you like
• Restaurants that you dislike

PRONUNCIATION

> ## 🎧 Reduced Forms of Words: Questions with *Do* and *Did*
>
> When people speak quickly, two or three words often become reduced. They are pushed together so that they sound like one word. Here are some examples of reduced forms in questions with *do* and *did*.
>
> | Examples: | Long Forms | | Reduced Forms |
> |---|---|---|---|
> | | **Why do you** want that? | → | **Whydya** want that? |
> | | **What do you** mean? | → | **Whaddya** mean? |
> | | **What did you** say? | → | **Whaja** say? |
> | | **Where did you** say you were going? | → | **Whereja** say you were going? |
> | | **Who did you** speak to? | → | **Whoja** speak to? |
> | | **When did you** leave? | → | **Whenja** leave? |
> | | **How did you** get here? | → | **Howja** get here? |

🎧 **E. REDUCED FORMS OF WORDS: QUESTIONS WITH *DO* AND *DID*** People say the reduced forms but write the long forms. Listen to the conversation. You'll hear the reduced forms of some words. Write the long forms on the lines.

A: _____Where did you_____ say you were going?
₁

B: I said I was going to get some lunch at the Student Union.

A: _____ want to eat at the Student Union? The food is terrible.
₂

B: I like the chili soup there.

A: _____ say?
₃

B: I like the chili soup.

A: _____ mean? That stuff's terrible!
₄

B: That's *your* opinion. I happen to like it.

WORDS IN PHRASES

Noun Phrases for Types of Food

Noun phrases are a combination of two or more words. In a sentence, they act like a noun. Noun phrases can be an adjective + a noun, or a noun + a noun.

When you learn noun phrases, it's important to remember the combinations of words *together*.

Examples: **Mexican food** is good for you.
            adj.   noun

            I like **health food.**
                 noun   noun

Here are some more noun phrases for types of food:

Mediterranean ⎫
Thai ⎬ food
Chinese ⎪
French ⎪
(etc.) ⎭

fast food
vegetarian[1] food
junk food

[1]**vegetarian** = without meat

 Which of the phrases above are adjective + noun combinations? Which are noun + noun combinations?

PUT IT TOGETHER

ASKING FOR AND GIVING MORE INFORMATION

In small groups, choose topics from the list below and talk about them. Ask for more information (reasons and examples) using the expressions in the boxes on pages 118 and 120. If possible, use noun phrases for types of food.

Examples: **A:** I like Indian food.
           B: Why?
           A: Because it's spicy.
           C: And it's good for you.
           A: What do you mean?
           C: It's got a lot of complex carbohydrates.
           B: Such as . . . ?
           C: Such as rice and vegetables.

Topics
• Food that's good for you
• Food that's bad for you
• Nutrition myths
• My favorite dish
• The best food is _____ because _____
• My favorite restaurant
• Food for a holiday or celebration in my culture
• My favorite junk food

PART ④ BROADCAST ENGLISH The Mediterranean Diet

BEFORE LISTENING

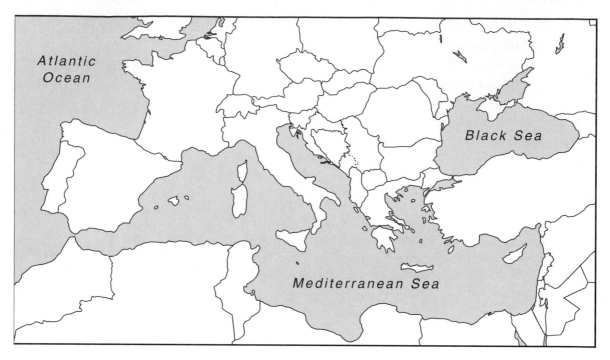

The Mediterranean region

A. BRAINSTORMING You are going to hear a radio program about the diet of the people in the Mediterranean region. Before you listen, look at the map. In small groups, write in the box below the names of the Mediterranean countries that you know.

Mediterranean Countries
Greece
Italy

Then think about the foods of the Mediterranean region. In the box on page 125, write the names of any Mediterranean foods that you know. Some examples are in the pictures on page 125.

Eggplant

Artichokes

Olive Oil

Garlic

Mediterranean Foods
eggplant olive oil

B. THINKING AHEAD Before you listen, think about the Mediterranean diet. With a partner, discuss this question. Write your answer on the line.

In your opinion, is the diet of the Mediterranean region healthy or unhealthy? Explain your answer.

Now test your knowledge of the Mediterranean diet. Which statements are true? Which statements are false? Fill in T for *True* or F for *False*. Do you and your partner agree on all the answers?

1. The Mediterranean diet includes a lot of fruits and vegetables.　　(T)　　(F)

2. It includes a lot of grains, such as pasta and bread.　　(T)　　(F)

3. It includes a lot of meat.　　(T)　　(F)

4. It includes a lot of butter and milk.　　(T)　　(F)

5. People who eat a Mediterranean diet seem to live longer.　　(T)　　(F)

C. VOCABULARY PREPARATION The words and phrases in the box below are from the radio program. Before you listen, read the words and phrases and their definitions. Then write the correct words and phrases on the lines.

Words/Phrases	Definitions
altered	changed
consume	eat
endorsed	approved
in abundance	in large quantities
incidence	occurrence; happening
intrigues	interests very much
life expectancy	the number of years a person is expected to live
linked	connected
safeguarding	keeping safe
sound	healthy

1. The Mediterranean diet _____ nutrition researchers. They wonder why the food of the Mediterranean makes people healthier than the food of other regions such as northern Europe and the United States.

2. Researchers have discovered that Greeks have a long _____. One study showed that they live about 10 years longer than people in the United States do.

3. Many people _____ more sugar than they should.

4. Some Mediterranean countries grow grapes _____. These countries are major wine producers.

5. Fruits and vegetables shouldn't be _____ too much; if you add sugar or salt or overcook them, they aren't as good for you.

6. Nutrition experts have _____ the recommendation to eat five servings of fruits and vegetables a day. They agree that it's a good idea.

7. There is a higher _____ of heart disease in the United States than in the Mediterranean region.

8. Avoiding stress is one way of _____ your health.

9. Mediterranean people have a very _____ diet. They eat a lot of fruits and vegetables every day.

10. According to "Nutrition Myths," eating sugar has not been _____ to any disease.

LISTENING

A. LISTENING FOR THE MAIN IDEA: SECTION 1 Listen to Section 1 of the radio program. Listen for the answer to the question below. Write your answer on the lines.

Why might people in the Mediterranean region be healthier than northern Europeans, Americans, and the Japanese?

_____

_____

Now compare your answer with a partner's answer.

B. LISTENING FOR DETAILS Listen to Section 1 again. How is life in the Mediterranean region different from life in other places? Check (✓) the things that describe Mediterranean people and those that describe non-Mediterranean people.

Descriptions	Mediterranean People	Non-Mediterranean People
have less stress	✓	_____
walk less	_____	_____
drive more	_____	_____
eat a lot of fat	_____	_____
eat a lot of vegetables	_____	_____
live in a clean environment	_____	_____

Test-Taking Strategy

Listening for Reasons

When you are listening to someone present an argument (a position or idea that he or she wants you to agree with) on standardized tests, remember that the reasons that support the argument are important information. Listen for facts, examples, **statistics** (information in number form), or **anecdotes** (stories). These will try to convince you that the argument is true.

C. LISTENING FOR REASONS Listen to Section 1 again. Why is the Mediterranean diet healthy? Listen for reasons and write them on the lines.

_____   _____

_____

Now compare your answers with a partner's answers.

D. LISTENING FOR DETAILS Listen to a part of Section 1 again. This time, listen for the names of foods that you can find at a Mediterranean market. Write the foods on the lines

_____   _____

_____

E. LISTENING FOR THE MAIN IDEA: SECTION 2 Listen to Section 2. Listen for the answer to the following question. Write your answer on the lines.

Why are Americans trying to eat a healthier diet? _____

_____

Listening Strategy

Listening for Numerical Information

Speakers often give important supporting information as quantities or statistics (numbers that represent something). Listen carefully for number expressions with the word *percent* and for fractions such as *one-fifth*.

Examples: Jane eats **two** servings of vegetables every day. **(Quantity)**
Thirty percent of Xenrovians are overweight. **(Statistic)**

F. LISTENING FOR NUMERICAL INFORMATION Listen to a part of Section 2 again. This time, listen for numerical information: statistics and quantities. Write the numerical words and expressions on the correct lines below. Use the items in the box.

fifth	five or more	two or less
~~50 percent~~	third	

Byar: All the way from the mouth on down through the stomach, and the colo-rectum, and also lung

cancer and many other internal organ cancers, uh, risk is reduced by _____*50 percent*_____ or
                                                                                                    1

so, for people who eat _____ servings a day of fruits and vegetables, compared
                                                       2

to many people who are out there who eat _____ a day. And I think that's a
                                                                               3

very important difference.

Host: With cancer now responsible for a _____ of all deaths in America, the
                                                                          4

fight against it is shifting to prevention. Scientists estimate that what we eat accounts for at least a

_____ of all cancers.
              5

Guessing the Meaning from Context: *Such As*

As you learned in Chapter 1 (page 27), you can often guess the meanings of new words from their contexts, the words around them. One way to guess the meaning of a new word is to listen for an example. The expression *such as* often introduces an example.

Example: Food that contains complex carbohydrates, **such as** pasta, bread, and cereal, can give you energy.

In the sentence above, the examples that follow *such as* (pasta, bread, and cereal) help you understand *complex carbohydrates*.

Sometimes the unknown word *is* the example. In this case, the explanation that helps you understand the unknown word comes first.

Example: The National Cancer Institute endorses plans for eating more fruits and vegetables, **such as** the "5-a-Day" recommendation.

In the sentence above, you can guess that the *"5-a-Day" recommendation* is a plan for eating more fruits and vegetables.

G. GUESSING THE MEANING FROM CONTEXT: *SUCH AS* Listen to some sentences from the radio program. Listen for the expression *such as*. Write the meanings of the words below.

1. chronic illness: _____

_____

2. antioxidants: _____

_____

AFTER LISTENING

A. DISCUSSION In small groups, discuss these questions.

1. According to the radio program, why is the Mediterranean diet healthy? Summarize the information in your own words. Then answer this question: Do you agree that it is healthy? Explain your answer.

2. How does your diet compare to the Mediterranean diet?

3. What other ethnic or regional diets (Chinese, Mexican, Japanese, Middle Eastern) are healthy, in your opinion?

4. What ethnic or regional diets are unhealthy, in your opinion?

5. In your opinion, what other diets are healthy or unhealthy (for example, vegetarian, low-fat, or high-protein)?

B. DISCUSSING YOUR PREDICTIONS Work with the same partner as you did for Activity B on page 125. Look at your answers for that activity. Do you want to change any answers about the Mediterranean diet?

PART ⑤ ACADEMIC ENGLISH Basic Principles of Nutrition

BEFORE LISTENING

👪 **A. THINKING AHEAD** You are going to listen to a lecture about nutrition. Before you listen, in small groups, discuss these questions.

1. What are the nutrients in food?

2. What is the connection between food and health?

3. What are some rules or guidelines about diets? In other words, what foods should we eat? How much of them should we eat?

Listening Strategy ◖◗◖◗

Previewing: Asking Questions Before You Listen

In Chapter 2 (page 75), you learned that it is a good idea to ask questions *while* you listen to a lecture. It is also a good idea to ask questions *before* you listen. This helps you to think ahead so you can focus on the lecture.

Example: You are going to hear a lecture about vegetarian diets. Before you listen, you might ask: What do vegetarians eat? Are vegetarian diets healthy?

B. PREVIEWING: ASKING QUESTIONS BEFORE YOU LISTEN Look at the outline for the lecture on pages 132–135 and think about your discussion from Activity A. What *don't* you know about nutrition? Write at least three questions about the subject.

Question 1: _____

Question 2: _____

Question 3: _____

C. VOCABULARY PREPARATION The words and phrases in the box below are from the lecture. Before you listen, read the words and phrases and their meanings. Then write the correct words and phrases on the lines.

Words/Phrase	Meanings
associated with	connected to
decreasing	making smaller
essential	important
profound	great
promotes	helps

1. Diet has a _____ effect on health. In fact, it is so important that everyone should understand the basics of nutrition.

2. Vitamin C is _____ to good health. Without it, you can become ill.

3. Protein _____ tissue repair: It helps tissue (such as the heart and the lungs) to heal itself.

4. Too much fat in the diet is _____ heart disease. In fact, many studies prove the relationship.

5. You can make your diet healthier by _____ the amount of salt in your food. A diet with less salt is better for your heart.

LISTENING

Listening Strategy

Getting the Main Ideas from the Introduction

You can get important information from the introduction to a lecture. In the introduction, lecturers often tell you the main idea of the lecture, including the topics that they will **cover** (discuss). When you hear the introduction to a lecture, listen for expressions such as:

Today, I'm going to discuss/talk about . . .
Today's lecture will cover . . .
This lecture is on . . .

Example: **Today, I'm going to talk about** the advantages and disadvantages of nutritional supplements.

A. GETTING THE MAIN IDEAS FROM THE INTRODUCTION Listen to the introduction to the lecture. Answer the questions below. Write your answers on the lines.

1. What is the lecture about? _____

2. What four topics will the lecturer cover?

   Topic 1: _____

   Topic 2: _____

   Topic 3: _____

   Topic 4: _____

Now compare your answers with a partner's answers.

B. TAKING NOTES: USING AN OUTLINE Listen to the lecture. It's in four sections. You will listen to each section twice. Fill in as much of the outline as you can. Don't worry if you can't fill in everything. (You'll hear the whole lecture again later.)

Basic Principles of Nutrition

Section 1

Introduction

I. Introduction to Nutrients

    A. Definition: substances from food, provide body with energy, help growth and repair of body tissues

    B. Classes of nutrients

        1. carbohydrates Examples: sugars, starches

        _____ (Purpose: give energy)

        2. fats Examples: oil _____

        (Purpose: _____)

        3. proteins—build _____

        4. vitamins _____

        5. minerals _____

        6. water

Section 2

II. The Connection Between Nutrition and Disease

    A. Nutrition plays a role in 4 of the 10 causes of _____

    _____

B. Diseases include heart disease, high blood pressure, diabetes, and _____

_____

C. The government has developed _____

_____

in order to _____

III. Dietary Guidelines for Americans

Salt and soy sauce contain sodium

A. Eat _____

B. Maintain _____

C. Choose _____

D. Choose _____

E. Use _____

F. Use salt and sodium only in _____

G. If you drink _____

Section 3

IV. Planning a Healthy Diet

A. Five food groups

1. _____

2. _____

3. Fruits

4. _____

5. _____

B. Diet planning principles

   1. Balance: eat right amount of foods from each group

   2. Variety: _____

   3. Moderation: _____

C. Smart food shopping

Legumes

   1. Read _____
_____

   2. Choose _____
_____

   3. Important fruits and vegetables are _____
_____

   4. Legumes are _____
_____

   5. Select lean meats, fish, and poultry, and low-fat milk products

Section 4

V. Nutritional Aspects of Ethnic Diets

A. The meaning of food

   1. people eat for pleasure; to be part of family and social situations

   2. culture influences eating habits

     a. eating traditional cultural foods makes people feel _____
_____
_____

     b. ethnic diets are characteristic of _____
_____

     c. the term *foodways* means _____

B. Mediterranean

   1. the diet includes _____

   _____

   2. most of the fat comes from _____

   _____

   3. people consider the diet to be _____

   _____

C. Chinese

   1. the diet includes _____

   _____

   2. it's low in _____

   and high in _____

   3. it's a good diet when _____

   _____

Source: Adapted from a lecture by Dr. Deborah E. Blocker, DSc, MPH, RN

Listening Strategy

Listening for Categories and Definitions

Sometimes you can predict when a lecturer is about to explain some very important information. Key words and expressions let you know that important information (such as categories and definitions) is coming. When this happens, you need to take good notes. Expressions that introduce categories include the following:

There are [number] types/classes/kinds of . . .
X is/can be divided into [number] groups/classes/categories

Examples: **There are two kinds of** dietary fat: animal fat, such as butter, and vegetable fat, such as olive oil.
Dietary fat can be divided into two classes: animal fat, such as butter, and vegetable fat, such as olive oil.

Expressions that introduce categories or definitions include:
X means Y
X is/are Y
X refers to Y

Examples: "Foodways" **means** the habits, customs, and beliefs people in a certain culture have about food.
The habits, customs, and beliefs people in a certain culture have about food **are** *foodways*.
"Foodways" **refers to** the habits, customs, and beliefs people in a certain culture have about food.

C. LISTENING FOR CATEGORIES AND DEFINITIONS Listen to the lecture again. Listen for the expressions that introduce categories and definitions or explanations. Write your answers to the questions on the lines.

1. How many classes of nutrients are there? _____

2. There are five food groups. What do foods in each group have in common?

_____

_____

3. What does *balance* mean in diet planning?

_____

_____

D. CHECKING YOUR NOTES Check your notes. Listen to the lecture again. Fill in any missing information.

AFTER LISTENING

A. USING YOUR NOTES In small groups, use your notes to discuss these questions about the lecture.

1. What are nutrients? Give examples of each type of nutrient.

2. What is the connection between nutrition and disease?

3. What dietary guidelines do government and other agencies recommend for Americans?

4. What should you consider when you plan your diet? (Think about food groups, principles, and shopping.)

5. What does *foodways* mean?

6. Describe the diet of both of these ethnic groups: Mediterranean and Chinese.

B. REVIEWING IDEAS Work with a partner. Look back to your questions in Activity B on page 130. Can you answer the questions now?

C. DISCUSSION In small groups, discuss these questions.

1. *The Five Food Groups:* The Five Food Groups is a program from the United States Department of Agriculture. The examples in the lecture are from the North American diet. Give an example for each food group from another culture or type of cuisine.

2. *Dietary Guidelines for Americans:* Do you agree with these? Do the guidelines seem international to you, or are they best for Americans only? Are these guidelines good for other ethnic groups? Explain your answer.

3. *Nutritional Aspects of Ethnic Diets:* The lecturer is critical of some aspects of ethnic diets. Do you agree with her, or is she mistaken, in your opinion?

Critical Thinking Strategy

Comparing Sources of Information

Sometimes you get information on a topic from more than one place. For example, you may get information from a professor and from a textbook.

Sometimes the information may not seem to agree. This is because specialists in certain fields often have different **theories** (opinions), or because ideas change over time. You may want to ask your professor about this. Or you may look for more information in other places. You should look for current information. You should look for information from experts in the field. For example, a recent book by a nutritionist should give correct information on nutrition.

 D. MAKING CONNECTIONS: COMPARING SOURCES OF INFORMATION Discuss these questions with a partner.

1. Both the radio program in Part 4 and the lecture gave information about the Mediterranean diet. Look at your notes. Look back at Part 4. Did the lecture give you any new information about the diet?

2. The radio program said that the Mediterranean diet was low in fat. The lecturer, however, said the Mediterranean diet was actually high in fat, but the fat was from olive oil. Read the following passage from a book by a nutritionist. What are your ideas about fat and the Mediterranean diet now?

> The Mediterranean diet has fat—olive oil. Research shows that olive oil is rich in a type of fat that does not raise "bad" cholesterol. "Bad" cholesterol is the kind that leads to heart disease. In addition, olive oil has a lot of vitamin E. This vitamin protects the heart from "bad" cholesterol.

 E. COMPARING SOURCE INFORMATION Do Internet research on the Mediterranean diet. Try to find the most current information on the diet. Compare your findings with the ideas and theories in this chapter.

Try doing a search with the following key words:

- Mediterranean diet
- Mediterranean diet latest research
- Mediterranean diet + fat

Make sure that you evaluate the source of the information that you find on the Internet. For example, URLs (website addresses) that include .edu may have better information than URLs that end in .com. This is because only .edu indicates that the website belongs to an educational institution such as a university. Therefore, the information may be more reliable.

PUT IT ALL TOGETHER

You are going to **collaborate** (work together) in small groups to create a meal that will both taste good to people from different ethnic groups and be healthy.

A. TAKING A SURVEY Talk to four classmates. Ask the following question. Write your classmates' answers in the chart.

• What are your favorite foods in each of these food groups?
  a. Bread, cereals, and other grain products
  b. Vegetables
  c. Fruits
  d. Meat, fish, poultry, and alternatives (alternatives are protein from plants such as soybeans)
  e. Milk, cheese, and yogurt

Breads, Cereals, and Other Grain Products	Vegetables	Fruits	Meat, Fish, Poultry, and Alternatives	Milk, Cheese, and Yogurt

Taking Turns

When you collaborate in a group, it's important to take turns talking. If you like to talk, make sure to give the quieter group members a chance to speak. You can help them by asking them for their opinions. If you don't like to talk, force yourself to make at least one comment. If you are shy, sometimes it helps to write down your ideas first, and then say them.

Here are some ways to help quiet group members have their turn:

Sam, what do you think?
Well, I've said enough. Sam, what's your opinion?
Let's see what someone else thinks. Sam?

B. CREATING A MEAL PLAN

Step 1

Form small groups. Share the findings from your survey. Make sure that everyone in the group has a chance to talk. Use the survey results to create a meal with dishes from each of the five groups. Choose dishes that your classmates like. Write a meal plan using the chart on page 140.

Step 2

List the nutrients of each dish on your meal plan. In other words, indicate the amount of protein, fat, carbohydrates, and vitamins and minerals in each item.

To find out the nutrients for the items on your menu, try the following:

• Use the nutrition information that appears on most food packaging in the United States (see the example at the right).
• Get the information from a book on nutrition at the library.
• Find nutrition information on the Internet. Here are some websites that might be useful:

  —United States Department of Agriculture http://www.usda.gov
  —British Nutrition Foundation
  http://www.nutrition.org.uk/
  —Nutrition Australia
  http://www.nutritionaustralia.org/
  —Health Canada
  http://www.hc-sc.gc.ca/hppb/nutrition/labels/

After you do the research, review your meal plan. Do you want to change some items for a healthier meal?

Nutrition Facts		
Serving Size 1/2 cup (56g)		
Servings per Container 8		
Amount per Serving		
Calories 200 Calories from Fat 10		
		% Daily Value*
Total Fat 1g		**2%**
Saturated Fat 0g		**0%**
Cholesterol 0mg		**0%**
Sodium 0mg		**0%**
Total Carbohydrate 41g **14%**		
Dietary Fiber 2g		**8%**
Sugars 1g		
Protein 7g		
Vitamin A 0% • Vitamin C 0%		
Calcium 0% • Iron 10%		
Thiamin 35% • Riboflavin 15%		
Niacin 20% • Folic acid 30%		

*Percent Daily Values are based on a 2,000 calorie diet. Your daily values may be higher or lower depending on your caloric needs.

	Calories:	2,000	2,500
Total Fat	Less than	65g	80g
Sat Fat	Less than	20g	25g
Cholesterol	Less than	300mg	300mg
Sodium	Less than	2,400mg	2,400mg
Total Carbohydrate		300g	375g
Dietary Fiber		25g	30g

Calories per gram
Fat 9   Carbohydrate 4   Protein 4

Nutrition label from a
package of pasta

Meal Plan	
Dishes	**Nutrients**

C. DISCUSSING MEAL PLANS Share your meal plan with the class. Have the class vote on the best meal. Discuss why it is the best.

UNIT ② VOCABULARY WORKSHOP

Review vocabulary items that you learned in Chapters 3 and 4.

A. MATCHING Match the definitions to the words and phrases. Write the correct letters on the lines.

Words and Phrases	Definitions
_____ **1.** acquired	**a.** get and bring back
_____ **2.** consume	**b.** way of eating
_____ **3.** detail	**c.** eat or drink
_____ **4.** diet	**d.** keep
_____ **5.** fetch	**e.** not active
_____ **6.** grasp	**f.** take and hold onto
_____ **7.** intrigue	**g.** got; received; learned
_____ **8.** maintain	**h.** animal that other animals hunt
_____ **9.** prey	**i.** interest very much
_____ **10.** sedentary	**j.** small point

B. SENTENCE HALVES Match the first half of the sentences with the second half. Write the correct letters on the lines.

_____ **1.** A person who is **skeptical**	**a.** will probably be very old someday.
_____ **2.** A person with a high **life expectancy**	**b.** is an expert who approves it.
_____ **3.** A **colleague**	**c.** isn't sure that something is true.
_____ **4.** A person who **endorses** a diet	**d.** lives through a bad situation.
_____ **5.** A person who **survives**	**e.** is a person in your profession.

C. HIGH FREQUENCY WORDS In the box below are some of the most common words in English. Fill in the blanks with words from the box. When you finish, check your answers in the reading on page 85.

asleep	curled	hit	hunt	ocean	swept
baby	female	hungry	male	park	terrible

Strange but True

In the early 2000s, something amazing happened in Kenya's Samburu National

_____. A young _____ lion adopted a baby oryx (a
        1   2

kind of antelope) as her own. Normally, oryxes are *prey* for lions; lions eat them. However, this lion

protected the _____ oryx from other predators. The oryx felt safe enough to
               3

rest _____ up next to the lion. The lion did not
       4

_____ and went _____ for many days because she did
       5   6

not want to leave the oryx alone, unprotected. Finally, after 16 days, when the young lion was

_____, the oryx was killed by another lion. However, since that time, the same
       7

young lion has never hunted oryxes, and she has adopted several other baby oryxes.

In early 2005, a baby hippo almost died in the _____ tsunami that
                                        8

_____ South Asia and East Africa. He was _____
       9   10

down a river, into the Indian _____, and then onto a beach. He survived, but
                              11

his mother did not. Baby hippos are very close to their mothers, so this little hippo looked around for

another mother. He found a 100-year-old _____ tortoise. They established a
                                        12

close relationship. They ate, slept, and walked together. If a human came close to the tortoise, the

hippo became very aggressive, apparently protecting his new friend.

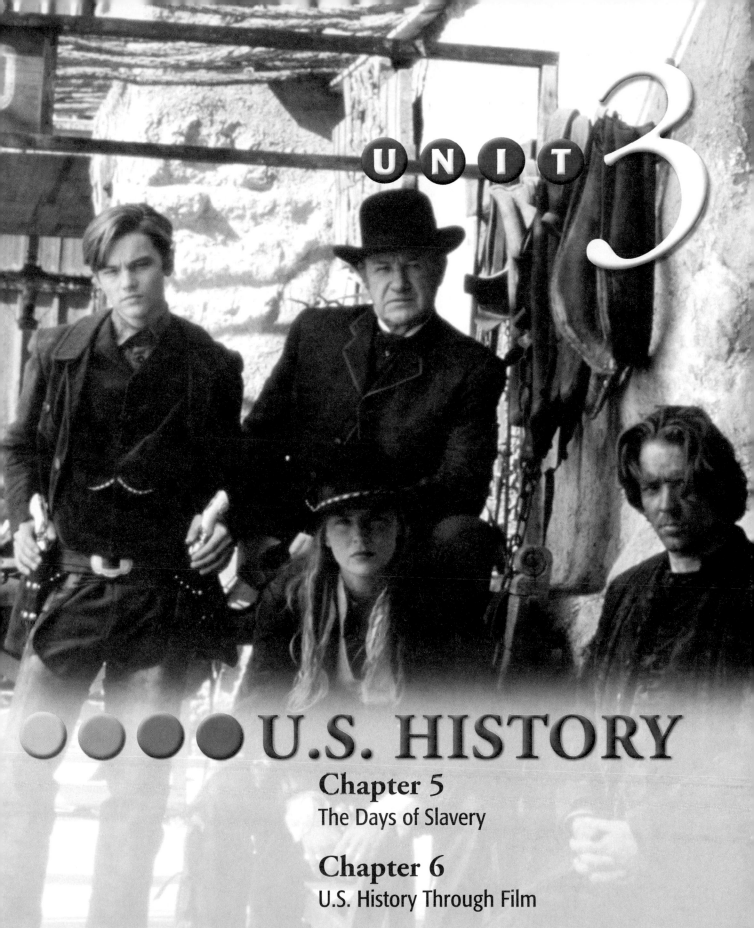

UNIT 3

●●●●● U.S. HISTORY

Chapter 5
The Days of Slavery

Chapter 6
U.S. History Through Film

The Days of Slavery

Discuss these questions:
• Look at the picture. Where are these people?
• What might they be doing?
• What do you know about slavery in the United States?

Slave traders kidnapping—capturing and taking by force—Africans, 1600s

Slaves working on a plantation, 1700s

A. USING PICTURES You are going to read about African Americans and slavery. Look at the pictures and read the **captions** (words that describe pictures) above. Discuss this question with a partner:
• What do the pictures tell you about the history of African Americans and about slavery in the United States?

B. THINKING AHEAD In small groups, share any other information that you have about slavery. Discuss these questions:

• In the past, what societies had slavery? When did it exist? Why did it exist?
• Does it exist anywhere today?

C. READING Read about African Americans and slavery. As you read, think about this question:

• What has life been like for most African Americans since the first Africans came to America?

African Americans and Slavery

The Beginnings of Slavery (1600s)

In 1619, a Dutch ship brought 20 Africans to the first American colony in Jamestown, Virginia. It's possible that these first African immigrants to the New World were indentured servants (people who agree to work for a period of time without money to pay for their trip to America), not slaves.

5   However, by the end of the 1600s, slave traders had kidnapped thousands of Africans. They brought them to the American colonies on crowded slave ships. There was little food. Many died. Those who survived had no freedom. They had to work without pay mainly on large farms called plantations.

Life Under Slavery (1700s–1800s)

Slavery was an important part of the economy in the American colonies,
10   especially in the South. Southern plantation owners used African slaves to grow tobacco and rice, so the cost of growing the crops was low. The southern colonies sold these crops in Europe and became very wealthy.

Enslaved African Americans had
15   terrible lives. Their owners could sell them at any time. They worked from sunrise to sunset. Children over the age of 10 did hard work in the fields along with adults. Most slaves lived in cabins with dirt floors.
20   Many slept on straw beds with only one blanket each. Ten to 12 people often lived together in one tiny cabin.

Slaves could not leave the plantation without permission. They could not learn
25   to read or write. Their owners could whip them for small mistakes and hang them for more serious ones.

A slave cabin

The United States became independent from Great Britain (England) in 1776. Although many Northerners did not have slaves and were against slavery, slavery was legal in all the Northern states. Many religious groups in the North, such as the Quakers and the Mennonites, were against slavery.

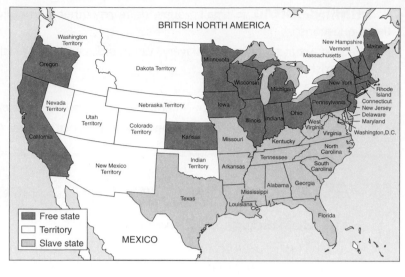

States with slavery and states without slavery in the early 1800s

Slavery became illegal in one Northern state after another. However, even free African Americans in the North experienced discrimination (unfair treatment). Southern states refused to end slavery. Their economies depended on it. In the 1830s, movements against slavery began. Nat Turner, a slave, led a violent rebellion in Virginia in 1831. Both abolitionists (people against slavery) and freed slaves helped to organize the Underground Railway. The Underground Railway was a system to help slaves escape to the North. Harriet Tubman escaped from slavery and helped others do the same on the Underground Railway. Frederick Douglass also escaped from slavery. For most of his life, he worked against slavery by giving speeches for abolitionist groups.

Abraham Lincoln, a northern Republican, became president in 1860. Lincoln did not believe in slavery. Many Southerners thought that Lincoln would end slavery. As a result, several Southern states seceded (separated) from the United States. This was one cause of the Civil War, the war between the North and the South. It lasted from 1861 to 1865. On January 1, 1863, during the war, Lincoln signed the Emancipation Proclamation. This law freed all enslaved African Americans.

The Civil Rights Movement (1950s–1960s)

Even after the Civil War, African Americans still experienced discrimination. For example, in the first half of the 20th century, African Americans in many parts of the United States could not go to the same schools as white Americans, could not buy homes in the same neighborhoods as whites, and in many states, could not vote.

African Americans fought for equality and civil rights throughout the 20th century. In 1955, a dressmaker named Rosa Parks was arrested. Why? In Montgomery, Alabama, she refused to sit in the back section of a city bus—the section for African Americans. Her arrest led to many other civil rights actions. One of the most important was the "March on Washington." In 1963, Martin Luther

King, Jr., a religious leader, led a march of two hundred thousand people from all over the country to Washington, D.C.

75   In 1964, Congress passed the Civil Rights Act. It made discrimination against African Americans illegal. In the South, African Americans still could not vote, and in 1965, Congress passed the Voting Rights Act. This led to many changes in the South. For example, by the 1970s, over 1,000 African Americans held public office in Southern states.

80

Source: *The American Journey* (Appleby, Brinkley, McPherson and The National Geographic Society)

The Civil Rights Movement: The March on Washington, 1963

Critical Thinking Strategy

Using a Timeline

A timeline is a kind of graphic organizer. It shows events in history in **chronological** (time) order. When you study history, using a timeline can help you identify and remember important events.

Here's one type of timeline: a horizontal line with dates on it. You put important events next to each date.

Event 1   Event 2   Event 3   Event 4   Event 5

1980   1990   2000   2010   2020

D. USING A TIMELINE Look back at the reading on pages 147–149. Complete the timeline of events in African-American history.

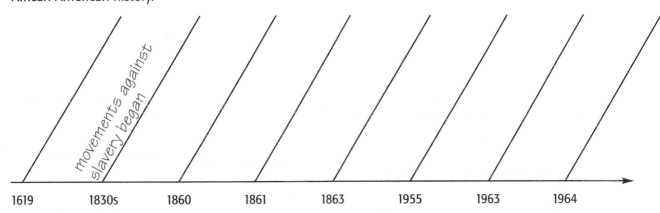

movements against slavery began

1619   1830s   1860   1861   1863   1955   1963   1964

E. VOCABULARY CHECK Read the definitions below. Use the line numbers to find the words and phrases in the reading on pages 147–149. Write the correct words and phrases on the lines.

<u>**Definitions**</u>   <u>**Words and Phrases**</u>

1. land controlled by another country (Line 1)   _____

2. stayed alive (Line 7)   _____

3. a financial system; a system of earning and   _____
   spending money (Line 9)

4. plants for food or other uses (Line 12)   _____

5. forced to be a slave (Line 14)   _____

6. needed (Line 47)   _____

7. a fight against a government or a powerful   _____
   organization (Line 48)

8. was held by the police for possibly committing a   _____
   crime (Line 68)

9. had political jobs; for example, were representatives _____
   or governors (Lines 82–83)

F. DISCUSSION In small groups, discuss these questions.

1. What important events took place in other parts of the world between 1619 and 1865?

2. What important events took place in other parts of the world between 1865 and 1965?

3. What societies in history have treated certain groups unfairly? Talk about them.

4. Is there a person in the history of another country who worked to end unfair treatment of a certain group of people? Talk about him or her.

G. JOURNAL WRITING Choose *one* of these topics.
• Write about anything that you know about slavery in the United States.
• Write about anything that you know about African-American history.
• Describe unfair treatment of a group of people in the United States or any other country, in the present or in the past.
• Describe a famous person from any country or time who worked to end unfair treatment of a certain group of people.

Write about the topic for five minutes. Don't worry about grammar and don't use a dictionary. Just put as many ideas as you can on paper.

PART ② SOCIAL LANGUAGE About That Assignment

BEFORE LISTENING

A. THINKING AHEAD You are going to listen to Chrissy talk to a professor. Before you listen, get more information about the antislavery movement.

Look for the answers to these questions:
• Who was *against* slavery in the United States?
• Who was *for* slavery? What were their reasons?

Follow these steps:

1. Get into two groups, Group A and Group B.

2. Read the paragraph in the box for your group only.

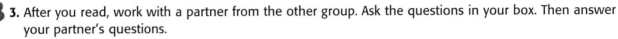**3.** After you read, work with a partner from the other group. Ask the questions in your box. Then answer your partner's questions.

4. Then share information as a class.

Group A

Read this paragraph. Use it to answer Group B's questions.

Northern Attitudes toward Slavery

    Some Northerners were against slavery, but not all. In fact, most Northerners discriminated against blacks. Some Northerners simply didn't want slavery to come to new parts of the country. Others had stronger feelings: They wanted all slavery to end. These people were called abolitionists. Free blacks, such as Sojourner Truth and Frederick Douglass, had even stronger feelings. They wanted not only freedom for black people but also equal treatment.

Source: "Northern Attitudes toward Slavery" (Drewry and O'Connor)

Ask someone in Group B these questions.
1. How did Southerners feel about abolitionists?
2. What were some of the reasons in favor of slavery?
3. What was one of the causes of the American Civil War (the war between the states)?

Group B

Read this paragraph. Use it to answer Group A's questions.

Southern Attitudes toward Slavery

Many Southern whites hated the abolitionists. Southern leaders tried to keep abolitionists and their ideas out of their states. Most Southerners favored slavery. They had many arguments for it. They believed it was necessary for the economy of the South and also for the whole country. They argued that slavery existed in many societies in the past. This difference between the North and the South about slavery was one of the causes of the American Civil War, the war between the states in the 1860s.

Source: "Southern Attitudes toward Slavery" (Drewry and O'Connor)

Ask someone in Group A these questions.

1. How did Northerners feel about slavery?
2. How did most Northerners feel about blacks?
3. What did abolitionists want?

B. VOCABULARY PREPARATION Read the sentences below. The words and phrases in red are from the conversation. Match the definitions in the box with the words and phrases in red. Write the correct letters on the lines.

a. examine carefully	c. part	e. strongly interested
b. geographical areas	d. presented in an organized way	

_____ **1.** The assignment asks you to **analyze** the causes of the American Civil War.

_____ **2.** Chrissy got an "A" on her presentation because her ideas were **well laid-out**.

_____ **3.** Most members of the antislavery movement were from the northern **regions** of the United States, especially New England states like Massachusetts.

_____ **4.** Some women were involved in the antislavery movement; in fact, many of them played a very important **role** in freeing blacks.

_____ **5.** Why were some women **motivated** to work against slavery? Perhaps it was because they were interested in women's rights.

LISTENING

A. LISTENING FOR THE MAIN IDEA Listen to the conversation. As you listen, try to answer this question:
• Why is Chrissy talking to the professor?

B. LISTENING FOR DETAILS Listen to part of the conversation again. Listen twice, if necessary. Listen for the answers to the questions below. Write your answers on the lines.

1. What class is Chrissy in? _____

_____

2. Why didn't Chrissy get the assignment? _____

_____

3. What time in history is Chrissy supposed to write about? _____

_____

4. Where can Chrissy get the information that she needs for her assignment? _____

_____

Now compare your answers with a partner's answers.

C. LISTENING FOR CATEGORIES

Listen to part of the conversation again. Listen for three different groups of abolitionists. Write the names of the groups on the lines.

Group 1: _____

Group 2: _____

Group 3: _____

Now compare your answers with a partner's answers.

AFTER LISTENING

A. INFORMATION GAP Work with a partner. Student A works on page 204. Student B works on page 208. Don't look at your partner's page. You are going to review the names of the people in the three different groups of abolitionists that Dr. Taylor discusses. Student A has some of the names; Student B has the rest. Ask and answer questions to complete your charts.

B. DISCUSSION In small groups, discuss these questions.

1. What new information about slavery did you learn so far in this chapter?

2. What new information about U.S. history did you learn so far in this chapter?

PART ③ THE MECHANICS OF LISTENING AND SPEAKING

LANGUAGE FUNCTIONS

Introducing Yourself to Someone Who Doesn't Remember You

Because people don't always remember names, sometimes you have to introduce yourself again to someone who already knows you. To reintroduce yourself, add extra information. Here are some examples.

Examples: Hi. I'm Dawn. **I'm in your history class.**
Hi. I'm Dawn Wu. **We met last week.**
Hello. **You may not recognize me.** My name is Dawn.

Responding to an Introduction

Sometimes a person introduces him- or herself again and gives you extra information to help you remember. There are several ways to respond to this kind of introduction. Here are some examples.

Examples: **Oh, yeah, sure.** Hi, Dawn.
Hi, Dawn. **How have you been?**
Oh, yes, hello, Dawn.
Hi, Dawn. **Nice to see you again.**
Oh, yes, Dawn. **I'm sorry. I didn't recognize you at first.**

A. LISTENING TO INTRODUCTIONS Listen to the conversations. Write the words and expressions that you hear on the lines.

1. A: Hi, I'm John. I'm _____.

　　B: Oh, yeah, sure. Hi, John.

2. A: Hello. You _____. My name is John.

　　B: Oh, yes, hello, John.

3. A: Hi. I'm John Martinez. We met last week.

　　B: Hi, John. _____.

4. A: Hi. I'm John.

　　B: _____.

5. A: Hi, I'm John. I'm in your English class.

　　B: I'm sorry. _____.

B. INTRODUCING YOURSELF Work with a partner. One person is Student A. The other person is Student B. Follow the directions in the boxes below. Take turns. Then exchange roles and repeat the activity.

Student A

Introduce yourself to Student B in each of the following ways.

Situation 1: You met him or her at a party last week.
Situation 2: You're in Student B's American history class.
Situation 3: Last week, you **bumped into** (accidentally hit while walking) Student B and all his or her books and papers fell onto the floor.

Student B

Situation 1: You remember meeting Student A at the party last week.
Situation 2: At first you don't recognize Student A.
Situation 3: At first you don't remember Student A, but he or she reminds you of what happened last week. Then you remember.

Identifying Yourself on the Phone

When you make a phone call, there are many ways to **identify yourself** (say who you are). Here are some examples.

Examples: **Hi. It's Maria.**
Hi. It's Maria Taylor.
Hello. This is Maria Taylor.

Which example above is informal? Which do you use when you don't know the person you are calling very well?

C. IDENTIFYING YOURSELF ON THE PHONE Listen to the phone conversations. Write the words and expressions that you hear on the lines.

1. **A:** _____?

   B: Hi. It's Dawn Wu. Is this Jim?

   A: _____, Dawn.

2. **A:** Hello?

   B: Hi, Jim. _____.

   A: Oh, hi, Dawn.

3. **A:** Hello?

   B: Hello. _____.

   A: _____, Dawn.

PRONUNCIATION

🎧 /I/ vs. /i/

Some students have problems with the sounds /I/ and /i/. They may not hear the difference between the two sounds, or they may not be able to pronounce the two sounds correctly.

Examples:

/I/	/i/
bit	beat
sick	seek
his	he's
live	leave
dip	deep
pick	peek
Sit down.	Have a seat.

🌏 What are the different spellings for the /i/ sound above? (These are the most common spellings for this sound.)

🎧 **D. HEARING THE DIFFERENCE BETWEEN /I/ AND /i/** Circle the words that you hear.

1. bit   beat

2. bin   bean

3. pick   peek

4. his   he's

5. pick   peak

6. sit   seat

7. it   eat

8. live   leave

9. dip   deep

10. mitt   meat

👥 **E. PRONOUNCING /I/ AND /i/** Work with a partner. Say one of the words in each of the pairs above. Your partner will underline the word he or she hears. Check your partner's answers to see if they match what you said. If they don't, try again. Then exchange roles.

👥 **F. PRONOUNCING /I/ AND /i/ IN CONVERSATIONS** Now use words with those sounds in conversations. Interview your classmates. Use the questions in the chart on page 158. If a classmate answers *yes*, write his or her name in the right column. Which student collects the most names?

Example: **A:** Do you like to read history books?
                B: Yes. I like to read about world history.
                A: Great. What's your name?
                B: Mark. M-A-R-K.

Questions	Classmates
Did you live on a farm?	
Do you like to read history books?	
Do you remember the dates of the American Civil War?	
Do you like the color green?	
Do you like to eat fast food?	
Do you like meat?	
Can you name one abolitionist?	
Do you stay home when you are sick?	

WORDS IN PHRASES

Verb Phrases for Meeting People

Here are some verb phrases (verbs + prepositions) for talking about meeting people, seeing people, and visiting people. They can be useful when you introduce yourself to and meet people. When learning verb phrases, it's important to remember the verb and the preposition(s) *together*.

Expressions		Definitions		Examples
bump into	→	meet unexpectedly	→	I **bumped into** Chrissy yesterday.
drop by	→	visit; come/go to without an appointment	→	**Drop by** my office after class.
drop in (on)	→	visit; come/go to	→	**Drop in on** my class sometime.
meet up (with)	→	meet; get together	→	Let's all **meet up** after class.
run into	→	meet unexpectedly	→	I **ran into** Rachel at school.
stop by	→	visit; come/go to briefly	→	**Stop by** my office after class.
stop in	→	visit; come/go to	→	I'll **stop in** to say *hello* later.

PUT IT TOGETHER

INTRODUCING YOURSELF Work with a partner. Take turns acting out these situations. One student is Student A; the other is Student B. For each situation, use the expressions that you learned in this part of the chapter. Remember to pronounce words with /I/ and /i/ correctly. Also, try to use verb phrases for meeting people. Then exchange roles.

Student A

1. You are an American history professor. A student comes to your office. You don't remember the student until he or she adds information.

2. You are an American history professor. A student comes to your office. You don't remember him or her at all.

3. You need to ask a classmate about something from yesterday's history assignment. You spoke to the person one time before a class. Your classmate doesn't remember you and doesn't remember anything about the assignment.

4. You need to ask a classmate about something from yesterday's history assignment. You met this person at a party last week. Your classmate remembers after you add some information.

5. You call a friend that you know well on the phone and ask about yesterday's homework.

6. You call someone that you don't know well–your teacher–and ask about yesterday's homework.

Student B

1. You come into your American history professor's office. He or she doesn't remember you. You add more information about yourself: you came to his or her office last week. Then he or she remembers you.

2. You come into your American history professor's office. He or she doesn't remember you. You add more information about yourself. He or she still doesn't remember you.

3. A classmate that you don't remember at all asks you about something from yesterday's history assignment. You don't remember anything about the assignment.

4. A classmate asks you about something from yesterday's history assignment. At first, you don't remember anything about the classmate. Then you remember after your classmate adds some information. You remember the assignment was to read Chapter 3.

5. A friend that you know well calls you on the phone to ask about yesterday's homework.

6. You are a teacher. A student that you don't know well calls you to ask about yesterday's homework.

PART 4 BROADCAST ENGLISH
Music of the Underground Railroad

BEFORE LISTENING

Test-Taking Strategy

Previewing: Brainstorming Possible Vocabulary

If you know something about the topic that you are going to listen to on a standardized test, you might be able to prepare for listening by quickly brainstorming possible vocabulary about the topic.

Example: You think: The test section is on slavery. I may hear some words about slavery as I listen. Some words may be *plantation, master, fields, escape,* and *abolitionists.*

A. PREVIEWING: BRAINSTORMING POSSIBLE VOCABULARY You are going to hear a radio program about the Underground Railroad. Before you listen, study vocabulary about railroads. Answer these questions with a partner.

1. What runs on railroad tracks? _____

2. What does a **conductor** on a railroad do? _____

3. Why do railroads need tunnels? _____

B. BACKGROUND READING Read about a part of African-American culture—music called **spirituals**.

Spirituals

   Spirituals (or faith songs) are part of the folk tradition of African Americans. Spirituals express strong feelings. They express the religious beliefs of the

people. Many of these songs come from the days of slavery. African Americans sang spirituals in church. They also sang them in the fields. Some people think
5 that spirituals express the slaves' wish for freedom and escape. Some people even think that slaves used the songs to send secret messages about escaping. They think that the songs told about times for escapes and plans for escapes.

Many of the songs, however, also have a real religious meaning. For example, the song "Steal Away" talks about Judgment Day. On Judgment Day,
10 Christians believe that the dead will come back to life, and all good people will go to a better life in heaven. Many ideas of escape come from stories from the Bible, the holy book of Christians. For example, the people in the Bible wanted to escape from slavery in Egypt and go back to their homeland. Many slaves felt that this was similar to their own situation.

C. COMPREHENSION CHECK In small groups, discuss these questions.

1. What are spirituals?

2. What are some ideas about why people sang them?

D. VOCABULARY PREPARATION Read the sentences below. The words and phrases in red are from the radio program. Match the definitions in the box with the words and phrases in red. Write the correct letters on the lines.

> **a. give positive feelings**
> **b. last a long time**
> **c. level of meaning; part**
> **d. a political group that represents people of many races and backgrounds**
> **e. strong; clear**
> **f. staying with something for a long time; not giving up**

_____ **1.** Faith songs **are enduring**; people still enjoy them many years after they were first sung.

_____ **2.** The words in these songs have two meanings. When you know both meanings, the song has another **dimension** to it.

_____ **3.** When I hear old songs, I have very clear memories of my past. These **vivid** memories make me forget about the present.

_____ **4.** Many spirituals **are affirming**; in other words, they make the singers feel good about themselves and about life.

_____ **5.** **Perseverance** is the key to success. If you stop trying, you won't reach your goal.

_____ **6.** Jesse Jackson calls his organization the "**Rainbow Coalition**" because it includes people from different cultures.

LISTENING

A. LISTENING FOR THE MAIN IDEA: SECTION 1 Listen to Section 1 of the radio program. After you listen, write the answer to this question on the line.

What do Kim and Reggie Harris sing about?

_____

 Now compare your answer with a partner's answer.

Listening Strategy

Being Prepared for an Important Explanation

You often hear interviews when you listen to broadcast (radio and TV) English. Sometimes the interviewer will let you know that an important explanation is coming. He or she may even ask for an explanation. Listen for expressions such as these.

Examples: (Can you) give us a brief explanation of . . .
(Can you) tell us exactly what was . . .
(Can you) remind our listeners of . . .

B. BEING PREPARED FOR AN IMPORTANT EXPLANATION Listen to Section 1 again. This time listen for an expression that lets you know an explanation is coming. Then listen for the answer to this question. Write your answer on the lines.

What was the Underground Railroad?

_____

C. GUESSING THE MEANING FROM CONTEXT Listen to part of Section 1 again. You can guess the meanings of some of the words in the radio program from context. Listen for clues in the words around them. Listen for the following words and phrases and then guess their meanings. Fill in the correct bubbles.

1. "sheroes"

   Ⓐ a kind of song

   Ⓑ a female hero

   Ⓒ a railroad conductor

2. resources

   Ⓐ historical characters

   Ⓑ bodies of water

   Ⓒ money or other things of value

3. a role model

   Ⓐ a good person to learn from or to imitate

   Ⓑ a train conductor

   Ⓒ the movement of a train

4. code songs

   Ⓐ songs about water

   Ⓑ songs with a secret message

   Ⓒ short songs

D. LISTENING TO A DESCRIPTION Listen to part of Section 1 again. This time listen for the answer to this question. Write your answer on the lines.

What kind of person was Harriet Tubman, according to Reggie Harris?

_____

_____

_____

Compare your answer with a partner's answer.

E. LISTENING FOR EXAMPLES: SECTION 2 Kim and Reggie Harris explain how faith songs were actually codes that helped slaves to escape. Listen to Section 2 of the radio program and answer the questions below.

1. How was the song "Wade in the Water" a tool for people who wanted to get to freedom?

_____

2. Why could slaves sing these code songs even when the master was listening?

_____

3. According to an anecdote, Harriet Tubman sang "Steal Away" in front of her master. What did the master think the song was about? What was the song *really* about?

_____

_____

Harriet Tubman

Now in small groups, compare your answers.

AFTER LISTENING

A. DISCUSSION In small groups, discuss these questions.

1. How did faith songs help the people on the Underground Railroad?

2. What did you find the most interesting about the radio program that you heard?

3. Tell your group about some traditional songs that you know. Do they have codes? If so, explain what the codes mean and why you think the songs exist.

B. APPLYING INFORMATION Work with a partner. Look at the picture and read part of another spiritual below. It's a code song, like "Wade in the Water." How did this song help slaves who were trying to escape? (Hint: A gourd is a vegetable. In the past, people made bowls from gourds and attached sticks to them. They used gourds to get water to drink.)

". . . the river ends between two hills
Follow the drinking gourd
There's another river on the other side
Follow the drinking gourd. . ."

Now share your answers with the class.

The constellation Ursa Major, also called The Big Dipper

PART ⑤ ACADEMIC ENGLISH The Underground Railroad

BEFORE LISTENING

Routes of the Underground Railroad

A. THINKING AHEAD You learned a little about the Underground Railroad in Parts 1 and 4. Now you are going to listen to a lecture about it. Before you listen, think about the Underground Railroad experience. Imagine that you are an escaping slave. Then in small groups, discuss these questions:

• What is the best time of day to escape?
• Where will you get supplies (for example, food)?
• Who will help you escape?
• How will you feel?

B. VOCABULARY PREPARATION The words and phrases in the box are from the lecture. Before you listen, read the words and phrases and their definitions. Then write the correct words and phrases on the lines.

Words/Phrases	Definitions
denounced	strongly criticized
first-hand	personal; direct
the maximum distance	the greatest distance
network	organization; collection
raised funds	collected money
significant	important
supported	believed in and helped

1. The Underground Railroad needed money, so abolitionists _____ for the movement.

2. Abolitionists _____ slavery at public meetings. This helped people to realize how bad slavery was.

3. Escaped slaves' _____ experiences, such as Henry "Box" Brown's amazing story of his escape, helped change people's minds about slavery.

4. Ten to 20 miles was _____ a person had to walk daily on the Underground Railroad.

5. The Underground Railroad was a _____ of people who wanted to free slaves.

6. Harriet Tubman and other freed slaves _____ the Underground Railroad.

7. The Underground Railroad was a _____ part of the antislavery movement because both African Americans and whites believed in and helped it.

C. VOCABULARY PREPARATION: WORDS IN PHRASES Read the sentences below. The verb phrases in red are from the lecture. Match the definitions in the box with the verb phrases in red. Write the correct letters on the lines.

a. criticize	b. first appeared	c. get freedom	d. know how to get

_____ **1.** The term "Underground Railroad" probably **came into existence** in the 1830s.

_____ **2.** Ex-slaves such as Frederick Douglass took every chance to **speak out against** slavery at public meetings.

_____ **3.** Songs with secret messages helped escaping slaves **find their way** north.

_____ **4.** Both whites and African Americans worked to **win freedom** for enslaved people.

LISTENING

A. GUESSING THE MEANING FROM CONTEXT Listen to parts of the lecture. Listen for the following words and then guess their meanings. Fill in the correct bubbles.

1. conductors

  Ⓐ people who raised money to support the movement

  Ⓑ people who helped slaves on their journey of escape

  Ⓒ people who spoke out against slavery

2. Quakers

  Ⓐ a religious group

  Ⓑ another name for the Underground Railroad

  Ⓒ people who kept slaves

3. the Fugitive Slave Law

    (A) a law that said that all escaped slaves must go to Canada

    (B) a law that said that all escaped slaves must receive a job and a place to live

    (C) a law that said that all escaped slaves must be returned to their masters

B. TAKING NOTES: USING AN OUTLINE Listen to the lecture. It's in four sections. You will listen to each section twice. Fill in as much of the outline as you can. Don't worry if you can't fill in everything. (You'll hear the whole lecture again later.)

The Underground Railroad

Section 1

I. The Underground Railroad

    A. It helped slaves _get their freedom_ _____

        _____

    B. Not an actual railroad, but a _____

        _____

    C. The Underground Railroad began

        1. when: _____

        2. how: _____

Section 2

II. Groups Involved in the Underground Railroad

    A. Individuals

        1. _Former slaves_ _____

        2. Free blacks who were _____

        3. White _____

        4. _____

    B. Groups

        1. _Abolitionists_ _____

        2. _____

    C. Reasons that whites were involved: gave them a chance to _____

        _____

The Underground Railroad, by Charles T. Weber, 1850s

III. A Trip on the Underground Railroad

    A. Supplies: _____

    B. Time of day: _____

    C. Guides: _____

    D. Stations: _____

    E. When slaves arrived in the North, they _____

    F. Henry "Box" Brown's story: _____

    _____

Section 4

IV. The Significance of the Underground Railroad

    A. It was a way to _____ the system of slavery

    B. It proved that African Americans were willing to _____

    _____

    _____

Source: Adapted from a lecture by Frances Jones-Sneed, Ph.D.

Listening Strategy

Listening for Examples in Groups

You listened for groups (or categories) of individuals who were involved in the Underground Railroad when you took notes on page 167. It's also important to listen for the examples within these groups. In this case, the examples are names of people.

Names are important in history, but it is often difficult to write them when you hear them because they may be difficult to spell. Professors sometimes write names on the board as they speak. It's your job, however, to connect the names with other information, such as the group they belong to.

When you take notes on categories of information, it's a good idea to make a chart. Put the category name at the top, and leave room below for the information that goes in each category.

Example:

Northern States	Southern States
New York	Virginia
Connecticut	North Carolina
New Hampshire	South Carolina

 C. LISTENING FOR EXAMPLES IN GROUPS Listen to part of the lecture again. It's about the groups who were involved in the Underground Railroad. The lecturer gives examples of people in each group. As you listen, put each name in the correct category.

William Wells Brown	Francis E. W. Harper	Henry Highland Garnet
Harriet Beecher Stowe	Levi Coffin	Charles Lenox Remond
~~Frederick Douglass~~	William Lloyd Garrison	the Grimké sisters
Sojourner Truth	William Jones	Harriet Tubman

Former Slaves	Free Black Abolitionists
Frederick Douglass	

White Abolitionists	Quakers

Listening Strategy

Listening for Dates

On page 149, you learned that dates are important in history lectures, and you learned how to make a timeline. When you hear dates, it's important to listen for two things: What is the date? What happened on the date? A timeline helps you do this.

When you listen for dates, also listen for prepositions of time such as *in, on,* and *by*. They let you know that a date or other time expression might follow.

Examples: **In** 1803 (a year, month, or other unit of time)
By 1860 (= in 1860 or before)
On March 16, 1865 (on a specific day)
the time that the war ended (a general time)
during the 17th century (within a period of time)

D. LISTENING FOR DATES Listen to parts of the lecture again. Listen for the following dates. Listen for prepositions of time. Use the timeline to take notes on what happened at these times.

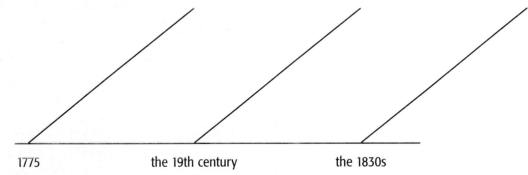

1775   the 19th century   the 1830s

E. CHECKING YOUR NOTES Listen to the entire lecture again. Check your notes. Fill in any missing information in your outline or your graphic organizers (the name chart and the timeline).

AFTER LISTENING

A. USING YOUR NOTES Work with a partner. Use your notes to answer these questions about the lecture.

1. When did the Underground Railroad start?

2. Why was it probably called a "railroad"?

3. Why were whites involved in the Underground Railroad?

4. What was a trip on the Underground Railroad like?

5. What happened when slaves arrived in the North?

6. Why was the Underground Railroad an important part of the antislavery movement?

B. MAKING CONNECTIONS In small groups, discuss this question.
• What information in the radio program in Part 4 and the lecture in Part 5 was similar?

PUT IT ALL TOGETHER

 Form small groups. You are going to give a presentation with your group. Your group will present information about a movement (such as the Underground Railroad or the abolitionists) that people started because they wanted to end a bad situation for themselves or another group. It can be a movement from any country, culture, or time in history.

You should include the following information:

• The background or history of the movement
• Important people in the movement
• The results of the movement: Was it successful? Why or why not?

Speaking Strategy

Working Cooperatively

Students sometimes must do assignments *in groups*. The best way to do this is to divide the assignment into separate tasks. Choose who in the group will do each task. Be honest about your interests and abilities. (For example, if you like don't like to talk in front of the class, offer to do research.) Then make a schedule. Be a responsible group member. Do a good job and do it on time.

Here are some examples of jobs that group members can have:

• leader
• researcher
• note taker
• time keeper
• speaker/reporter

Step 1

Brainstorm possible groups or movements to talk about. Choose one that most group members are interested in. Decide who will do which parts of the assignment. Here's one way to divide up the tasks:

Example:

Presentation Parts	Researchers	Speakers
1. The History	Victor	Evan
2. The People	Jennifer	Tanya
3. The Results	Brandon	Chrissy

Step 2

Do research on your topic. Do research in the library and on the Internet. Learn as much as you can. If you do Internet research, the following key words might be helpful:

- freedom movements
- human rights
- human rights movements

- civil rights
- civil rights movements

The following websites might also be helpful:

- Amnesty International
- Human Rights Watch

- National Civil Rights Museum

Step 3

Take notes as you do research. Organize your ideas. Use an outline like the one below.

I.   The Movement (name): _____

II. Background/History

Date	What Happened

III. Important People in the Movement

Name	Why Important/What They Did

IV. Results (Successful? Why or why not?)

_____

_____

_____

Step 4

Give your presentation to the class.

Speaking Strategy

Giving and Getting Feedback

Whenever you give a presentation or speak in front of others, it's a good idea to ask for feedback—information on how well you did. When you give feedback, it's a good idea to use neutral language and to make positive suggestions for improvement. When you do this, you don't hurt people's feelings and you give real help.

Example: Sam, I liked your presentation, but I think you could look at the audience more. Why don't you try this technique: Look at your notes, read one or two points, and then look up at the audience as you say them.

Step 5

After each group has given its presentation, take turns giving feedback. As a class, discuss these questions:

1. Were all areas of information covered (history, people, results)?

2. Did the group do enough research?

3. Was the information well organized?

4. Did the speakers speak clearly?

5. Did the speakers make eye contact?

CHAPTER 6

U.S. History Through Film

Discuss these questions:
- What do you think is happening in the picture? Who might these people be?
- This is a scene from a movie. What kind of movie might it be?
- Do you like to watch movies that take place in the past?

Far and Away, an immigration story

The Missing, a "modern" western

The Searchers, a classic western by John Ford

 **A. THINKING AHEAD** Look at the pictures. Discuss these questions with a partner.

1. Have you seen any of these movies? If so, tell your partner about them.

2. In what period of history does each movie take place? What might each movie be about?

3. What historical events are often depicted in movies?

B. READING Read about three films by the American director Ron Howard. As you read, try to answer these questions:
• What historical event does each film depict?
• What values does each film reflect?

Ron Howard's Vision of U.S. History

Introduction

The movies of any country reflect its values and tell its history. Any film in any country falls into a certain **genre**, or type. Some of these genres are **universal**—in other words, found all over the world. Comedies, dramas, musicals, and action/adventure movies, for example, are fairly universal. Some

5 genres are specific to a certain country, such as Japanese *anime*. Some films fall into more than one genre. Ron Howard is an American film director who works in several genres. The films that he has created are particularly American: they reflect both the values and history of the United States. Among them are two historical dramas and one western.

Far and Away

10 Howard's 1992 film *Far and Away* is one of his historical dramas. It is a romantic story of two Irish people who immigrate to America during the potato famine of 1845. At this time in Ireland, many families were dying of hunger. Potatoes were the most important part of the diet of poor Irish, and the potato crop had failed. Added to this, rich landlords required high rents, so many

15 people were left homeless. Because of these economic hard times, many Irish people were looking for a new country to settle in. In *Far and Away*, Nicole Kidman plays the role of Shannon Christy, the daughter of a rich Protestant landlord. Tom Cruise plays Joseph Connelly, a poor Catholic farmer, landless after his landlord **evicts** his family from their home. These two people, from

20 very different social classes, make the **journey** to America and meet in Boston.

The film focuses on these two characters through many terrible **hardships** as they follow their dream of owning land in the new country. At times, this seems impossible. Simple *survival* is even difficult. However, at the end, good wins over **evil**. The two characters come together over a piece of land in

25 Oklahoma, which becomes a **symbol** of disappearing **boundaries** (borders) between social classes. As with many American historical dramas, true love, hard work, and perseverance lead to a happy ending.

The Missing

The **western** is an action genre that generally takes place during the second half of the 19th century. It involves the opening of the **frontier**—the huge

30 undeveloped area west of the Mississippi river—to people coming from Europe. Typical westerns involve a cowboy (the hero) who saves a beautiful young woman—or perhaps a whole town—from the "bad guys."

Westerns were popular in the past, but by the 1960s, movie studios were not making them any longer. They almost didn't allow Ron Howard to make his film, *The Missing*, in 2003. It takes place in the American southwest of the 1880s. Its story is similar to a classic western from 1956 called *The Searchers*. In both movies, there is a kidnapping: the "bad guys" violently take a young woman from her family, and the hero goes off to find and save her. However, *The Missing* is different from traditional westerns in one way: the "hero" is actually a *heroine*—the mother of the missing girl, who goes on a long, difficult trip in search of her missing daughter.

Apollo 13

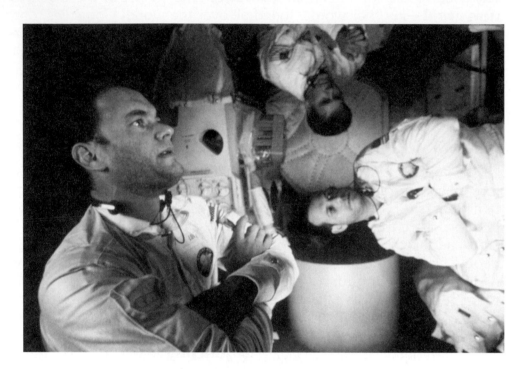

Photo from *Apollo 13*

One of Howard's historical dramas that takes place in more modern times is *Apollo 13*. It is the true story of a 1970 trip to the moon by three **astronauts**. Before they actually landed on the moon, there was an accident on the space ship. The three men were in terrible danger and almost died in space, before their return to Earth. In the film, the three men are the heroes who travel to the "new frontier"—space.

Like *Far and Away* and *The Missing*, *Apollo 13* is the story of a journey into a strange and dangerous place. All three films are about American history and reflect American values: honesty, **courage**, family, hard work, and perseverance. Of course, these values are not *only* American. They are universal. This may be why Ron Howard's films are popular in other countries, too.

C. VOCABULARY CHECK Read the definitions below. Find words and phrases in **bold** in the reading that match the definitions. Write the correct words and phrases on the lines.

Definitions	Words and Phrases
1. type or kind	_____
2. found everywhere in the world	_____
3. throws someone out of his or her home	_____
4. long trip	_____
5. difficulties	_____
6. bad	_____
7. something that represents or stands for something else	_____
8. borders or lines	_____
9. action film about the American west	_____
10. undeveloped area	_____
11. people who explore space	_____
12. being unafraid	_____

D. COMPARING AND CONTRASTING Look over the list of **themes** (subjects) and values in the box below. They are from the three Ron Howard films in the reading on pages 177–178. Match the words and phrases in the box to the correct films. Write them in the chart below.

courage	~~family~~	honesty
danger on a trip to the moon	a female hero (heroine)	immigrants to the U.S.
disappearing social classes	finding a family member	journey
the dream of owning land	hard work	perseverance

Far and Away	The Missing	Apollo 13	All three films
	family	family	

1. In what ways are the three Ron Howard films similar?

2. Do you know of other movies with the same themes or values? Which ones?

3. What films from other countries tell about historical events?

Speaking Strategy 🔵🔵🔵

Talking about Symbols

You read this sentence in the passage:

> The two characters come together over a piece of land in Oklahoma, which becomes a **symbol** of disappearing boundaries (borders) between social classes.

When you discuss topics such as films, poetry, art, or history, you often need to ask about or explain **symbols**–objects that stand for or represent something else.

There are several ways to ask about symbols.

Examples: What **is** the shared land **a symbol of**?
What does the flag **represent**?
What do the colors **stand for**?
What does an eagle **symbolize**?

The same words can be used to explain a symbol.

Examples: The shared land **is a symbol of** disappearing social classes.
The flag **represents** the country.
The colors **stand for** the blood of the people and the vegetation of the land.
An eagle **symbolizes** several countries.

Sometimes a symbol has a different meaning to different people.

Examples: **To Christians**, a cross symbolizes their religion.
A cross symbolizes the four directions **to Native Americans**.

F. TALKING ABOUT SYMBOLS Look at the chart below and think of what each symbol means to you. Then write one more symbol in the last row. Now ask three of your classmates their opinions of the symbols. Write their answers in the chart.

Example: **A:** What does a flag symbolize to you?
   B: To me, a flag symbolizes patriotism.

Symbols	Classmate 1	Classmate 2	Classmate 3
A star			
A tree			
A road			
Blue			
Red			
A dove			
A white flag			
Other:			

G. JOURNAL WRITING Choose *one* of these topics.

• One of the films from the reading
• Your favorite historical film
• Something that you know about Native Americans
• Something that you know about cowboys

Write about the topic for five minutes. Don't worry about grammar and don't use a dictionary. Just put as many ideas as you can on paper.

PART ② SOCIAL LANGUAGE Hollywood and Stereotypes

BEFORE LISTENING

The image of the cowboy as hero from
The Magnificent Seven (1960)

The image of Native Americans as "bad guys" in
Flaming Frontiers (1938)

More recent films such as *Dances with Wolves* (1990)
show European Americans learning to understand
the culture of Native Americans.

A. THINKING AHEAD Look at the pictures on page 182. In small groups, discuss these questions.

1. Have you seen any of these westerns—movies about the western United States in the 19th century? Have you seen other westerns? If so, which ones? Did you like them?

2. In old westerns, who were usually the "good guys"? Who were the "bad guys"?

3. How are recent westerns different from older ones?

B. GUESSING THE MEANING FROM CONTEXT Read the sentences below. The phrase and word in red are from the conversation. Find a phrase or word in the context (the sentences around the phrase and word) with the same meaning. Write it on the line.

1. **A:** So what movie should we watch? Maybe a mystery? Or do you **feel like** a drama?

   B: No. I'm not in the mood for a drama. Nothing serious. How about a comedy?

   Meaning: _____

2. They asked their grandfather for advice because he was very **wise**. He always knew the most intelligent thing to do.

   Meaning: _____

LISTENING

A. LISTENING FOR THE MAIN IDEA Listen to the conversation. As you listen, try to answer this question:
• Do Tanya and Jennifer agree about *Dances with Wolves*? Why or why not?

B. LISTENING FOR STRESSED WORDS Listen to part of the conversation again. In Chapter 3 (page 89) you learned to listen for stressed words. Put an accent mark (') over each stressed word or word part that you hear. When you finish, compare your marks with those of other students.

1. **Jennifer:** That's a sád movie!

   Tanya: Uh-huh.

2. Jennifer: This is the third time I've seen it, and I cry every time.

3. Tanya: You want some ice cream?

4. Jennifer: Ice cream? How can you think about ice cream now, after *Dances with Wolves?*

5. Tanya: Well, I'm hungry, and I feel like some mint chocolate chip.

6. Jennifer: You didn't think that movie was depressing?

7. Tanya: Not really. I mean, I know it was supposed to be sad, but I just didn't think it was very good.

8. Jennifer: But think about all those cowboy and Indian movies from the past. The cowboys were always the good guys; the Indians* were always the bad guys, and—

9. Tanya: True, but—

Jennifer: Isn't it nice to finally see the Indians as the good guys?

10. Tanya: I'm not sure. I mean, I know those old movies were pretty terrible. But this really isn't any better. It just takes away one stereotype and puts a new stereotype in its place.

*Many people use the term *Native American* instead of *Indian*.

C. LISTENING FOR A DEFINITION Tanya gives a definition of a stereotype. Listen again and then write her definition on the lines. You'll hear her definition twice.

Stereotype: _____

_____

D. LISTENING FOR EXAMPLES OF STEREOTYPES Listen for some stereotypes of Native Americans from old movies and from new ones. Write them in the chart. You'll hear the list of stereotypes twice.

From Old Movies	From New Movies

E. LISTENING FOR REASONS Listen to the conversation again. Jennifer thinks there is something good about the movie. Tanya thinks there is something bad about it. What do they think? Write your answers on the lines.

Jennifer thinks it's good because _____

_____

Tanya thinks it's bad because _____

_____

AFTER LISTENING

A. GATHERING IDEAS In small groups, prepare for a discussion about stereotypes of different groups of people. Think about these questions. Write down your ideas.
- What are some of the stereotypes of people in movies?
- Are they positive (good) or negative (bad) stereotypes?

B. DISCUSSING STEREOTYPES In small groups, discuss these questions.

1. What are some movie stereotypes of different groups of people? Are these stereotypes positive or negative?

2. In what ways are these stereotypes not realistic (or simply incorrect)?

Now report one of your stereotypes to the class.

PART ③ THE MECHANICS OF LISTENING AND SPEAKING

PRONUNCIATION

🎧 Verbs Ending in –ed

There are three ways to pronounce -ed on the end of a word: /t/, /d/, or /ɪd/.

1. After a voiceless consonant sound (/p/, /k/, /ks/, /s/, /tʃ/, /ʃ/), pronounce -ed as /t/.

   Examples: *rop**ed***   *pick**ed***   *ax**ed***   *kiss**ed***   *pitch**ed***   *wish**ed***

2. After a voiced consonant sound (/b/, /g/, /dʒ/, /l/, /m/, /n/, /ŋ/, /r/, /v/, /z/) or a vowel sound (as in *play*), pronounce -ed like a very quiet /d/.

   Examples: *climb**ed***   *wagg**ed***   *chang**ed***   *pull**ed***   *show**ed***   *play**ed***

3. When the verb ends in the /t/ or /d/ sound, the pronunciation of -ed is /ɪd/. (You need to add a vowel sound.)

   Examples: *start* → *start**ed***   *trade* → *trad**ed***

A. HEARING VERBS ENDING IN –ed

Listen to each past tense verb. Is the ending pronounced /t/, /d/, or /Id/? Use both your listening ability and the three rules from the box on page 185 to help you decide. Check (✓) the correct pronunciation. You'll hear each verb two times.

		/t/	/d/	/Id/			/t/	/d/	/Id/
1.	turned	____	✓	____	10.	saved	____	____	____
2.	dropped	____	____	____	11.	passed	____	____	____
3.	laughed	____	____	____	12.	repeated	____	____	____
4.	poured	____	____	____	13.	loved	____	____	____
5.	needed	____	____	____	14.	watched	____	____	____
6.	explained	____	____	____	15.	pointed	____	____	____
7.	joked	____	____	____	16.	looked	____	____	____
8.	agreed	____	____	____	17.	studied	____	____	____
9.	killed	____	____	____	18.	appreciated	____	____	____

B. REPEATING VERBS ENDING IN –ed

Listen and repeat each word.

/t/	/d/	/Id/
worked	worried	treated
crossed	answered	rented
washed	handled	sounded
fixed	climbed	listed

C. PRONOUNCING VERBS ENDING IN –ed

Work with a partner. Decide on the pronunciation of these words. Practice saying the words below and write /t/, /d/, or /Id/ on the lines.

____ 1. hoped	____ 8. wanted	____ 15. packed
____ 2. accepted	____ 9. covered	____ 16. pushed
____ 3. liked	____ 10. painted	____ 17. nodded
____ 4. happened	____ 11. traded	____ 18. thanked
____ 5. included	____ 12. carried	____ 19. represented
____ 6. played	____ 13. traveled	____ 20. toured
____ 7. called	____ 14. added	____ 21. listened

Now listen and correct your answers.

WORDS IN PHRASES

Giving an Opinion

There are several ways to express an opinion. Here are some expressions for giving your opinion:

I think . . .   It seems to me that . . .

In my opinion, . . .   If you ask me, . . .

Follow these expressions of opinion with an independent clause* to form complete sentences.

Examples: **I think** it was a sad movie.
It seems to me that the ending wasn't realistic.
In my opinion, there are too many stereotypes in movies.
If you ask me, they should make more modern westerns.

*An *independent clause* is a clause that contains a subject, a verb, and sometimes an object. It is a sentence in a sentence.

 D. WORDS IN PHRASES Work with a partner. Tell your partner your opinion about two of the topics below. Use the expressions from the box above.

- English spelling
- A popular movie star
- A recent exam in your class
- A good subject to major in

LANGUAGE FUNCTION

Agreeing and Disagreeing

There are various ways to express agreement. Here are some expressions for agreeing:

True.   Well, that's true.
Yeah.   I see your point.
That's a good point.   Yeah, I guess you have a point.

Example: **A:** It's good to see Native Americans as the "good guys."
B: **I see your point.**

Often when you don't agree with everything someone says, you still agree with one small point. Or sometimes, to be polite, you say that you agree before saying "but . . ." and then disagreeing. If so, you probably begin in the same way.

Example: **A:** It's good to see Native Americans as the "good guys."
B: **I see your point, but** it's still a stereotype. Nobody is *all* good or *all* bad.

 E. AGREEING AND DISAGREEING Work with a partner. Student A gives an opinion about each of the topics below. Student B agrees or disagrees using the expressions from the box above. Then exchange roles and repeat the activity.

- A good animal to have as a pet
- A wonderful food
- A TV commercial that you don't like
- A good way to learn English quickly

INTONATION

◯ Showing Disagreement with Intonation

People often say that they agree when they don't actually agree. They use the same words, but their intonation is different. You expect them to add "but . . . ." You can often "read their mind"—know what they are *really* thinking—from their intonation.

Example: **A:** It's good to see Native Americans as the "good guys."

　　　　　　B: Yeah, I guess you have a point . . .
　　　　　　　　True . . .
　　　　　　　　Yeah . . .
　　　　　　　　That's a good point . . .
　　　　　　　　Well, that's true . . .
　　　　　　　　I see your point . . .

◯ **F. UNDERSTANDING INTONATION** Listen to the conversations. Pay attention to the second person's intonation. Does this person truly agree? If so, circle *Agree*. Or do you think that this person will say "but . . ." and then disagree? If so, circle *Disagree*.

1.	Agree	Disagree	**5.**	Agree	Disagree
2.	Agree	Disagree	**6.**	Agree	Disagree
3.	Agree	Disagree	**7.**	Agree	Disagree
4.	Agree	Disagree	**8.**	Agree	Disagree

◯ **G. USING INTONATION** Listen again. Repeat the second person's response. Pay special attention to intonation.

PUT IT TOGETHER

GIVING AND RESPONDING TO OPINIONS Work with a partner. Follow the directions below. As you do this activity, remember to pronounce the past endings correctly.

• Student A gives an opinion about each of the following topics.
• Student B either agrees or disagrees. (Use the expressions on page 187.) Student B expresses the true meaning only with intonation.
• When you finish, exchange roles and repeat the activity.

Example: **A:** I think *Dances with Wolves* was a great movie.
　　　　　　B: Yeah.

Topics
• A current movie (choose one)
• A movie from the past (choose one)
• A current story in the news (choose one)
• An event from history (choose one)

• Irregular verbs in English
• A stereotype that bothers you
• Anything else (You choose!)

PART ④ BROADCAST ENGLISH
Hollywood Westerns Make a Comeback

BEFORE LISTENING

A **gunslinger** from a western movie

A **cop** from a modern **urban crime thriller**

A **knight** from ages past battling a **dragon**

A. THINKING AHEAD You are going to hear a radio program about westerns and how they are popular again, after many years of not being popular. In small groups, discuss these questions.

1. What **characteristics** (qualities or features) do gunslingers, cops, and knights share? How might they be similar?

2. Who was probably the **target audience** for westerns; in other words, who went most often to see these movies?

3. In the 1950s and 1960s, there were western films called "**spaghetti westerns**." What country might these be from? Explain your answer.

4. Why do you think westerns became less popular in the 1980s and 1990s?

5. Do you know any movie stars who were very popular in the past, then were not popular, then **made a comeback**—became popular again?

6. What are some movies that are **out** (in movie theaters) now?

7. Think about your family's **roots**—where your family came from. Did your grandparents and great-grandparents have urban or **agrarian** (farming) roots?

B. VOCABULARY PREPARATION The words and phrases in the box below are from the radio program. Before you listen, read the words and phrases and their definitions. Then write the correct words and phrases on the lines.

Words/Phrases	Definitions
box office	the financial success of a film (literally, the place at a theater where you buy tickets)
despot	a terrible and cruel ruler; a dictator
fading into the sunset	disappearing; used literally and figuratively (At the end of a traditional western, the hero rides off into the distance, toward the sunset.)
generation	all the people who are a certain age
romanticize	make something seem better than it really is
shootout	a fight with guns

1. Many people have a difficult childhood, but adults often _____ this time in their lives.

2. This project is _____. I'll have to look for a new job pretty soon.

3. Most of us use the Internet regularly, but our great-grandparents' _____ couldn't even imagine computers.

4. At the end of the movie, there's a big _____, and only the hero is left standing.

5. I loved that movie, but it failed at the _____. I guess most people didn't go to see it.

6. In the movies, the good guys fight a _____ who is causing trouble, and that solves all the problems.

LISTENING

A. LISTENING FOR THE MAIN IDEA: SECTION 1 Listen to Section 1 of the radio program. As you listen, try to answer this question:
• Hollywood westerns seem to be popular again. Why did they disappear for a while?

B. LISTENING FOR THE MAIN IDEA: SECTION 2 Listen to Section 2 of the radio program. As you listen, try to answer this question:
• What characteristic do cowboys and cops share with knights of old times?

C. LISTENING FOR DETAILS: SECTION 1 Listen to Section 1 again. Write the answers to these questions.

1. Who has always been the target audience for westerns? _____

2. Between 1903 and the beginning of World War II (early 1940s), how many movies were westerns?

_____

3. The director Walter Hill has made westerns that "failed at the box office." He has also "made other kinds of movies." What did he once say about *all* his movies? _____

_____

D. LISTENING FOR DETAILS: SECTION 2 Listen to Section 2 again. Write the answers to these questions.

1. How are cops like gunslingers? _____

_____

2. What is "the story [that] the western always tells"? _____

_____

AFTER LISTENING

A. COMPREHENSION CHECK Compare your answers in Activities A–D with a partner's answers.

B. DISCUSSION In small groups, discuss these questions.

1. Have you ever seen a western? If so, tell your group about it.

2. Are there any other film genres that used to be popular but aren't now?

3. What are some film genres that are popular now?

4. What are the target audiences (age? gender?) for different kinds of films?

BEFORE LISTENING

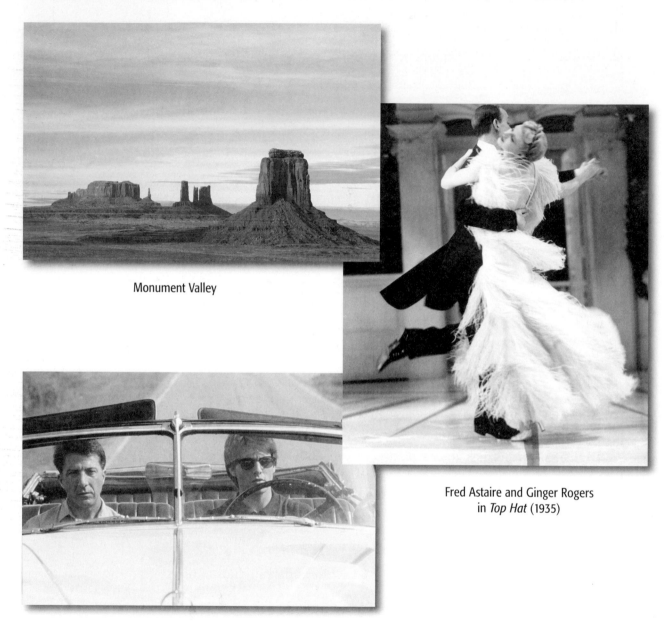

Monument Valley

Fred Astaire and Ginger Rogers
in *Top Hat* (1935)

Dustin Hoffman and Tom Cruise in *Rain Man* (1988)

👥 **THINKING AHEAD** You are going to hear a lecture about U.S. history as seen through film. In small groups, discuss these questions before you listen.

1. What film genres do you already know about? What are characteristics of each one?

2. Look at the photos above. What might the genre be for each?

Review: Taking Lecture Notes

When you listen to a lecture, it's important to take good notes and not "just listen." Even on standardized tests (such as the TOEFL® iBT), you need to take notes as you listen. To take good notes, follow these suggestions.

• Don't write complete sentences.
• Write anything that the lecturer repeats, writes on the board, or emphasizes.
• Write dates, names, and definitions of new words or terms.
• Take notes in various forms, depending on the type of lecture or part of the lecture. For example, you can use:
      –a formal outline
      –an informal outline
      –a numbered list
      –a graphic organizer, such as a chart or a causal chain
• Listen for signal words such as *first, second, third, next, finally*.
• Listen for important ideas. The lecturer often signals these with expressions such as *The point is that . . .* or *The main idea here is . . .*

LISTENING

🎧 **A. TAKING LECTURE NOTES: USING AN OUTLINE** Listen to the lecture. It's in three sections. You will listen to each section twice. As you listen, take notes in the various forms below and on pages 194–195. Fill in as much of the information as you can. Don't worry if you can't fill in everything. (You can listen to the whole lecture again later.)

U.S. History Through Film

Section 1

1. <u>New Term</u>   <u>Definition</u>

    _____ = _____

                                                    _____

2. <u>Characteristics of film in the same genre:</u>   <u>Meaning</u>

    setting _____ = _____
    theme _____ = _____
    period _____ = _____
    plot _____ = _____
    characters _____ = _____
    _____ = _____

3. Why is immigration a "natural subject" for American films? _____
    _____

Section 2

1. <u>New Term</u>   <u>Definition</u>

    the Wild West   where? _____

                         when? _____

2. History: What was happening?

Cause	**Effect/Cause**	**Effect**
railroad was built across the country		

land   gold   silver   adventure   no law

3. Four elements of westerns:

    _____

    _____

    _____

    _____

4. Three iconic images from westerns:

    _____

    _____

    _____

Section 3

1. **History:**

   Period: _The Great Depression_____

   Years: _____

   1. _stock market crashed:_____ (when?)

   2. _____

   3. _Prohibition =_____

   _____

   4. _W.P.A. (Works Progress Administration):_____

   _____

2. **Film Genres from the Great Depression**

Genres	Examples	Iconic Images
1.	*42nd Street* *Top Hat* *Singing in the Rain* *A Chorus Line* *Chicago*	
2.	*Public Enemy* *Bonnie and Clyde* *The Godfather*	
3.	*It Happened One Night* *The Grapes of Wrath* *Rain Man* *Thelma and Louise*	

B. CHECKING YOUR NOTES Before listening to the lecture again, read the questions on page 196. Use your notes from pages 193–195 to help you answer the questions. Then listen to the lecture again. Fill in any gaps in your notes and any questions that you left blank.

AFTER LISTENING

A. USING YOUR NOTES Use your notes to find the answers to these questions. Write the answers on the lines.

1. What is an iconic image? _____

_____

2. What are four film genres from the lecture? _____

_____

3. What are examples of iconic images from these genres? _____

_____

4. When and where was "the Wild West"? _____

_____

5. What happened during the period of the Wild West? _____

_____

6. When was the Great Depression? _____

_____

7. What happened during the Great Depression? _____

_____

B. MAKING INFERENCES Discuss these questions with a partner:
• Is the lecturer's style formal or informal? Why do you think this?
• What does the shootout in western movies symbolize?

Critical Thinking Strategy

Synthesizing

When you **synthesize** information, you put together information from different sources—for example, from both a textbook and a lecture. Often, you also need to analyze this information in a fresh, new way. Synthesizing is important on many academic exams.

C. MAKING CONNECTIONS: SYNTHESIZING In the radio program in Part 4, you heard from the movie director Walter Hill, who makes mostly westerns but has also made urban crime dramas such as *48 Hours*, *Streets of Fire*, and *Trespass*. He "once famously said that *all* his movies are westerns." What did he mean?

In a small group, discuss this question. Make a list of everything that you learned about westerns from Parts 1, 2, and 4, and from the lecture in Part 5. How are urban crime dramas similar to westerns?

PUT IT ALL TOGETHER

In this activity, you'll study iconic images in film.

Choose *one* project—Project A, below, or Project B on page 198. You can do Project A if the students in your class come from the same country. You can do Project B if there are students from different countries at your school.

Speaking Strategy

Taking a Survey

When you take a **survey**, you interview several people and ask them for information or for their opinion. Follow these suggestions:

- Open each interview by saying something such as:
  Hi. Could I ask you a few questions?
  Hello. Do you mind answering a few questions?
  Hi. I have a few quick questions for you. Is that O.K.?
- Listen carefully to their answers and record them on a chart.
- If they don't understand one of your questions, ask it in a different way or give an example.
- If you don't understand something, ask for clarification. You might say:
  Excuse me?   I'm sorry. I don't understand.
  What was that again?   Could you explain that?
  Could you please repeat that?
- If you don't agree, don't argue! There are no right or wrong answers on a survey.
- Smile and thank them for their help.

Project A

You will watch an American film and analyze it.

Step 1
Outside class, rent one of these films and watch it. You can do this alone or with a small group. If you work with a small group, you'll need to agree on a time and place to watch it. As you watch it, take notes. Write all of the images that you think might be iconic.

- *It Happened One Night*
- *Far and Away*
- *Top Hat*
- *The Godfather*
- *The Grapes of Wrath*
- *Dances with Wolves*

Step 2
After you watch the film, do an Internet search about it. (If you're working with a small group, each student should choose a different website.) Find an analysis of the film. You can use a search engine and type in the title of the film and the word *analysis*. (This might be called a "review" or "summary.") This analysis will explain something about the film. What can you learn? Take notes.

Step 3

Form groups with students who saw different movies. Tell them about the movie that you saw. Discuss these questions.

1. Who are the main characters? What are they like?

2. What do you think are some of the iconic images?

3. What does the film express about American history?

4. What does it express about American culture (what values are important)?

Project B

Your teacher will arrange for your class to interview students in another class. Ask them about movie genres and iconic images in movies from their cultures. (However, they probably don't know the terms *genre* or *iconic image*, so you will use other words.)

Step 1

Interview three students. Record their answers on the chart below.

	Student's Culture: _____	Student's Culture: _____	Student's Culture: _____
What is an important or very popular movie in your culture? (What is the title?)			
What kind of movie is it? (For example, a drama? Musical? Comedy?)			
What does it express about your culture?			
When you think of this movie, what image (picture) comes into your mind?			

 Step 2

In small groups, discuss your survey results. What movie genres are popular? In what cultures? What can you learn about the cultures from these movies? What are some iconic images?

UNIT 3 VOCABULARY WORKSHOP

Review vocabulary items that you learned in Chapters 5 and 6.

A. MATCHING Match the definitions to the words. Write the correct letters on the lines.

Words	Definitions
_____ **1.** boundary	**a.** very bad, morally
_____ **2.** evil	**b.** found everywhere in the world
_____ **3.** first-hand	**c.** long trip
_____ **4.** hardship	**d.** direct
_____ **5.** journey	**e.** subject
_____ **6.** perseverance	**f.** fight against the government
_____ **7.** rebellion	**g.** border
_____ **8.** region	**h.** determination; not giving up
_____ **9.** theme	**i.** difficulty
_____ **10.** universal	**j.** area

B. WORDS IN PHRASES Fill in each blank with a word from the box to complete the phrase. Use two of these words more than once.

into	office	out	target

1. Her father was the president of the country, but she has never **held public** _____.

2. I **bumped** _____ a friend in the supermarket yesterday.

3. The _____ **audience** for that film is between the ages of 18 and 25.

4. That movie didn't do very well at the **box** _____. It lost a lot of money.

5. More and more people began to **speak** _____ **against** slavery.

6. At the end of a traditional western, the cowboy **fades** _____ **the sunset**.

C. HIGH FREQUENCY WORDS In the box below are some of the most common words in English. Fill in the blanks with words from the box. When you finish, check your answers in the reading on page 147.

crops	especially	rice	slaves	terrible
dirt	mistakes	slavery	straw	

Life Under Slavery (1700s–1800s)

_____ was an important part of the economy in the American colonies,
          1

_____ in the South. Southern plantation owners used African
          2

_____ to grow tobacco and _____, so the cost of
          3   4

growing the _____ was low. The southern colonies sold these crops in Europe
                          5

and became very wealthy.

Enslaved African Americans had _____ lives. Their owners could sell them
                                                          6

at any time. They worked from sunrise to sunset. Children over the age of 10 did hard work in the

fields along with adults. Most slaves lived in cabins with _____ floors. Many
                                                                                  7

slept on _____ beds with only one blanket each. Ten to 12 people often lived
                    8

together in one tiny cabin.

Slaves could not leave the plantation without permission. They could not learn to read or write. Their

owners could whip them for small _____ and hang them for more serious ones.
                                                          9

APPENDIX 1: INFORMATION GAP ACTIVITIES

Activity G, page 34
Student A

Ask about the location of these buildings:

a. Beth's Health Spa

b. City Theater

c. Three Sisters Stereo Store

d. Northeast Senior Center

Example: **A:** Where's Sam's Store?

B: It's on Gareth Avenue. It's the second building from the corner.

Answer your partner's questions. Use the location of the buildings on the map below.

Activity A, page 58
Student A

Ask your partner questions to complete this catalog page. Then answer your partner's questions.

Example: **A:** Where is the Parma ham from?
B: It's imported from Italy.

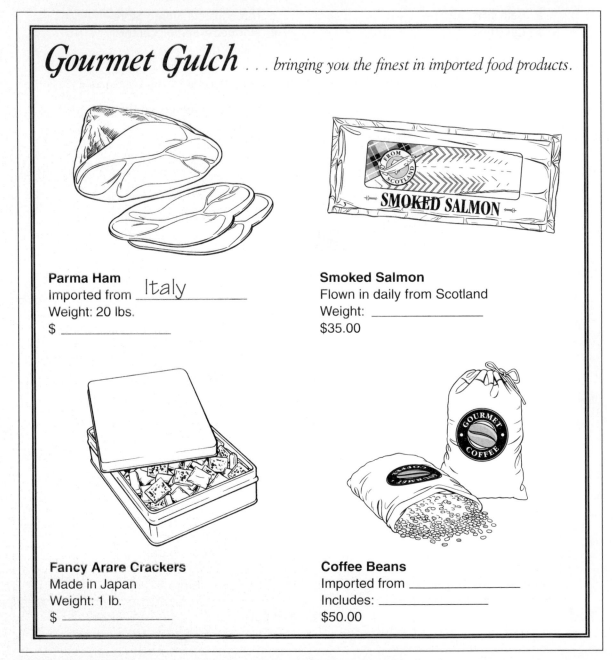

Gourmet Gulch . . . *bringing you the finest in imported food products.*

Parma Ham
Imported from ___Italy___
Weight: 20 lbs.
$ _____

Smoked Salmon
Flown in daily from Scotland
Weight: _____
$35.00

Fancy Arare Crackers
Made in Japan
Weight: 1 lb.
$ _____

Coffee Beans
Imported from _____
Includes: _____
$50.00

Note: The abbreviation lb. = pound; the abbreviation lbs. = pounds.

Ask your partner these questions about the fruit drink. Write the answers on the label.

• Is the measurement for vitamin D in international units or milligrams?
• How much vitamin E is there?
• What's another name for vitamin B-6?
• What mineral has 25 milligrams?
• How much iron is there?

Example: **A:** What is another name for beta carotene?
B: Vitamin A.

Now answer your partner's questions about the fruit drink. Use the information on the label.

SuperPower
Protein Drink ☆☆☆

Includes all of these important vitamins and minerals!

Beta carotene (<u>Vitamin A</u>)	10,000 IU
Vitamin D	400 ____
Vitamin C	150 mg
Vitamin E	____ IU
Vitamin B-1 (thiamin)	25 mg
Vitamin B-2 (riboflavin)	25 mg
Vitamin B-6 (_____)	25 mg
_____	25 mg
Magnesium	7.2 mg
Zinc	15 mg
Copper	20 mg
Iron	____ mg

Notes: IU = international units
mg = milligrams
The first seven items are vitamins; the last five are minerals.

Activity A, page 154
Student A

Example: **A:** What woman was an abolitionist?
B: Lucretia Mott.
A: How do you spell that?
B: L-U-C-R-E-T-I-A M-O-T-T.

Free Blacks	Women	New England Poets
Frederick Douglass	<u>Lucretia Mott</u>	John Greenleaf Whittier
_____	the Grimké sisters	_____

Activity G, page 34
Student B

Answer your partner's questions. Use the location of the buildings on the map below.

Ask about the location of these buildings:

e. Southwest Health Food Store   g. City Youth Center
f. Secondhand Things Thrift Store   h. Griffith Bath Supplies

Example: **A:** Where's Sam's Store?
                B: It's on Gareth Avenue. It's the second building from the corner.

Activity A, page 58
Student B

Answer your partner's questions. Then ask your partner questions to complete this catalog page.

Example: B: How much does the Parma ham weigh?
A: It weighs 20 pounds.

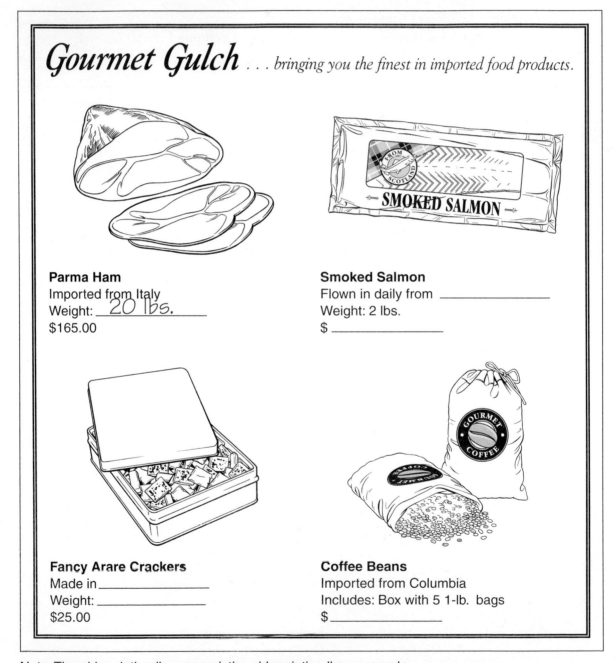

Gourmet Gulch . . . *bringing you the finest in imported food products.*

Parma Ham
Imported from Italy
Weight: _20 lbs._
$165.00

Smoked Salmon
Flown in daily from _____
Weight: 2 lbs.
$ _____

Fancy Arare Crackers
Made in _____
Weight: _____
$25.00

Coffee Beans
Imported from Columbia
Includes: Box with 5 1-lb. bags
$ _____

Note: The abbreviation lb. = pound; the abbreviation lbs. = pounds.

Activity A, page 118
Student B

Answer your partner's questions about the fruit drink. Use the information on the label below.

Now ask your partner these questions about the fruit drink. Write the answers on the label.

• What's another name for vitamin B-1?
• What's another name for riboflavin?
• How much magnesium is there?
• What mineral has 15 milligrams?
• How much copper is there?

Example: **A:** How much vitamin C is there?
            B: One hundred and fifty milligrams.

SuperPower Protein Drink ☆☆☆

Includes all of these important vitamins and minerals!	
Beta carotene (Vitamin A)	10,000 IU
Vitamin D	400 IU
Vitamin C	_150_ mg
Vitamin E	100 IU
Vitamin B-1 (_____)	25 mg
_____ (riboflavin)	25 mg
Vitamin B-6 (pyridoxine)	25 mg
Calcium	25 mg
Magnesium	____mg
_____	15 mg
Copper	____mg
Iron	10 mg

Notes: IU = international units
mg = milligrams
The first seven items are vitamins; the last five are minerals.

Activity A, page 154
Student B

Example: A: What woman was an abolitionist?
B: Lucretia Mott.
A: How do you spell that?
B: L-U-C-R-E-T-I-A M-O-T-T.

Free Blacks	Women	New England Poets
_____	Lucretia Mott	_____
Sojourner Truth	_____	James Russell Lowell

APPENDIX 2: AUDIO SCRIPT

Getting Started
Introduction to Academic Life

C. Listening to a Lecture: Section 2 (page 5)

Lecturer: For your freshman and sophomore years in the United States (but not in Canada), you'll take mostly general education requirements. General education requirements are basic classes in many different subjects—an introduction to biology, history, art, psychology, anthropology, English, and so on. All students must take the general education requirements. There's no escape! However, there is also space for you to take electives. Electives are classes that you choose to take. It's a good idea—and this is important—to choose electives in a number of different subjects that interest you. This is the time to explore, to discover new things.

Soon you'll need to decide on a major. Your major is your main area, your main field of study. In your first two years—your freshman and sophomore years—you'll take some classes in your major but not many. In your third and fourth years—your junior and senior years—almost all of your classes will be in your major. When you graduate, you will have a degree in your major. For example, you might have a B.A. in history or a B.S. in chemistry.

Introduction to Listening and Speaking

D. Understanding the Intonation of Tag Questions (page 11)

1. They're busy, aren't they? *[Falling Intonation]*
2. This bus goes to Brand Street, doesn't it? *[Rising Intonation]*
3. It was a great movie, wasn't it? *[Falling Intonation]*
4. This bus doesn't go to Riverside, does it? *[Falling Intonation]*

5. The biology books are over there, aren't they? *[Rising Intonation]*
6. The food at this party is fabulous, isn't it? *[Falling Intonation]*
7. The test wasn't very hard, was it? *[Falling Intonation]*
8. The homework was interesting, wasn't it? *[Falling Intonation]*
9. We didn't have to do Chapter 5, did we? *[Rising Intonation]*
10. The history department isn't offering History 207 this term, is it? *[Falling Intonation]*

E. Understanding the Intonation of Tag Questions (page 12)

1. **A:** Boy, it's hot today, isn't it? *[Falling Intonation]*
   B: Yeah, it really is.
2. **A:** This bus doesn't run on time too often, does it? *[Rising Intonation]*
   B: No, it doesn't.
3. **A:** They're pretty slow at fixing the air conditioning around here, aren't they? *[Falling Intonation]*
   B: They sure are.
4. **A:** They look nice, don't they? *[Falling Intonation]*
   B: Yeah, they do.
5. **A:** You haven't ever taken Business 251, have you? *[Rising Intonation]*
   B: No, I haven't.

G. Listening for the Main Idea (page 14)

Penkava: O.K., we go to Daniel in Hollywood, Florida. Hi there, Daniel.

Daniel: How are you?

Penkava: O.K. How are you?

Daniel: Good. I'm calling because I think I have a somewhat interesting, uh, vantage point. I mean, my one piece of advice, and it's hard for some, 'cause I don't know how much I'd be listening to this if I was sort of entering college and just real excited to have my parents, as someone put it, drop off the radar screen. But, um, but really just study what you like and, uh, things will fall into place.

Penkava: Well, Daniel, thanks for your call and your advice.

H. Understanding Fast or Difficult English
(page 15)

Levine: By the way, I think that's a great piece of advice. I remember meeting a young woman, and I asked her what she was majoring in. She said business, and I said, "Hey, that's great. How do you like it?" She said, "I absolutely hate it." And I said, "What would you rather be majoring in?" And she said "Dance," and I said, "Why don't you major in dance?" And her answer was: "Money is nice, poor is not nice, and I want nice." The sad part about this young woman was she gave up all of her dreams. Too many people give up their dreams too early.

Chapter 1: Career Planning
Part 2 Social Language

A. Listening for the Main Idea (page 26)

B. Listening for Details (page 26)

Evan: Hi, how are you doing?

Speaker 1: Hi, I'm well, thanks.

Evan: What's your name?

Speaker 1: Kay.

Evan: Well, I'm doing an interview for Campus TV. Would you mind if I asked you a couple of questions?

Speaker 1: No, that's fine, go ahead.

Evan: What advice, if anything, would you give to students starting in college?

Speaker 1: Um, I would advise them not to be afraid to ask questions that they think are silly or stupid because chances are other people have the same questions, and if you don't ask, you never get the answers.

Speaker 2: I think the most important thing is to, um, manage your time well, to, um, apply yourself after classes, to put in an equal effort, like, review classes as much as—if the class is an hour and a half, you study for at least an hour and a half just to review things.

Speaker 3: So, I guess the advice that I would take from somebody would be to choose their school wisely and to realize that that's going to be your future right there.

Speaker 4: Take classes in areas that you would never think you would be interested in—um, learning about, um—totally just using it as a time to open yourself up to other things and other ideas.

Evan: What advice can you give to students just beginning college?

Speaker 5: Meet new people. And, ah, really learn new things, not just from books but from, you know, the people and—

Evan: Be open-minded?

Speaker 5: Yes, be more open minded—that's what I meant to say. Yeah, that's it.

Speaker 6: I would say, you know, take full advantage of the resources that are available to you. Meet as many different people as possible from as many different backgrounds.

Speaker 7: Oh, just beginning college, probably be academically prepared and, you know, don't get sucked in by social pressures.

Evan: Don't party too much.

Speaker 7: That's right.

Speaker 8: I think that college students should remember that they're here to learn, not just to party.

Speaker 9: Don't worry about what major you're going to have 'cause invariably it changes.

Speaker 10: Relax. Stop worrying so much about my career, my future, and enjoy what you're learning.

Speaker 11: Have fun.

Evan: Have fun.

Speaker 11: Don't take it all that seriously.

C. Guessing the Meaning from Context
(page 27)

1. **Speaker 1:** Um, I would advise them not to be afraid to ask questions that they think are silly or stupid because chances are other people have the same questions, and if you don't ask, you never get the answers.

2. **Speaker 2:** I think the most important thing is to, um, manage your time well, to, um, apply yourself after classes, to put in an equal effort like, review classes as much as—if the class is an hour and a half, you study for at least an hour and a half just to review things.

3. **Speaker 7:** Oh, just beginning college, probably be academically prepared and, you know, don't get sucked in by social pressures.

   Evan: Don't party too much.

   Speaker 7: That's right.

D. Listening for Specific Ideas (page 27)

1. **Speaker 1:** Um, I would advise them not to be afraid to ask questions that they think are silly or stupid because chances are other people have the same questions, and if you don't ask, you never get the answers.

2. **Speaker 2:** I think the most important thing is to, um, manage your time well, to, um, apply yourself after classes, to put in an equal effort like, review classes as much as—if the class is an hour and a half, you study for at least an hour and a half just to review things.

3. **Speaker 5:** Meet new people. And ah—

   Evan: Be open-minded?

   Speaker 5: Yes, be more open-minded—that's what I meant to say. Yeah, that's it.

4. **Speaker 9:** Don't worry about what major you're going to have 'cause invariably it changes.

Part 3 The Mechanics of Listening and Speaking

A. Following Directions (page 31)

1. **A:** Excuse me. Can you tell me where the college library is?

   B: Sure. Just go down a block. Make a left at the college entrance. It's right there on your right.

   A: Thanks.

   B: You're welcome.

2. **A:** Excuse me. Could you tell me how to get to a drugstore?

   B: A drugstore. Um, sure. Go down First Street one block. Make a left on Gareth Avenue.

   A: Left on Gareth. O.K.

   B: Then go down Gareth three blocks. There's a drugstore on the corner of Fourth and Gareth.

   A: Fourth and Gareth.

   B: Right.

   A: Thanks a lot.

   B: Uh-huh.

3. **A:** Excuse me. Can you tell me where to find a bookstore?

   B: The college bookstore?

   A: No. Just a regular bookstore.

   B: Well, go down College Drive two blocks and make a left. There's a bookstore across from the park—across from the college.

   A: Thanks a lot.

   B: No problem.

4. **A:** Excuse me. Could you tell me where to find a bank?

   B: Uh, yeah. Go down College Drive two blocks . . .

   A: Two blocks . . .

   B: Yeah. Then make a right on Third Street. Go about a block, a block and a half. There's a bank in the middle of the block. On Third.

   A: Thanks.

   B: Uh-huh.

5. **A:** Excuse me. Can you tell me how to get to the Career Planning Office at the college?

B: Sure. Go down College Drive to the entrance. Turn left. Go past the Admissions Building. Make another left on Valley Walk. Career Planning is across from Admissions.

A: On the corner of Campus Way and Valley Walk?

B: That's right.

A: Well, thanks.

B: You're welcome.

B. Understanding Interjections (page 32)

1. **A:** It's in the College Library.

B: Huh?

2. **A:** Do you mean, "Try to enjoy your classes?"

B: Uh-huh.

3. **A:** I think the test is tomorrow.

B: Uh-uh.

4. **A:** I think the test is tomorrow.

B: Uh-oh.

5. **A:** Thanks for all your help.

B: Uh-huh.

6. **A:** Do you like it?

B: Uh-huh.

E. Hearing the Difference Between /θ/ and /s/ (page 33)

1.	sank	**7.**	force
2.	sings	**8.**	thigh
3.	thaw	**9.**	theme
4.	thick	**10.**	tense
5.	path	**11.**	eighth
6.	worse	**12.**	some

Part 4 Broadcast English

A. Hearing the Medial T (page 37)

1.	30	**3.**	15
2.	40	**4.**	60

5.	17	**10.**	15
6.	18	**11.**	60
7.	19	**12.**	70
8.	13	**13.**	18
9.	40	**14.**	90

B. Hearing the Medial T in Sentences (page 37)

1. Almost 50 percent of the class can speak another language.

2. William started college when he was 40.

3. Roughly 30 percent of all high school graduates went to college.

4. Zach's family moved to Kenya when he was 14.

5. The average age is 13.

6. Many students lived in dormitories 50 years ago.

7. Becky graduated 15 years ago.

8. Ethan got married when he was 90.

9. A person who is 30 or 40 can enjoy college more than someone who is 18 or 19.

C. Hearing the Medial T Followed by /N/ (page 38)

1. I was bitten by some insect yesterday.

2. Do you know where I can find a drinking fountain?

3. I bought a blue cotton shirt.

4. Are you certain of that?

5. I have a mountain of homework tonight.

D. Listening for the Main Idea: Section 1 (page 38)

Penkava: Arthur Levine, talk to us a bit about this historically. Has, has there been a marked change in how we approach higher education over, say, the last 50 years?

Levine: Oh, sure. Uh, college is real different these days. Fifty years ago we had, oh, roughly 15 percent of all high school graduates going to college. We're now up to 65 percent of all high school graduates. So it's become a rite of passage.

What we're finding now is 50 years ago the majority of college students would have been men. A majority are now women. Fifty years ago, a majority of college students would have been 18 to 22; the average age is now over 25. Fifty years ago, the average college student would have been white; today a third of all college—20-odd percent of all college students are of color. Uh, fifty years ago, a majority—almost all—college students would have been full-time; today 42 percent are part-time. So it's a very different mix of people we're going to see on campus these days.

E. Taking Notes: Using a Graphic Organizer (page 38)

Levine: Uh, college is real different these days. Fifty years ago we had, oh, roughly 15 percent of all high school graduates going to college. We're now up to 65 percent of all high school graduates. So it's become a rite of passage. What we're finding now is 50 years ago the majority of college students would have been men. A majority are now women. Fifty years ago, a majority of college students would have been 18 to 22; the average age is now over 25. Fifty years ago, the average college student would have been white; today a third of all college—20-odd percent of all college students are of color. Uh, fifty years ago, a majority—almost all—college students would have been full-time; today 42 percent are part-time. So it's a very different mix of people we're going to see on campus these days.

F. Listening for the Main Idea: Section 2 (page 39)

Penkava: Well, Anne Matthews, what advice would you offer somebody so that there'd be a greater chance that something would click in their mind when they were in that lab, when they were in that class, so that—that they could gain something from this, from their college years, Anne Matthews?

Matthews: Oh, I would—I—I'd have a couple of piece of ad—pieces of advice. I'd say, take enough quarters for laundry. Talk to strangers, because this is the big chance to meet people very unlike you. I would say talk to professors, go to office hours. If you find a class that appeals to

you, even ask them for extra reading. They'll—they'll kiss your feet in amazement and joy. I would say try everything, you know, Thai dance, botany, South American history—'cause no one cares if you turn out to be not any good at it. You know, you're in college and you're supposed to be experimenting. And my last piece of advice to a student on the younger end of the range, uh, the 17- or 18-year-old, would be: think about dropping out—because very often those years of 18, 19, and 20, uh, campuses are forced to do a lot more babysitting than they probably should. It's people who are 20, 30, 40 that really enjoy and get a great deal out of the undergraduate investment.

G. Listening for Numbers (page 39)

Matthews: And my last piece of advice to a student on the younger end of the range, the 17- or 18-year-old, would be: think about dropping out—because very often those years of 18, 19, and 20, uh, campuses are forced to do a lot more babysitting than they probably should. It's people who are 20, 30, 40 that really enjoy and get a great deal out of the undergraduate investment.

H. Listening for Details (page 39)

Matthews: I would say try everything, you know, Thai dance, botany, South American history—'cause no one cares if you turn out to be not any good at it. You know, you're in college and you're supposed to be experimenting.

I. Listening for the Main Idea: Section 3 (page 39)

J. Listening for Details (page 40)

Penkava: 1-800-989-8255. 1-800-989-TALK. Jeff in Pullman, Washington. Hi there, Jeff.

Caller: Hi. Um, I'm a graduate student and a TA, so I thought I could make a couple more suggestions that might be helpful.

Penkava: Sure.

Caller: Um, first off, um, it is good to seek out professors. And, uh, I would also add that it's good to talk to your teaching assistants—they oftentimes have a little more time available, and they're generally pretty excited and want to work with students.

Penkava: Mm-hm.

Caller: And the other suggestion I would make is, um, not to worry too much about grades the first couple of years, you know. Bs are good enough. But try to take the time to explore the material and, uh, enjoy yourself, at least the first couple of years.

Penkava: Well, Jeff, thanks for your advice.

Caller: Thank you.

Part 5 Academic English

A. Understanding New Words (page 45)

1. In this lecture, I'm going to discuss five keys to academic success for ESL students. Now, by the word *academic* I mean "college or university."

2. First, self-assessment. This is a process. In this process, you discover and understand four things about yourself.

3. In this process, you discover and understand four things about yourself: your interests (things that you like to do), your skills (things that you do well), your values (things that you believe in), and your personality.

4. In this process, you discover and understand four things about yourself: your interests (things that you like to do), your skills (things that you do well), your values (things that you believe in), and your personality.

5. Transition is the process of moving from college to the world of work.

B. Taking Notes: Using an Outline (page 46)

C. Checking Your Notes (page 48)

Section 1

Lecturer: O.K. Let's get started. Welcome to Valley College. I'm the director of the Career Office here at the college, and we want to help you to be successful in your classes here, um, both now and when you finish ESL and start all your other classes. In this workshop, I'm going to discuss five keys to academic success for ESL students. Now, by the word *academic* I mean "college or university." So what will make you a successful student here at Valley College?

First, self-assessment. This is a process. In this process, you discover and understand four things about yourself: your interests (things that you like to do), your skills (things that you do well), your values (things that you believe in), and your personality. It's important to understand yourself very well so that you can make good choices about your major and your future career. The Counseling Office can give you a self-assessment test, or you can use a computerized self-assessment program at the Computer Lab or Career Office.

Now, the second key to academic success is setting a goal. A goal is a carefully planned purpose. What goal do you hope to reach this year, next year, in four years? Now, after you set your goal or goals, you need a plan of action. In other words, what steps are you going to take, what do you have to do, to reach your goal?

Section 2

Lecturer: The third key to college success is knowing the college culture and environment. Now, for ESL students, this is very, very important because ESL students often don't understand the system of higher education in the United States. And I can't emphasize this enough: you *absolutely must* become familiar with this college and what it offers. Now, how can you do this? Study a map of the college. Find out where the offices and services are. Study your college catalog. Read the explanations of the services at the college. Ask a lot of questions! Let me say this again: *ask a lot of questions.* It's important to know about your college. Why? Because you need to know where to go for help when you have a problem. Also, even when you *don't* have a problem, there are many services that can make your college life more fun, more enjoyable, richer.

Section 3

Lecturer: Now, the fourth key to success in college is developing academic skills. ESL students usually know that they have to study hard, right? But they often don't know *how* to "study hard." They might not have the skills. Here are just some of the skills that you need: First, you need to do all of the reading before you come to class each day. Second, you need to find key points in the reading and highlight them with a highlighter—yellow or orange or green. Next, you need to make notes on important new words and their definitions. Fourth, you need to take good lecture notes and write down any questions that you think of. Fifth, it's important to form a study group with a few students in each class. In this study group, you can review and compare your lecture notes.

Sixth, it is also important to make good use of academic services at the college. Here are three: Student Services offers special workshops on subjects such as note-taking and using your time well. The Math Lab has tutors who can give you individual help. The Writing Center also offers tutors who can help you with your essays and research.

Section 4

Lecturer: The fifth key to success is transition. Transition is the process of moving from college to the world of work. If you have a part-time job now, you've already started this process. Great. The best part-time job, of course, is one that gives you experience in your field of interest, in your major. Now, in addition, you need to visit us here at the Career Office at the college. It's here you can learn several things: how to write your résumé, how to look for a job, how to find careers that relate to your major, and how to prepare for a job interview. Then you're ready to move from school to work. O.K. Any questions?

Chapter 2: The Global Economy
Part 2 Social Language

A. Listening for the Main Idea (page 55)

B. Listening for Details (page 56)

Chrissy: Hey, Brandon. What's up? I *love* your glasses. Are they new?

Brandon: Yeah. I got them at that designer discount place downtown.

Chrissy: They are really cool. I'd like some like that. Who made them?

Brandon: It says "Olivier Renaud." Sounds French. Nope, wait a minute. It says "Made in China."

Chrissy: Huh. That's like a lot of stuff these days. See these shoes?

Brandon: Yeah.

Chrissy: Don't they look cool?

Brandon: Nice.

Chrissy: Yeah, I thought they looked very fashionable, but if you look closely—

Brandon: Hey, they're plastic!

Chrissy: They're made in China, too, and—they were only thirty bucks!

Brandon: Cool.

Chrissy: Yeah. I noticed you can get great-looking copies of designer stuff that's made overseas. China, Korea—

Brandon: Hey, speaking of stuff made overseas, have you seen that new ad for Super Mints?

Chrissy: Um, I don't know.

Brandon: It's really wild. There are all these odd couples—an old lady and a little boy, a woman and her dog, two guys—and one wants to kiss the other.

Chrissy: Oh, yeah, but the other refuses because the one that wants a kiss has bad breath!

Brandon: Yeah, it's done in wild colors and settings, like a music video. I was so curious, I bought some. I noticed they're from England; I was wondering if the commercial is British, too. It just didn't look American.

Chrissy: I don't know. I think they remake commercials for the country they want to sell the product in 'cause you have to appeal to the local market. You've got to relate the product to local values.

Brandon: Yeah, and there's stuff you can do in commercials in other countries that you *sure* can't do here.

Chrissy: Hey, that's right! I saw this commercial in a movie theater last summer in France. It was just for yogurt, but they showed this woman's—

Brandon: Whoa, we're going to have to pick this up later. I'm going to be late for class.

Chrissy: All right. Hey, Brandon, what did you do with those Super Mints? You could use some!

Brandon: *Chrissy!*

C. Listening for Descriptive Language
(page 56)

D. Listening for Supporting Information
(page 57)

Brandon: Hey, speaking of stuff made overseas, have you seen that new ad for Super Mints?

Chrissy: Um, I don't know.

Brandon: It's really wild. There are all these odd couples—an old lady and a little boy, a woman and her dog, two guys—and one wants to kiss the other.

Chrissy: Oh, yeah, but the other refuses because the one that wants a kiss has bad breath!

Brandon: Yeah, it's done in wild colors and settings, like a music video. I was so curious, I bought some. I noticed they're from England; I was wondering if the commercial is British, too. It just didn't look American.

Chrissy: I don't know. I think they remake commercials for the country they want to sell the product in 'cause you have to appeal to the local market. You've got to relate the product to local values.

Brandon: Yeah. And there's stuff you can do in commercials in other countries that you *sure* can't do here.

Part 3 The Mechanics of Listening and Speaking

C. Greeting People You Know (page 60)

1. **A:** Hi! What's up?
   B: Oh, nothing much.
2. **A:** Hi. How's it going?
   B: Great!
3. **A:** Hi. How have you been?
   B: Not bad.
4. **A:** Hi. How are you?
   B: Hi! Just great.
5. **A:** Hi. What have you been up to lately?
   B: I've been really busy studying.

D. Responding to Greetings: General
(page 60)

1. How are you?
2. How's it going?
3. What did you do last night?
4. What's up?
5. How are you doing?
6. What's new?

G. Reduced Forms of Words (page 62)

A: Hi. Whasup?

B: Hi. Not much. Howzit going with you?

A: I dunno. I've been busy lately. Whatuv you been up to?

B: I've been busy, too. How ya doing in English?

A: Not bad, but it's a lotta work.

Part 4 Broadcast English

A. Listening for the Main Idea (page 68)

Siegel: There was a time not too long ago when most clothing bought in the U.S. was made in the U.S. No longer. Take T-shirts, for example. Most shirts on sale in American stores today come from such countries as Honduras, Vietnam, and, more and more often, China. Chinese companies have spent the last decade learning how to perfect the cheap manufacture of quality T-shirts. And with the expiration of apparel quotas, China is expected to dominate the world T-shirt market. This week we're running a series inspired by the book *The Travels of a T-shirt in the Global Economy* by Pietra Rivoli, a professor at Georgetown University. We asked her to show NPR's Adam Davidson around Shanghai, where many T-shirts are sewn.

Davidson: The Huangpu River, a tributary of the Yangtze, has been a cotton and textile water highway for almost a hundred years. Pietra Rivoli is on a boat looking out at Shanghai, China's busiest and fastest-growing city.

Rivoli: The cotton for a typical, uh, T-shirt that was made in China might have left west Texas, uh, and gone to California and then to Long Beach probably, the big port on our West Coast, and traveled all the way here.

Davidson: Much of the U.S. cotton arriving at the port of Shanghai is knit into cloth and then sewn into T-shirts, and this is exactly what Shanghai workers have been doing for most of the last hundred years: making T-shirts and other apparel. But things have been changing rapidly in recent decades. Shanghai has become the financial center of mainland China. Instead of cotton mills, the banks of the Huangpu are crowded now with exciting postmodern skyscrapers that house things like banks, ad agencies, hip restaurants, and absurdly expensive shops.

The city has a newness and wealth that rivals New York, London, and Tokyo. Rivoli says none of this would be here, though, if the textile mills hadn't come first.

Rivoli: Because once you have one kind of factory, you can diversify into other kind of factories, and your workforce gains skills, and you get this infrastructure that you see here that allows the ships to come in and out, and it allows trade to flourish. So it really started—what you see here today, which is really a fantastically modern city—was started by the investment of especially the British and the Japanese and the cotton factories that they built.

Davidson: As Chinese workers do better, though, there is a price to pay on the other side of the world. Greg Burgess used to work at one of the many T-shirt plants in Florence, Alabama. It closed a couple years ago. It couldn't compete with all those cheap Chinese imports. Burgess remembers the day he realized Florence's economy was in trouble.

Burgess: I was actually at Wal-Mart with my wife, and she was trying some clothes on. And I just walked over to a rack of shirts. There was, like, six shirts on this rack, and I just flipped through, and not one tag said 'Made in the USA.' And I knew then. And, I mean, these were from all different countries: Mexico, Sri Lanka, Dominican Republic, China. And I knew right then. I said, 'Not one shirt out of six in the U.S.' Then we knew it was time to start looking for something else.

B. Listening for Details (page 68)

Rivoli: The cotton for a typical, uh, T-shirt that was made in China might have left west Texas,

uh, and gone to California and then to Long Beach probably, the big port on our West Coast, and traveled all the way here.

C. Identifying a Causal Chain (page 69)

Davidson: The city has a newness and wealth that rivals New York, London, and Tokyo. Rivoli says none of this would be here, though, if the textile mills hadn't come first.

Rivoli: Because once you have one kind of factory, you can diversify into other kind of factories, and your workforce gains skills, and you get this infrastructure that you see here that allows the ships to come in and out, and it allows trade to flourish. So it really started—what you see here today, which is really a fantastically modern city—was started by the investment of especially the British and the Japanese and the cotton factories that they built.

D. Listening for an Anecdote (page 69)

Davidson: As Chinese workers do better, though, there is a price to pay on the other side of the world. Greg Burgess used to work at one of the many T-shirt plants in Florence, Alabama. It closed a couple years ago. It couldn't compete with all those cheap Chinese imports. Burgess remembers the day he realized Florence's economy was in trouble.

Burgess: I was actually at Wal-Mart with my wife, and she was trying some clothes on. And I just walked over to a rack of shirts. There was, like, six shirts on this rack, and I just flipped through, and not one tag said 'Made in the USA.' And I knew then. And, I mean, these were from all different countries: Mexico, Sri Lanka, Dominican Republic, China. And I knew right then. I said, 'Not one shirt out of six in the U.S.' Then we knew it was time to start looking for something else.

Part 5 Academic English

A. Taking Notes: Using an Outline (page 73)

B. Checking Your Notes (page 75)

Section 1

Lecturer: All right. Let's begin. Today's lecture is on a case study involving a marketing campaign initiated by the Quaker Oats Company several years ago. *[Points to board.]* Quaker Oats Company.

O.K. Now, in the United States, everyone knows Quaker Oats Company for its good-tasting, high-quality food products. For many years, millions of cereal eaters have enjoyed its Quaker Oatmeal as a wholesome, nutritious breakfast food. And yet Quaker, which is noted for good marketing practices in the United States, experienced a major problem when it tried to introduce a new product into a foreign market.

What was the product? Snapple. *[Points to board.]* Snapple had been a popular beverage in the United States for several years. Now, the Snapple line of beverages included a wide assortment of iced tea and fruit-flavored drinks. Many of these drinks contained bits of fruit pulp and seeds of fruits such as strawberries and bananas used to make these drinks. And American customers liked the fresh, clean, thirstquenching taste of these drinks. The fruit pulp and the seeds at the bottom of the containers indicated that these drinks were made from fresh fruits, another highly desirable trait to American customers. The fruit pulp and seeds generated a *positive* attitude toward Snapple in the minds of American customers. As a result, this favorable attitude created an increasing demand for Snapple.

So, in January 1994, Quaker Oats introduced the line of Snapple iced tea and fruit-flavored beverages into Japan. These drinks, popular with many different segments of the U.S. beverage market, were not successful in Japan. Exactly three years later—in January of 1997—Quaker stopped shipping Snapple to Japan. Snapple, which was successfully marketed in the United States, failed after only three years in Japan. The question is: How could a major consumer-goods marketer like Quaker misunderstand the market so badly?

Section 2

Lecturer: When Quaker introduced Snapple in many Japanese retail stores, it used point-of-purchase displays. *[Points to board.]* Now, these displays featured attractive, attention-getting signs and a wide selection of Snapple drinks.

These displays generated a large amount of customer traffic. Shoppers walking through stores went out of their way to visit the displays. However, while customer interest in Snapple was high, first-time sales were lower than anticipated. Repeat sales, that is, sales to customers that had already made an initial purchase of a Snapple drink, were also lower than anticipated.

It had soon become apparent that Snapple fruit drinks had an image problem with Japanese customers. Here's why: In 1994, most Japanese preferred clear beverages. In fact, in Japan, clarity denotes purity. The Japanese fruit drink customer felt that a clear fruit drink was both high quality and wholesome. Japanese consumers were quite interested in Snapple at first, walking up to the displays and examining the individual containers of Snapple. However, as customers examined the Snapple more closely, they noticed the fruit seeds and pulp at the bottom of the containers. This made them think that Snapple, while interesting, was not a high-quality, wholesome drink. And, if it was not a high-quality drink, why should they buy it?

When the Quaker Oats Company heard about this situation, the marketing people simply did not believe that the information correctly indicated Japanese customers' true feelings about Snapple. So, their response was something like this: "The seeds and pieces of fruit pulp indicate that real fruit was used to make the drinks, and is therefore a sign of quality. Strawberry and banana seeds are so small that no one can detect their presence in a fruit drink as it is consumed. In time, the Japanese customers will realize this. The sales of Snapple will continue to increase as more and more customers realize that Snapple, with its seeds and fruit pulp, is a high-quality drink." So, what was wrong with this thinking?

Section 3

Lecturer: Quaker may have made several important marketing mistakes when it introduced Snapple to Japan. Here are some ideas on what mistakes Quaker may have made. First, it seems as if little market research was done. *[Points to board.]* Quaker didn't try to understand the likes and dislikes of fruit juice customers in Japan. Now, market research is conducted before a product is introduced into a new market, to discover the potential new customers' likes and dislikes. Snapple was a successful product in the United States, but Japan was a new market for Snapple. Therefore, Quaker needed to treat Japan like any *other* market and conduct a thorough study of the marketplace and its potential customers before it tried to sell Snapple in Japan.

Simple research into customer likes and dislikes would have shown that the Japanese had a strong dislike of fruit pulp and seeds in fruit drinks. So one mistake of Quaker was probably simply not knowing customers and what they like and dislike before introducing a new product into a new market. Now, this can be even more important when the new market is in another country. Frequently the customers in the potential new market have different attitudes, opinions, and beliefs. These must be identified and incorporated into the marketing planning before the new product is introduced.

Let's say Quaker management *knew* about the Japanese customers' preference for clear beverages. But it still decided to market Snapple with the fruit pulp and seeds anyway. If so, Quaker needed to develop a marketing campaign that addressed this problem. It needed to develop advertising and promotional efforts to change Japanese customers' perception about fruit and pulp from negative to positive. In other words, Quaker's advertisements could have said this: "Snapple fruit drinks contain fruit and seeds; but these really indicate quality and flavor."

Well, perhaps over time, Japanese customers would have changed their minds and, and have developed a liking for Snapple with its fresh fruit pulp and seeds. This way, Quaker would have a marketing advantage over other fruit drinks in Japan, which were clear. Snapple would have been the only drink with pulp and seeds. However, Quaker didn't use their advertising and promotional efforts to change customers' perceptions about the fruity pulp and seeds. So this probably was Quaker's second marketing mistake.

Section 4

Lecturer: A third potential mistake Quaker management made may have been due to the marketing of Snapple in the United States. Snapple was first sold along the East Coast in the United States. As it was sold in more and more

parts of the United States, Snapple began to use up more and more of its management and financial resources. *[Points to board.]* Management and the financial resources.

Management did not feel that they could afford either the time or the money to build production facilities to produce two lines of fruit drinks: one with fruit and seeds for sale in the United States, and one without fruit and seeds for sale in Japan. Management felt that one type of drink, with fruit and seeds, could be successfully sold in two different markets. And so, it appears as if the Japanese market got the types of Snapple fruit juices that were most convenient for Snapple to manufacture, and not the types that were typically preferred in Japan.

Well, that wraps up the Snapple case study. Are there any questions before we move on?

C. Asking Questions (page 75)

Lecturer: A third potential mistake Quaker management made may have been due to the marketing of Snapple in the United States. Snapple was first sold along the East Coast in the United States. As it was sold in more and more parts of the United States, Snapple began to use up more and more of its management and financial resources. *[Points to board.]* Management and the financial resources.

Management did not feel that they could afford either the time or the money to build production facilities to produce two lines of fruit drinks: one with fruit and seeds for sale in the United States, and one without fruit and seeds for sale in Japan. Management felt that one type of drink, with fruit and seeds, could be successfully sold in two different markets. And so, it appears as if the Japanese market got the types of Snapple fruit juices that were most convenient for Snapple to manufacture, and not the types that were typically preferred in Japan.

Well, that wraps up the Snapple case study. Are there any questions before we move on?

Chapter 3: Animal Behavior
Part 2 Social Language

A. Listening for the Main Idea (page 88)

B. Listening for Details (page 88)

Brandon: Mmmm.

Tanya: Cream?

Brandon: Ah, no thanks.

Tanya: You coming down with something? Sounds like you got a cold.

Brandon: No, it's weird. It just started. I don't know what it is.

Jennifer: Well, I have a surprise. His name's Charlie.

Brandon and Tanya: Aw!

Tanya: Wait a minute. Is it gonna live here with us?

Jennifer: Not "it," he. Isn't he adorable?

Tanya: Yeah, he's adorable. Is he gonna live here with us?

Jennifer: Just for a few weeks, while Mr. Jensen's out of town. We're babysitting, uh, catsitting.

Tanya: Well, I'm not catsitting. You're catsitting.

Jennifer: O.K., O.K., O.K., I'll take care of him. But you'll like him. He's really smart. And he understands a lot.

Brandon: Yeah, you can tell. That cat's got a real intelligent face.

Tanya: Oh, come on.

Brandon: You see? I think you hurt his feelings. Don't listen to her.

Jennifer: Cats are very sensitive. You know, sometimes when a cat does something kind of stupid—I don't know, falls off a table or something—and everybody laughs? You can just tell that the cat feels really embarrassed. It hates to be laughed at.

Tanya: I don't buy that. Why do people always think that animals have the same emotions that humans have?

Jennifer: Because they do. And maybe they understand a lot more than we realize.

Brandon: Yeah, there are a zillion stories about how smart animals are.

Jennifer: Like dolphins. You know, sometimes they save a swimmer in the ocean who gets in trouble and can't swim back to the beach. They come right up, get right under the swimmer, and push him up to the surface. I don't understand it, but somehow they know.

Brandon: Yeah, and elephants. Man, they're great animals.

Jennifer: And whales. I love whales.

Tanya: Well, it appears that one animal lover in this room is allergic to cats.

Brandon: You think?

Tanya: You mean you don't know?

Brandon: No. I've never had a cat. Maybe I am allergic.

Jennifer: I'm so sorry, Brandon. I didn't know.

Brandon: Me neither, obviously. Sorry, you guys. I got to get out of here. See you later.

Tanya: Bye.

Jennifer: Take care.

C. Listening for Stressed Words (page 89)

Jennifer: Cats are very sensitive. You know, sometimes when a cat does something kind of stupid—I don't know, falls off a table or something—and everybody laughs? You can just tell that the cat feels really embarrassed. It hates to be laughed at.

Tanya: I don't buy that. Why do people always think that animals have the same emotions that humans have?

Jennifer: Because they do. And maybe they understand a lot more than we realize.

Brandon: Yeah, there are a zillion stories about how smart animals are.

Jennifer: Like dolphins. You know, sometimes they save a swimmer in the ocean who gets in trouble and can't swim back to the beach. They come right up, get right under the swimmer, and push him up to the surface.

D. Understanding Emotion from Tone of Voice (page 90)

1. **A:** I'm going out of town. Could you take care of my cat for a few days?

   B: O.K. *[Person B agrees and is excited.]*

2. **A:** This is the *fourth* cat you've brought home. We *can't* have any more animals.

   B: O.K., O.K., O.K. *[Person B agrees unhappily.]*

3. **A:** My cat can obey commands. When I say sit, she sits.

   B: You're kidding. *[Person B is surprised, but believes person A.]*

4. **A:** Phil's parrot can talk. It can answer questions.

   B: You're kidding. *[Person B does not believe person A.]*

Part 3 The Mechanics of Listening and Speaking

A. Changing Statements Into Questions
(page 94)

1. He has a cat?
2. She doesn't believe you.
3. He went to Bermuda?
4. This isn't your cat?
5. I'm allergic to cats.
6. He went to Bermuda.
7. You've gone swimming with dolphins?
8. She doesn't believe you?

E. Reduced Forms of Words (page 96)

A: Are you gonna take Biology 121 next term?

B: I might. Is Dr. Hurst teaching it?

A: Yeah, I think so. You'll like 'er.

B: Well, Brandon says she's really hard.

A: Oh, don't listen to 'im. Besides, you know, you gotta take it before you take 152. And it's a required class. You can't get outta taking it some time.

Part 4 Broadcast English

A. Listening for the Main Idea: Section 1
(page 99)

B. Listening for Details (page 100)

Siegel: If you think your dog understands you and is getting better at it, scientists say you may be right. New research shows not only can dogs understand human speech, they can learn new words the same way children do. The finding is published in this week's issue of the journal *Science.* NPR's Jon Hamilton has the story.

Hamilton: Every species has its prodigies. In the dog world, one of these is a Border collie in Germany named Rico. He knows literally hundreds of words. Julia Fischer is a senior researcher at the Max Planck Institute for Evolutionary Anthropology in Leipzig. She and her colleagues learned about Rico several years ago while watching TV.

Fischer: There's a German program called *Wetten, Dass . . . ?;* that's something like "I betcha." And this is a show where people—everyday people can say, I can do amazing things. You know, I can tell the color of my crayons from just, you know, sucking on them.

Hamilton: Rico did something a little more interesting from a scientific point of view. He showed he could fetch any one of his 70 toys on command. Since then, Rico has acquired a lot more toys and added nearly 200 words to his vocabulary. Fischer and her colleagues have lots of videotapes of Rico working with his owner.

Unidentified Woman: Rico, *[German spoken]*

Hamilton: Skeptics out there should know that Rico isn't being prompted in any way.

Unidentified Woman: *[German spoken]*

Hamilton: What Fischer's team really wanted to know was whether Rico could learn new words the way children do. Fischer says if any dog could make the leap, it would be Rico.

Fischer: He's a workaholic. He's crazy. I mean, he just goes on and on and on and on, and the owner has to stop him. She has to go—she sees when he gets tired, so—you know, he has red eyes then. And he forgets to drink and eat. I mean, I've never seen that before in a dog.

Hamilton: So the scientists put seven of Rico's familiar toys and one new toy in a room. They asked Rico to fetch the new toy using a word for it that he'd never heard before. Rico brought back the right toy. More important, he often added its name to his vocabulary. A month later, Rico was able to remember a new toy's name about half the time even though he'd heard the word only once. Sue Savage-Rumbaugh is a biology professor at Georgia State University. She says that's a remarkable achievement.

Savage-Rumbaugh: We know now that the dog can rapidly associate new words with new objects, which is what children do right at the point that language takes off, becomes very complex, grammar production pops in. So the dog's on the borderline of very complex language ability.

C. Listening for the Main Idea: Section 2 (page 100)

D. Listening for Details (page 100)

Hamilton: Savage-Rumbaugh is also working on dog vocabulary these days, but she's best known for her work with apes that appear to have crossed that linguistic border. Her prize pupil is a bonobo named Kanzi, who, like Rico, has appeared in lots of videotapes.

Savage-Rumbaugh: Kanzi, can you put the pine needles in the refrigerator? Good job. Thank you.

Hamilton: Savage-Rumbaugh says Kanzi has provided the most convincing evidence yet that animals can learn not only words, but grammar.

Savage-Rumbaugh: Kanzi understands syntax; he understands novel sentences when he's heard them for the first time. Kanzi can overhear conversations in the other room and even report about what he's heard.

Hamilton: Such abilities challenge the theory that only modern humans have the capacity for language. Stuart Shanker of York University in Toronto is a co-author of an upcoming book called *The First Idea* about the ideas of the origins of symbols, language, and intelligence. Shanker says many species appear to have the potential to communicate with humans. Whether they actually do, he says, depends less on a specialized brain than on the sort of interactions they have with people.

Siegel: You can see video of Rico learning a new word—and there's more about animal communication—at our website, npr.org.

E. Making Inferences (page 101)

Hamilton: Savage-Rumbaugh is also working on dog vocabulary these days, but she's best known for her work with apes that appear to have crossed that linguistic border. Her prize pupil is a bonobo named Kanzi, who, like Rico, has appeared in lots of videotapes.

Savage-Rumbaugh: Kanzi, can you put the pine needles in the refrigerator? Good job. Thank you.

Part 5 Academic English

A. Taking Notes (page 105)

B. Checking Your Notes for Details (page 106)

Section 1

Lecturer: Good morning, everyone. I hope you all had a good weekend. Before we get started today can everyone please make sure their cell phones are turned off. O.K. Thank you very much. I appreciate that. Thanks. O.K. Over the weekend, besides the reading, I sincerely hope you considered the question that I'll be exploring today: What distinguishes humans from other animals? Oh, and please don't feel insulted that I am calling humans "animals," right? You understand that I am speaking biologically, yes? O.K. Good.

So. Our question for the day. Humans and non-humans *[writes on board]*. As you'll see, the answer has been changing, thanks to recent research and discoveries.

Today, we're going to cover only four areas: emotion, *[writes on board]*, that's one, tool use, *[writes on board]*, learning, *[writes on board]*, and language *[writes on board]*.

First, emotion: love, hate, anger, embarrassment, fear, even a sense of *fun.* Of course, humans experience emotion every day. Do we all agree? O.K.? O.K., what about animals? What do you think? How many of you have pets? O.K., well, most of us who have been around domestic dogs, cats, horses, and even birds think that these animals *also* have emotions, or at least *appear* to have emotions. For example, when a dog wags its tail *[moves hand back and forth]*, it's clear to us that the dog is happy, or enthusiastic. Similarly, it seems clear that dogs can express sadness, along with other emotions.

Many animals in the wild also seem to express emotion, such as enjoyment, fun. For example, otters sometimes slide down a small hill into the water *[slides hand down]*, swim back to the beach*[makes swimming motion]*, climb up the hill *[raises arms over head]*, and slide down again *[slides hand down]*, over and over. This appears to be for no other reason than *fun.* It's play behavior. Another very cute example of play behavior is in Australia, where parrots called "galahs" will fly to the top of a building that holds corn or grain. They grasp *[closes hand]* a support wire with their feet, then slide down to the ground *[slides hand down]*. Now, they do this over and over. There's a beauty in this play behavior, and it is easy to see that the animals enjoy it.

So it seems obvious to many people that animals do have emotions. But the problem is *proving* it, scientifically. Modern researchers who scientifically study emotions in humans believe that humans have emotions because they can *say* with *words* that they *do* have emotions *[points to board]*. But, because other animals can't speak in *words,* researchers aren't sure that they have emotions.

There is, however, a possible solution. For both humans and non-humans, scientists can watch their *nonverbal body language* such as facial expressions *[points to face]*, hand gestures *[shows hand]*. Scientists record different *sounds* that often seem to go *with* emotion—sounds that are not words, such as screams of anger. There have been many studies like this on humans. Now, when scientists do this type of study with other animals, they see the fact that the nonverbal language of humans is very similar to the nonverbal language of many other animals. However, there haven't yet been many studies on this.

Section 2

Lecturer: Now, how about tool use *[points to board]*? Of course, humans use tools *[writes on board]*. But other animals? Well, for many years, until fairly recently, the answer was "no." Scientists always used to say that one characteristic that distinguishes humans from other animals is tool use. In other words, only humans use tools. But then in the 1960s, a young researcher named Jane Goodall *[writes on board]* was observing chimps *[writes on board]* in a place called Gombe, in Tanzania, Africa. She made an amazing discovery. The chimps in that area take a thin branch from a tree or bush and use it to stick into a small hill where termites live. Why? These insects are important food for chimps. Good protein. But they're impossible to reach in their hills. But when the chimps pull the branch out, there are hundreds of termites on the branch. Dinner! So why did I call this discovery "amazing"? Because for the first time, a researcher saw the use of a tool by a non-human, in the wild, in nature *[writes on board]*. There have been many other such discoveries since then, but this was the first.

Section 3

Lecturer: O.K. On to learning *[points to board]*. Humans learn all the time, right? O.K., yeah, some learn more than others. But what about other animals? Scientists used to believe that only humans learn. This makes us different from other animals. But then . . . there was another amazing discovery on a beach in Japan. For a long time, scientists studied a group of macaques there *[writes on board]*. This is a kind of monkey. Anyway, the scientists watched these guys for a long time. They watched, for example, as every day the macaques ate sweet potatoes. But then, one day—and nobody will ever know why—one young female took her sweet potato down to the water and *washed off the sand before she ate it.* This had never happened before. And even more amazing . . . you know what happened after that? Her mother started washing her sweet potatoes. Then other young females washed theirs. Now this *whole group of macaques* is famous for washing their food. No other group does it. So what does this prove? Yes. *Learning. [Writes on board.]* O.K. O.K. One more example of learning in the wild (I mean, not a zoo, right?). Remember those chimps in Tanzania? They *learn* how to use that tool to get termites. They *learn by watching their mothers.*

Section 4

Lecturer: One more area. Language. Humans have it *[writes on board]*. But other animals? They make sounds, of course, and some of these sounds have meaning. But can they learn to understand and use *language*—not just *sounds*? Well . . . there have been a number of studies in recent years, with different kinds of animals. Oh, this reminds me . . . did any of you happen to hear that radio program about that dog in Germany, Rico? Yeah? Great. Well, you noticed that this dog is able to understand a lot of words and also understands some *syntax*—the order of words and how this order changes the meaning. But of course Rico doesn't *produce* language.

There are many other studies going on now, some with chimps, some with gorillas, some with parrots, you know, talking birds. The chimps and gorillas aren't able to actually *speak,* of course, because of their vocal tract *[indicates throat]* so in these studies, they learn sign language *[shows hand]*, you know, gestures with their hands—or a special computer language with symbols. Anyway, for homework, you're going to read about these studies, and we'll discuss them next time, but just to give you an idea about this . . . the research questions are, "Can non-human animals create new words, and can they put words together into new *original* sentences?" What do you think? Well, the answer is . . . to a certain degree, yes. There's a gorilla named Koko *[writes on board]* for example, who didn't know the word *ring [points to finger]*, so . . . she created the term "finger *[holds up one finger]* bracelet *[indicates wrist]*" instead. Pretty good, huh? Anyone could understand that, even though the term doesn't exist. Another example. There's a parrot named Alex *[writes on board]* who didn't know the word *apple,* and so he created a new word for it—*banerry*—a combination of *banana* and *cherry*—two words for fruit that he *did* know. One last example. There's a chimp named Kanzi *[writes on board]* who is able to create simple sentences such as "You, me, go out, hurry." So can we say that other animals learn language? Yes. It's limited, but it's there *[writes on board]*.

O.K. So what can we conclude from this? Well, we can't say much yet about emotion *[writes on board]*. But the other areas . . . humans and other animals are beginning to look pretty similar, huh? So what's the difference? Well, some animals can use simple tools but they can't build an airplane. Animals can learn, but they can't learn higher mathematics. Animals can learn some language, but "You, me, go out, hurry" is not exactly Shakespeare. So what can we conclude? In these four areas, humans and other animals have many of the same abilities. We are very similar. The difference? Humans do all of this *[indicates board]* more. The difference is only of *degree*. We do it all *more*.

O.K. That's it for today. You know the chapters to read tonight, right? O.K.

Chapter 4: Nutrition
Part 2 Social Language

A. Listening for the Main Idea (page 116)

B. Listening for Opinions (page 117)

Rachel: Hi, Ashley. Hi, Mike.

Ashley & Mike: Hi.

Rachel: Hey, that looks good. What is it?

Ashley: Uh . . . chili soup.

Rachel: That looks so good. What's the problem?

Ashley: Oh, this stuff's never spicy enough . . . And there's no hot sauce . . .

Mike: Hey, I told you—you should carry your own bottle of hot sauce 'cause you love it so much!

Ashley: Yeah. Man, do I miss my mom's kimchi! You ever had that?

Mike: Nope.

Rachel: No way! I don't like spicy food. You know that!

Ashley: Well, hot stuff's good for you—a lot better than most of the stuff people usually eat, like fast food.

Mike: Hey, that's right. Remember, we heard about this, in our nutrition class. Uh, a study that said Mexican food was bad for you, but they were studying, you know, the stuff that, you know, you get in a fast-food restaurant, not the real thing.

Rachel: Actually, I *do* like those fast-food *tacos* . . . they're not too spicy . . .

Mike: Anyways, *real* Mexican cuisine is supposed to be very healthy for you.

Rachel: How come?

Mike: Well, you, you get a lot of rice, and beans, and corn, and, and lotsa complex carbohydrates . . . not too much fat or meat . . . and, uh, the, uh, chili pepper is supposed to have a lotta vitamin C.

Rachel: Well, I don't worry too much about eating foods that are healthy anyway 'cause I take vitamins.

Ashley: Like what?

Rachel: Well . . . Uh, every day I take 1,000 milligrams of vitamin C, and, uh, 1,000 milligrams of E, B complex—

Mike: That sounds like a lot!

Rachel: I take herbs, too.

Ashley: Such as?

Rachel: Ginkgo, ginseng—

Mike: What are those for?

Rachel: They give you energy and help your brain, I think.

Mike: You don't sound too sure.

Ashley: Are there studies that prove this?

Rachel: To tell you the truth, I don't really know, but I *did* get an "A" on that nutrition exam we had last week!

Ashley: Ah! So, maybe they do some good after all!

C. Listening for Details (page 117)

Rachel: Well, I don't worry too much about eating foods that are healthy anyway 'cause I take vitamins.

Ashley: Like what?

Rachel: Well . . . Uh, every day I take 1,000 milligrams of vitamin C, and, uh, 1,000 milligrams of E, B complex—

Mike: That sounds like a lot!

Rachel: I take herbs, too.

Ashley: Such as?

Rachel: Ginkgo, ginseng—

Mike: What are those for?

Rachel: They give you energy and help your brain, I think.

Part 3 The Mechanics of Listening and Speaking

A. Asking for More Information: Reasons (page 119)

1. **A:** Chili pepper is supposed to be good for you.

   B: Why?

   A: It has a lot of vitamin C.

2. **A:** Eating too much sugar is supposed to be bad for you.

   B: Why do you say that?

   A: It can cause tooth decay.

3. **A:** Weight training is more important than eating a lot of protein.

   B: How come?

   A: It can help you build muscles.

4. **A:** I think gingko is good for you.

   B: What do you mean?

   A: It can give you energy.

5. **A:** Eating fat can make you fat.

   B: Excuse me, but what do you mean by that?

   A: Fat has a lot of calories.

B. Asking for More Information (page 120)

1. **A:** Everybody needs carbohydrates.

   B: How come?

   A: They give you energy.

2. **A:** I think it's important to take supplements.

   B: Excuse me, but why do you say that?

   A: Because most people don't eat a well-balanced diet.

3. **A:** Mexican food is very healthy.

   B: Whaddya mean?

   A: Well, you get a lot of complex carbohydrates.

4. **A:** Eating fat can make you fat.

   B: Excuse me, but what do you mean by that?

   A: Fat has a lot of calories.

5. **A:** Broccoli is better for you than iceberg lettuce.

   B: Whaddya mean?

   A: Broccoli has more vitamins and minerals.

E. Reduced Forms of Words: Questions with Do *and* Did (page 122)

A: Whereja say you were going?

B: I said I was going to get some lunch at the Student Union.

A: Whydya want to eat at the Student Union? The food is terrible.

B: I like the chili soup there.

A: Whaja say?

B: I like the chili soup.

A: Whaja mean? That stuff's terrible!

B: That's *your* opinion. I happen to like it.

Part 4 Broadcast English

A. Listening for the Main Idea: Section 1 (page 127)

B. Listening for Details (page 127)

C. Listening for Reasons (page 127)

Host: Take a trip to the Mediterranean, and you'll probably notice something more than the flavorful food. For decades, researchers have linked this region with good health. One nation that stood out is Greece, where scientists in the 1960s found one of the highest rates of adult life expectancy on earth.

Studies of the whole Mediterranean basin showed a lower incidence there of chronic illness, such as cancer and heart disease, than in northern Europe, Japan, and the United States. Less stress, fewer cars, and more walking, as well as a cleaner environment contributed to the atmosphere of well-being. But it was the Mediterranean *diet* that intrigued researchers most. People there consume on average lower amounts of harmful fats, and plentiful portions of grains and tender, fresh vegetables and fruits.

You'll find wooden carts overflowing with them in most any neighborhood marketplace, [such as] this one in the heart of Naples in southern Italy. There are deep purple eggplants ready for the roasting, plump, fruity tomatoes ready for anything, and pungent cloves of garlic, nature's way of drawing us to the dinner table— and just possibly, safeguarding us from disease. Tucked away in these vegetables and fruits at the microscopic level, scientists have identified a swirl of natural protective ingredients, such as antioxidants, that can help prevent illness. It's a whole secret pharmacy in your food. And worldwide, hundreds of studies show populations that consume fruits and vegetables in abundance have a much lower rate of cancer and other serious diseases.

D. Listening for Details (page 128)

Host: You'll find wooden carts overflowing with them in most any neighborhood marketplace, [such as] this one in the heart of Naples in southern Italy. There are deep purple eggplants ready for the roasting, plump, fruity tomatoes ready for anything, and pungent cloves of garlic, nature's way of drawing us to the dinner table— and just possibly, safeguarding us from disease. Tucked away in these vegetables and fruits at the microscopic level, scientists have identified a swirl of natural protective ingredients, such as antioxidants, that can help prevent illness. It's a whole secret pharmacy in your food. And worldwide, hundreds of studies show populations that consume fruits and vegetables in abundance have a much lower rate of cancer and other serious diseases.

E. Listening for the Main Idea: Section 2 (page 128)

Byars: All the way from the mouth on down through the stomach, and the colorectum, and also lung cancer and many other internal organ cancers, uh, risk is reduced by 50 percent or so, for people who eat five or more servings a day of fruits and vegetables, compared to many people who are out there who eat two or less a day. And I think that's a very important difference.

Host: With cancer now responsible for a fifth of all deaths in America, the fight against it is shifting to prevention. Scientists estimate that what we eat accounts for at least a third of all cancers. So a sound diet is now cited as powerful protection, and Americans are becoming more conscious about the benefits of healthy eating.

The National Cancer Institute, the surgeon general, and all major health authorities have endorsed the five-a-day recommendation: consume at least five daily servings of fruits and vegetables. A serving is about a half a cup of vegetables, or a whole piece of fruit. Americans typically eat only about two to three servings per day. Compare that to the Mediterranean, where, in southern Italy, for example, the average person eats a many as *11* servings per day.

Dr. Anna Ferraluzzi, of the National Institute of Nutrition, in Rome:

Ferraluzzi: Another aspect is that if you eat fruits and vegetables, you eat less of something else. Uh, if you go back to our Mediterranean diet, we start our meals . . . we have several-course meals—it's a classical one—and the first, uh, dish is a pasta dish or a soup dish, so this will occupy part of your appetite and your stomach space so that you probably will have a smaller helping of the second, uh, plate. And the second plate will be meat or another animal-based, uh, product. So the whole thing is linked together. Um, you definitely need also to have a d-di-uh-diet which is varied, and, uh, the, the basic composition of even of your fruits and vegetables still be such that it arrives on your dish without having been altered too much.

F. Listening for Numerical Information
(page 128)

Byars: All the way from the mouth on down through the stomach, and the colo-rectum, and also lung cancer and many other internal organ cancers, uh, risk is reduced by 50 percent or so, for people who eat five or more servings a day of fruits and vegetables, compared to many people who are out there who eat two or less a day. And I think that's a very important difference.

Host: With cancer now responsible for a fifth of all deaths in America, the fight against it is shifting to prevention. Scientists estimate that

what we eat accounts for at least a third of all cancers.

G. Guessing the Meaning from Context: Such As (page 129)

1. Studies of the whole Mediterranean basin showed a lower incidence there of chronic illness, such as cancer and heart disease, than in northern Europe, Japan, and the United States.

2. Tucked away in these vegetables and fruits at the microscopic level, scientists have identified a swirl of natural protective ingredients, such as antioxidants, that can help prevent illness.

Part 5 Academic English

A. Getting the Main Ideas from the Introduction (page 132)

Lecturer: Hello. Did everyone have a nice weekend? Good. Today I'm going to discuss some basic principles of nutrition. I'm going to cover the nutrients in food, the connection between nutrition and health, and how to plan a healthy diet. I'm also going to give you an overview of the nutritional aspects of two ethnic cuisines.

B. Taking Notes: Using an Outline (page 132)

C. Listening for Categories and Definitions (page 136)

D. Checking Your Notes (page 136)

Section 1

Lecturer: Hello. Did everyone have a nice weekend? Good. Today I'm going to discuss some basic principles of nutrition. I'm going to cover the nutrients in food, the connection between nutrition and health, and how to plan a healthy diet. I'm also going to give you an overview of the nutritional aspects of two ethnic cuisines.

Let's start with the principles of good nutrition. The food we eat, our diet, has a profound effect on our health. Good nutrition is essential for good health, but what is nutrition? Nutrition involves the nutrients in food and the body's handling of those nutrients. Nutrients are substances that are obtained from foods and used in the body to provide energy and to promote growth, maintenance, and repair of the body's tissues.

There are six classes of nutrients. They include carbohydrates, fats, protein, vitamins, minerals, and water. The carbohydrates include sugars, starches, and most types of dietary fiber. They are found in foods like breads, cereals, grains, and fruit. The fats include lard, oils, and cholesterol. Carbohydrates and fats provide the body with energy. Proteins are used to build and repair body tissues and are found in meat, milk, eggs, and beans. Vitamins and minerals are needed for proper body functioning.

Section 2

Lecturer: Many studies have shown the connections between nutrition and disease. In fact, nutrition plays a role in four of the ten leading causes of illness and death in the United States. Diseases associated with poor nutrition include heart disease, high blood pressure, diabetes, and obesity. Government and other agencies have developed diet recommendations to prevent disease, such as the Dietary Guidelines for Americans.

These guidelines are:

1. Eat a variety of foods.

2. Maintain a healthy weight.

3. Choose a diet low in fat, especially saturated fat and cholesterol.

4. Choose a diet with plenty of vegetables, fruits, and grain products.

5. Use sugars only in moderation.

6. Use salt and sodium in moderation.

7. If you drink alcoholic beverages, do so in moderation.

Section 3

Lecturer: Now, let's move on to the second main point of today's lecture: planning a healthy diet. To plan a healthy diet, people first need to understand the five food groups. Foods can be divided into groups, each group containing foods that are similar in nutrient content. The five food groups are: grain products like breads and cereals; vegetables; fruits; dairy products like milk and cheese; and meats, including fish, poultry, and protein substitutes like beans.

The second part of planning a healthy diet is understanding diet planning principles. It is not difficult to eat a healthy diet if you take the time to learn about nutrition and use the principles of balance, variety, and moderation. Balance means that you eat the right amount of foods from each of the food groups. For example, eating a diet that contained only milk and bread wouldn't be healthy. Variety is a similar concept. For good health, it is best to select foods from each of the groups each day. Moderation means that we should eat only as much food as we need and not overeat.

The third part of planning a healthy diet is smart shopping. Read food labels when shopping to help you make healthy food choices. Choose whole grain and enriched breads and cereals. Fresh green and yellow-orange vegetables are important, as well as yellow-orange and citrus fruits. Legumes (beans and peas) are nutritious and inexpensive. Select lean meats, fish and poultry with visible fat removed. Low-fat milk and milk products are recommended over full-fat versions.

Section 4

Lecturer: In the last part of today's lecture, we're going to take a look at the nutritional aspects of certain ethnic diets. Food has many meanings for people—it is not only a means of providing nutrients for the body. People eat for pleasure and as part of family and social situations. One of the greatest influences on eating habits is culture. People often experience feelings of pleasure and comfort when eating their traditional cultural foods. Ethnic diets are characteristic of particular racial, ethnic, and cultural groups.

The term *foodways* can be used when discussing ethnic diets. Foodways describe the food habits as well as the customs and beliefs about food in a particular culture.

There are positive and negative aspects to all types of diets, and any type of diet can be healthy as long as proper food choices are made.

Here are some examples of two ethnic diets: Mediterranean and Chinese.

People from countries that border the Mediterranean Sea, such as Greece and Italy, consume a diet which has been called the Mediterranean diet. This diet includes seafood, meats—especially lamb, chicken, and beef—cheese, fruits, and vegetables. This diet is quite high in fat; however, most of the fat comes from olive oil. Consuming a diet rich in olive oil has been associated with a lower risk of heart disease and the Mediterranean diet is considered to be a heart-healthy diet.

Chinese meals are built around rice, contain small amounts of meat, seafood, poultry, and eggs mixed with vegetables, and usually include soups and tea. The Chinese diet is low in fat and high in fiber. Chinese foods tend to be high in salt, which is not recommended. When the salt is reduced, Chinese food is a healthy diet choice.

So, in conclusion, good nutrition is essential to good health. Knowing what's in food and following a few basic guidelines can lead to better health not only today, but in the future.

Chapter 5: The Days of Slavery Part 2 Social Language

A. Listening for the Main Idea (page 153)

Chrissy: Uh, excuse me, Dr. Taylor?

Dr. Taylor: Hi, you're, uh . . .

Chrissy: Chrissy. I'm in your American History class.

Dr. Taylor: Right, Chrissy. Have a seat.

Chrissy: Thanks.

Dr. Taylor: What can I do for you?

Chrissy: Uh, it's about the assignment for next week.

Dr. Taylor: Mm-hm.

Chrissy: Unfortunately, I had to leave class about ten minutes early yesterday, so I didn't get the assignment. What exactly are we supposed to write about?

Dr. Taylor: Well, you're supposed to analyze the social issues that led to the rise of the antislavery movement of the early 1800s.

Chrissy: Gee, was that in the lecture?

Dr. Taylor: No, but have you read Chapter 3 yet?

Chrissy: Well, no, not yet.

Dr. Taylor: Well, that's all you have to do. It's very well laid out in that chapter. You need to look at the regions these people represented, and their role in society. For example, there were the New England abolitionists.

Chrissy: Oh, yeah, the poets, uh, James Russell Lowell and John Greenleaf Whittier.

Dr. Taylor: Right. What was their reason for supporting the abolition of slavery?

Chrissy: Right.

Dr. Taylor: And the whole role of women in the movement—Lucretia Mott and the Grimké sisters. You need to look at the role of women in American society at the time to explain what might have motivated women of that particular social class to participate in the movement.

Chrissy: Yeah, I see.

Dr. Taylor: And don't forget to mention the role of the free blacks who were involved.

Chrissy: Oh, yeah, like Frederick Douglass and Sojourner Truth.

Dr. Taylor: Right. So, you've got these three different— *[Phone rings.]* Excuse me. Hello? Oh, hi, Dr. Dorwick. No, um, could you hold for a moment please? I'm sorry, Chrissy, I'm going to have to take this call.

Chrissy: Oh, that's O.K. I think I understand what to do.

Dr. Taylor: Great!

Chrissy: Thanks so much. I really appreciate it.

Dr. Taylor: You're welcome.

Chrissy: Thanks again. Bye.

Dr. Taylor: Bye, bye. See you tomorrow . . . Hi.

B. Listening for Details (page 153)

Chrissy: Uh, excuse me, Dr. Taylor?

Dr. Taylor: Hi, you're, uh . . .

Chrissy: Chrissy. I'm in your American History class.

Dr. Taylor: Right, Chrissy. Have a seat.

Chrissy: Thanks.

Dr. Taylor: What can I do for you?

Chrissy: Uh, it's about the assignment for next week.

Dr. Taylor: Mm-hm.

Chrissy: Unfortunately, I had to leave class about ten minutes early yesterday, so I didn't get the assignment. What exactly are we supposed to write about?

Dr. Taylor: Well, you're supposed to analyze the social issues that led to the rise of the antislavery movement of the early 1800s.

Chrissy: Gee, was that in the lecture?

Dr. Taylor: No, but have you read Chapter 3 yet?

Chrissy: Well, no, not yet.

Dr. Taylor: Well, that's all you have to do. It's very well laid out in that chapter.

C. Listening for Categories (page 154)

Dr. Taylor: Well that's all you have to do. It's very well laid out in that chapter. You need to look at the regions these people represented, and their role in society. For example, there were the New England abolitionists.

Chrissy: Oh, yeah, the poets, uh, James Russell Lowell and John Greenleaf Whittier.

Dr. Taylor: Right. What was their reason for supporting the abolition of slavery?

Chrissy: Oh, right.

Dr. Taylor: And the whole role of women in the movement—Lucretia Mott and the Grimké sisters. You need to look at the role of women in American society at the time to explain what might have motivated women of that particular social class to participate in the movement.

Chrissy: Yeah, I see.

Dr. Taylor: And don't forget to mention the role of the free blacks who were involved.

Chrissy: Oh, yeah, like Frederick Douglass and Sojourner Truth.

Dr. Taylor: Right. So, you've got these three different—*[Phone rings.]*

Part 3 The Mechanics of Listening and Speaking

A. Listening to Introductions (page 155)

1. **A:** Hi, I'm John. I'm in your English class.

   B: Oh, yeah, sure. Hi, John.

2. **A:** Hello. You may not recognize me. My name is John.

   B: Oh, yes, hello, John.

3. **A:** Hi. I'm John Martinez. We met last week.

   B: Hi, John. Nice to see you again.

4. **A:** Hi. I'm John.

   B: Hi, John. How have you been?

5. **A:** Hi, I'm John. I'm in your English class.

   B: I'm sorry. I didn't recognize you at first.

C. Identifying Yourself on the Phone (page 156)

1. **A:** Hello?

   B: Hi. It's Dawn Wu. Is this Jim?

   A: Oh, hi, Dawn.

2. **A:** Hello?

   B: Hi, Jim. It's Dawn.

   A: Oh, hi, Dawn.

3. **A:** Hello?

   B: Hello. This is Dawn Wu.

   A: Hello, Dawn.

D. Hearing the Difference Between /I/ and /i/ (page 157)

1. bit	6. seat
2. bin	7. eat
3. pick	8. live
4. his	9. dip
5. peak	10. meat

Part 4 Broadcast English

A. Listening for the Main Idea: Section 1
(page 162)

B. Being Prepared for an Important Explanation (page 162)

Section 1

Kim and Reggie *[singing]*:

No more ox and blood for me

No more no more

No more ox and blood for me

Many thousand gone

No more pickin' corn for me

No more no more

No more pickin' corn for me

Many thousand gone . . .

Host: Kim and Reggie Harris have been singing and telling stories for nearly 20 years now. They met each other at summer camp in 1974, married in 1976, and began touring together in 1980. It was then they were asked to do a presentation at a school assembly. They decided that the Underground Railroad would be their subject.

Their first recording on that subject was called "Music of the Underground Railroad." Their second recording, following it, is called, "Steal Away: Songs of the Underground Railroad." Kim and Reggie Harris join us from the studios of Peachstate Public Radio. Welcome, both of you.

Kim: Thank you.

Reggie: Oh, thank you. It's great to be here.

Host: For those who might not know or remember what the Underground Railroad was, give us a brief explanation.

Kim: The Underground Railroad really was people who were working very hard in the cause of freedom during the days of slavery. Uh, it was really run by the free African American community, which makes a lot of sense since they had a lot to gain from helping their family and friends and people get out of slavery. But they also had help from people of different races who believed in freedom. So we love to say the

Underground Railroad was America's first Rainbow Coalition.

Host: Ah, it was not a train—it was people.

Kim: It was people.

Reggie: It was not a train. And we often say that, uh, in our performances, because, uh, you can talk about the Underground Railroad and the fact that it was people, and the enduring image is people digging tunnels, or, uh, taking a train to freedom. And, uh, so part of what we do is to dispel that myth.

Host: One of the things you like to say is that you like to sing songs of heroes and "sheroes." One of the sheroes you devote a song to on your new CD is Harriet Tubman. Now she was one of the main "conductors" on this railroad.

Reggie: She was, and, you know, Harriet Tubman is just such a fascinating character. A woman, you know, a black woman in the 1800s, uh, she couldn't read, she couldn't write, she had very few resources, if any. And she has become an enduring historical figure. We like to particularly tell young people that here is a great role model of someone who had very little going for her, and, and yet managed through sheer perseverance, and determination, and the love of her people to do something so great, that we're still talking about her today.

C. Guessing the Meaning from Context
(page 162)

1. One of the things you like to say is that you like to sing songs of heroes and "sheroes." One of the sheroes you devote a song to on your new CD is Harriet Tubman. Now she was one of the main "conductors" on the railroad.

2. She was, and you know, Harriet Tubman is just such a fascinating character. A woman, you know, a black woman in the 1800s— she couldn't read, she couldn't write, she had very few resources, if any. And she has become an enduring historical figure.

3. We like to particularly tell young people that here is a great role model of someone who had very little going for her, and, and yet managed through sheer perseverance, and determination, and the love of her people to

do something so great, that we're still talking about her today.

4. They were songs that were used as code songs. Uh, they were used as mapping songs. People could take a song like "Wade in the Water" and remember that you need to stay near water.

D. Listening to a Description (page 163)

Host: One of the things you like to say is that you like to sing songs of heroes and "sheroes." One of the sheroes you devote a song to on your new CD is Harriet Tubman. Now she was one of the main "conductors" on this railroad.

Reggie: She was, and, you know, Harriet Tubman is just such a fascinating character. A woman, you know, a black woman in the 1800s, uh, she couldn't read, she couldn't write, she had very few resources, if any. And she has become an enduring historical figure. We like to particularly tell young people that here is a great role model of someone who had very little going for her, and, and yet managed through sheer perseverance, and determination, and the love of her people to do something so great, that we're still talking about her today.

E. Listening for Examples: Section 2 (page 163)

Host: What was the significance of the music?

Reggie: The music was significant in that, first of all, it, it brought hope. Ah, the songs are—are songs of faith, and they are songs that, that, uh, gave people great hope, uh, in that faith. And yet, they were very practical songs as well. They were songs that were used as code songs, uh— they were used as mapping songs. People could take a song like "Wade in the Water," and remember that you needed to stay near water. Not only because you needed water to drink, but also because fish live in the water. So you could, on your escape, have something to eat. Uh, animals coming down to the water to drink, you might be able to catch one. Uh, essentially, you also needed to remember that you needed to wade in the water—you needed to walk through water whenever you could to kill your scent and so that you didn't leave tracks.

So they were, were songs with sort of two realities going on, uh, faith and, and keeping people, uh, focused on the fact that they wanted to get to freedom, but also providing them the tools to do exactly that.

Kim and Reggie *[singing]*:

Wade in the water

Wade in the water, children,

Wade in the water

God's gonna trouble the water

Who are those children all dressed in white?

God's gonna trouble the water

Must be the waters, get ready to fly

God's gonna trouble the water

Wade in the water

Host: Where would slaves have had the opportunity to, to sing a song like "Wade in the Water" to pass along that information without getting caught?

Kim: Well at times you could sing it, uh, while the master or the overseer was listening because they were faith songs. And many of the slaves were being encouraged to take up Christianity as their religion, and so at times you could sing it right when the master was listening. Other times you might just sing it at a secret meeting, or hum it to yourself to remind yourself and to remind others of these, uh, tools for freedom.

Host: There's a beautiful song. It's called "Steal Away." How is "Steal Away" connected to Harriet Tubman?

Kim: It was one of the songs that, that people like Harriet Tubman and also others who were preparing to escape could sing the night before they were leaving as a signal to let other people know that they would be going. And I guess there is an anecdote that says that she sang that song right walking past her master. She was humming and singing to herself:

Steal away to Jesus

Steal away home

I ain't got long to stay here . . .

And the anecdote says that he just, you know, nodded to her. She nodded to him and he didn't get it that she was going to be leaving soon.

Host: Huh.

Reggie: It was often believed that a singing slave was a happy slave. So many masters just sort of felt like if they were singing songs and singing in particular about going to heaven, or singing about God, then they were just happy and, uh, happy with their faith, so they left them alone.

Kim and Reggie *[singing]*:

Steal away

Steal away home

I ain't got long to stay

I ain't got long to stay here . . .

Host: These songs are still sung at religious gatherings, at community gatherings, civic gatherings around the country. Why are they still so popular?

Reggie: Part of it is their, their great power and their great beauty. I mean, they are truly wonderful songs. They are, in many ways, so—so very affirming to sing. And, uh, and they have remained part of, of the, uh, community of faith. I grew—I grew up singing these songs. I remember vivid memories of "Wade in the Water" at my church, uh, during baptism. And, uh, the choir just singing, and, and—which is sort of being taken almost to another place, listening to the words, uh, not even realizing at that time that it—that song in particular had a whole 'nother dimension to it.

Part 5 Academic English

A. Guessing The Meaning from Context
(page 166)

1. A number of former slaves, such as Frederick Douglass, Harriet Tubman, and Sojourner Truth, supported the Underground Railroad movement. Uh, you read about them in Chapter 23—right? That's Frederick Douglass, Harriet Tubman, and Sojourner Truth.

   They were well known for speaking out against slavery, and, uh, Tubman became one of the most famous conductors of the railroad. By "conductor," I mean that she actually helped the slaves on their journey of escape from the South to the North.

2. Another group organized in the antislavery movement were the Quakers. The Quakers were a religious group. They were the first to organize an antislavery society, way back in 1775, and they actively *discouraged* slaveholding by their members.

3. Slaves were free when they had reached the northernmost portion of their journey, where they would be supplied with food and a place to stay. But many did not feel safe even in the North because of the Fugitive Slave Law. This law said that slaves must be returned to their masters and that a person who helped slaves could also be jailed. So, some went on to Canada.

B. Taking Notes: Using an Outline
(page 167)

E. Checking Your Notes (page 170)

Section 1

Lecturer: Good morning. Nice to see you. Um. O.K. Today I'm going to talk to you about a little background on the Underground Railroad *[indicates board]*.

All right. Uh, the Underground Railroad was the name given to a movement in the United States during 19th century *[indicates board]*. The 1800s *[indicates board]*. It was a movement that helped slaves get their freedom. On the Underground Railroad, individuals escaped from slavery in the South to freedom in the North. There was no actual railroad or train on the Underground Railroad. Rather, it consisted of a series of houses that were called "stations." Slaves hid at these stations as they traveled from the South to the northern United States and sometimes even into Canada. More than 100,000 slaves escaped through the Underground Railroad.

The Underground Railroad began when individual slaves began to escape and find their way north. And, after a time, a number of northerners began to help the runaways, and the movement became organized.

Now, where did the term *Underground Railroad* come from? It's not known when the term was first used, but it probably came into existence shortly after railroads became popular in the 1830s *[indicates board]*. However, slaves were escaping to the North long before then.

Section 2

Lecturer: Many people were involved in the Underground Railroad. It included a network of former slaves, free blacks, white Americans, and Canadians. Two organized groups that were involved in running the Underground Railroad were the abolitionists *[indicates board]* and the Quakers *[indicates board]*. A number of former slaves, such as Frederick Douglass, Harriet Tubman, and Sojourner Truth, supported the Underground Railroad movement. You read about them in Chapter 23—right? That's Frederick Douglass, Harriet Tubman, and Sojourner Truth.

They were well known for speaking out against slavery, and Tubman became one of the most famous conductors of the railroad. Now, by "conductor," I mean that she actually helped the slaves on the journey from the South to the North. And there were also a number of free blacks who were abolitionists such as William Jones, Charles Lenox Redmond, Henry Highland Garnet, William Wells Brown, and Francis E. W. Harper. They organized and raised funds to support the movement.

Now, the abolitionists were blacks and whites that were part of an organized movement against slavery. The most famous of the white abolitionists was William Lloyd Garrison, who established the first antislavery newspaper. Another abolitionist was Harriet Beecher Stowe. Stowe was the author of *Uncle Tom's Cabin*. In it, Stowe described the horrors of slavery. Many people in the North read it, and it made them aware of the evil of slavery. Now, the Grimké sisters—that's G-R-I-M-K-E, with an accent on the *E*—they were also well known abolitionists. They denounced their own families' ownership of slaves and traveled around the country telling their story.

Another group organized in the antislavery movement were the Quakers *[indicates board]*. The Quakers were a religious group. They were the first to organize an antislavery society, way back in 1775, and they actively discouraged slaveholding by their members. They were also dedicated to helping ex-slaves by providing them with shelter, food, clothing, and money. Levi Coffin, a Quaker, he was known as "the president of the Underground Railroad" because of all the work he did in helping more than 3,000 slaves escape.

So, the Underground Railroad allowed white Americans a chance not only to speak out against the injustice of slavery but also to allow them to play an active role in *freeing* slaves.

Section 3

Lecturer: Now, what was a trip on the Underground Railroad like? Well, slaves would usually escape at night and travel along a route marked by others who had gone before them. Now, normally, slaves would take supplies from their masters for the journey. The slaves traveled at night. They used the North Star as a guide, and on cloudy nights, the moss that grew on the northern part of the trees helped to guide them in the right direction.

The stations were only ten to twenty miles apart because this was the maximum distance that most people could walk at one time. During the day, the conductors—the people helping the slaves—would hide them in their barns or in secret places like cellars or attics until it was dark and safe for the slaves to leave. Slaves were free when they had reached the northernmost portion of their journey, where they would be supplied with food and a place to stay. But many did not feel safe even in the North because of the Fugitive Slave Law *[indicates board]*. This law said that the slaves must be returned to their masters and that a person who helped slaves could also be jailed. So, some went on to Canada. Now, there are some unusual escape stories. One of the most famous was that of Henry "Box" Brown. He traveled from Richmond, Virginia, to Philadelphia, Pennsylvania as freight in a box. It took him twenty-six hours to reach his destination, but at the end, he was free.

Section 4

Lecturer: Now, why was the Underground Railroad significant in the antislavery movement? Well, there are two reasons. It's true that the Railroad was just one of the many strategies that abolitionists used to attack the system of slavery in the United States.

However, it was important because it proved that African Americans were not only committed to ending slavery, but also organized as a group to work against it. Of course, Harriet Tubman is the best example of the many African Americans who took action to win their own freedom. Her actions and those of other African Americans disproved the idea that slaves were unwilling to risk their lives for their own personal freedom or for the freedom of other slaves.

People who "traveled on the Underground Railroad" to freedom exposed the horrible system of slavery. Frederick Douglass's autobiography, along with the narratives of Venture Smith, William and Ellen Craft, and Henry "Box" Brown, are all good examples. Their first-hand experiences worked as a kind of antislavery publicity. Slaveholders viewed the Underground Railroad as a direct attack on the system of slavery. And the tremendous success of the Underground Railroad proved that the abolitionists were determined to destroy slavery.

O.K. I imagine there are plenty of questions. Um, O.K., uh, yes, Mike?

C. Listening for Examples in Groups
(page 169)

Lecturer: Many people were involved in the Underground Railroad. It included a network of former slaves, free blacks, white Americans, and Canadians. Two organized groups that were involved in running the Underground Railroad were the abolitionists *[indicates board]* and the Quaker.

A number of former slaves, such as Frederick Douglass, Harriet Tubman, and Sojourner Truth, supported the Underground Railroad movement. You read about them in Chapter 23—right? That's Frederick Douglass, Harriet Tubman, and Sojourner Truth.

They were well known for speaking out against slavery, and Tubman became one of the most famous conductors of the railroad. Now, by "conductor," I mean that she actually helped the slaves on the journey from the South to the North. And there were also a number of free blacks who were abolitionists such as William Jones, Charles Lenox Redmond, Henry Highland Garnet, William Wells Brown, and Francis E. W. Harper. They organized and raised funds to support the movement.

Now, the abolitionists were blacks and whites that were part of an organized movement against slavery. The most famous of the white abolitionists was William Lloyd Garrison, who established the first antislavery newspaper. Another abolitionist was Harriet Beecher Stowe. Stowe was the author of *Uncle Tom's Cabin*. In it, Stowe described the horrors of slavery. Many people in the North read it, and it made them aware of the evil of slavery. Now, the Grimké sisters—that's G-R-I-M-K-E, with an accent on the *E*—they were also well known abolitionists. They denounced their own families' ownership of slaves and traveled around the country telling their story.

Another group organized in the antislavery movement were the Quakers *[indicates board]*. The Quakers were a religious group. They were the first to organize an antislavery society, way back in 1775, and they actively *discouraged* slaveholding by their members. They were also dedicated to helping ex-slaves by providing them with shelter, food, clothing, and money. Levi Coffin, a Quaker, he was known as "the president of the Underground Railroad" because of all the work he did in helping more than 3,000 slaves escape.

D. Listening for Dates (page 170)

1. Another organized group in the antislavery movement were the Quakers. The Quakers were a religious group. They were the first to organize an antislavery society, way back in 1775, and they actively *discouraged* slave-holding by their members.

2. All right. The Underground Railroad was the name given to a movement in the United States during 19th century.

3. Now, where did the term *Underground Railroad* come from? It's not known when the term was first used, but it probably came into existence shortly after railroads became popular in the 1830s. However, slaves were escaping to the North long before then.

Chapter 6: U.S. History Through Film
Part 2 Social Language

A. *Listening for the Main Idea* (page 183)

E. *Listening for Reasons* (page 185)

Jennifer: That's a sad movie.

Tanya: Uh-huh.

Jennifer: This is the third time I've seen it, and I cry every time.

Tanya: You want some ice cream?

Jennifer: Ice cream? How can you think about ice cream now, after *Dances with Wolves?*

Tanya: Well, I'm hungry, and I feel like some mint chocolate chip.

Jennifer: You didn't think that movie was depressing?

Tanya: Not really. I mean, I know it was supposed to be sad, but I just didn't think it was very good.

Jennifer: But think about all those cowboy and Indian movies from the past. The cowboys were always the good guys, the Indians were always the bad guys, and—

Tanya: : True, but—

Jennifer: Isn't it nice to finally see the Indians as the good guys?

Tanya: I'm not sure. I mean, I know those old movies were pretty terrible. But this really isn't any better. It just takes away one stereotype and puts a new stereotype in its place.

Jennifer: What do you mean?

Tanya: Well, think about it. What's a stereotype, anyway? An idea about a group of people that's too simple, right? An idea that isn't realistic, right?

Jennifer: Yeah, but—

Tanya: So in the old movies, all the Indians were evil, lazy, violent, dirty, dangerous, stupid. And now, huh, they're all good, gentle, loving, and wise. Pretty picture, but it isn't realistic. Nobody is all bad or all good.

Jennifer: OK, I guess you have a point. But I think it's good for people to learn how horrible we were to the Indians in the last century—how we took the land, we killed the buffalo, we brought disease—

Tanya: Whoa, girl! What's this *we?* It wasn't *my* people that did that stuff. It was *your* people.

Jennifer: Yeah. OK. Anyway, people need to know how bad it was for the Indians.

Tanya: Until the big white movie star came and saved them, right?

Jennifer: I feel like some chocolate chip mint. How about you?

B. *Listening for Stressed Words* (page 183)

1. **Jennifer:** That's a *sad* movie.

    Tanya: Uh-huh.

    Jennifer: This is the *third* time I've seen it, and I *cry* every time.

2. **Tanya:** You want some *ice cream?*

    Jennifer: Ice cream? How can you think about ice cream *now,* after *Dances with Wolves?*

    Tanya: Well, I'm *hungry,* and I feel like some mint chocolate chip.

3. **Jennifer:** You didn't think that movie was *depressing?*

    Tanya: Not really. I mean, I know it was supposed to be sad, but I just didn't think it was very *good.*

4. **Jennifer:** But *think* about all those cowboy and Indian movies from the past. The cowboys were always the good guys, the Indians were always the bad guys, and—

    Tanya: True, but—

    Jennifer: Isn't it nice to finally see the Indians as the *good* guys?

    Tanya: I'm not sure. I mean, I *know* those old movies were pretty *terrible.* But this really isn't any better. It just takes away one stereotype and puts a *new* stereotype in its place.

C. *Listening for a Definition* (page 184)

Tanya: Well, think about it. What's a stereotype, anyway? An idea about a group of people that's too simple, right? An idea that isn't realistic, right?

D. Listening for Examples of Stereotypes
(page 184)

Tanya: So in the old movies, all the Indians were evil, lazy, violent, dirty, dangerous, stupid. And now, huh, they're all good, gentle, loving, and wise. Pretty picture, but it isn't realistic. Nobody is all bad or all good.

Part 3 The Mechanics of Listening and Speaking

F. Understanding Intonation (page 188)

G. Using Intonation (page 188)

1. **A:** He's a wonderful actor.
   B: True! *[Agree]*

2. **A:** That movie is completely unrealistic.
   B: I see your point . . . *[Disagree]*

3. **A:** The American government broke almost every promise to the Indians.
   B: Well, that's true. *[Agree]*

4. **A:** We should visit a reservation over summer vacation.
   B: Yeah! *[Agree]*

5. **A:** It's just another stereotype.
   B: That's a good point . . . *[Disagree]*

6. **A:** You know, the whites weren't the only ones who killed buffalo. The Plains Indians killed them all the time.
   B: Well, that's true . . . *[Disagree]*

7. **A:** You know, the government almost always moved Native Americans to reservations on really terrible land.
   B: That's a good point. *[Agree]*

8. **A:** Native American jewelry is beautiful, but it's very expensive.
   B: True. *[Disagree]*

Part 4 Broadcast English

A. Listening for the Main Idea: Section 1 (page 190)

C. Listening for Details: Section 1 (page 191)

Inskeep: The Hollywood western is making a comeback, or riding back into town, or getting back on the train, or however you want to put it. The movie *Open Range* is out. Director Ron Howard has a western coming out this fall. John Woo plans to makes a western about Chinese workers building the Transcontinental Railroad. Pat Dowell reports on the latest episode for an art form that dates back to the last days of the Old West itself.

Dowell: Audiences for westerns have always been male but they also used to be what is now Hollywood's target audience, teenage males who'll see a movie more than once. From 1903 when *The Great Train Robbery* was released up to World War II, audiences loved westerns so much that one out of every five movies made in the United States was a western. Director Walter Hill says the biggest reason that westerns started fading into the sunset in the 1960s was because the stories and the settings they romanticized began disappearing from living memory.

Hill: The broad audience was no longer identifying with their agrarian roots of American history, American past. And I think the generation before that, whether by direct experience or through their parents or grandparents, they had a great identity with what we use to call the making of the West and that being in touch with that history. And they weren't nearly as urban.

Dowell: Hill directed the western *The Long Riders* in 1980 and in the 1990s, *Geronimo* and *Wild Bill,* both of which failed at the box office. He's made other kinds of movies too, such as *48 Hours,* but he once famously said that all his movies are westerns.

B. Listening for the Main Idea: Section 2 (page 191)

D. Listening for Details: Section 2 (page 191)

Dowell: The *Wild Bunch,* one of the greatest westerns of all time, is about to be remade as an urban crime thriller. Walon Green earned an Oscar nomination for co-writing the original 1969 movie. Green won an Emmy writing for *NYPD Blue* and now produces the new TV *Dragnet.* Both cowboys and cops seem to him to share something with the knights errant of old.

Green: They come, they do some amazing service; they either kill a dragon, they kill the bad guy, whatever they do, and they move on. The traditional western hero—and probably my favorite western actually is *Shane,* and it's a great example of that—is that the western hero comes—he lives actually in this family but you know no matter how much they like him, he will not ever be part of the family.

[Audio from Shane*]*

Brandon De Wilde (As Joey Starrett): We want you, Shane.

Alan Ladd (As Shane): Joey, there's no living with, with the killing. There's no going back. Right or wrong, it's a brand. A brand sticks. There's no going back. Now you run on home to your mother and tell her—tell her everything's all right and there aren't any more guns in the valley.

Dowell: Like the gunslinger, cops are outsiders who come in to clean up the town but not socialize, says Green.

Green: They're the people that we bring them in when we need things done that either we can't do or they're too unpleasant to do. And we basically pay them or hire them or coerce them or whatever to do it. And they do it. And then when they've done it we don't particularly want to know them and they don't particularly want to know us.

Dowell: *Open Range* is a very traditional American western in the line of John Ford, says historian Scott Simmon. It harks back to the days before Clint Eastwood went to Europe to become a star in spaghetti westerns.

Simmon: Although *Open Range* tells a kind of traditional story, it's one that feels to me a little more dangerous to tell now which is that if you have a despot who is causing trouble, that if you get out your guns and have a shootout, the problems are solved and there's nothing really to be said afterwards.

You know, that's the story the western always tells and it's not particularly unique. But, you know, it's a question of whether it needs to be told again right now.

Dowell: The questions *Open Range* raises are still the old ones usually asked by the women in the movie: How long before they ride out of the valley and will all the guns go with them? For NPR News this is Pat Dowell.

Inskeep: It's 11 minutes before the hour.

Part 5 Academic English

A. *Taking Lecture Notes: Using an Outline* (page 193)

B. *Checking Your Notes* (page 195)

Section 1

Lecturer: O.K. Hi guys. Guys? Um, we need to get started here. O.K. Thanks.

As you know, this week we're on U.S. history as seen through film. Everyone likes movies, right? Well, one great thing about movies is that they can help you remember things you learn in class. You study some historical period or event in class, and a picture comes into your mind—an image from some movie you saw once maybe when you were a kid. These images—these vivid pictures that stay in your mind from movies—these are called *iconic images.* I'll say that term again 'cause you're gonna hear it a lot in this lecture. Iconic images. I-C-O-N-I-C. Got that? Good. Iconic images are a kind of symbol. They represent a bigger idea.

O.K., let me review from last time. Does everyone remember the word *genre?* Right. A genre is a type or *form* of film. Every film in the same genre shares certain similar, familiar characteristics. Did I go through this list last time? No? O.K., well, lemme give you a quick list of these characteristics. Films in the same genre have *one or more* of these. First, setting—in other words, where the movie takes place. Next, subject or theme—what it's about. Third, period. *When* does it take place? Fourth, plot or story. Next, certain familiar characters—you know, like the good guy, the bad guy, the beautiful young girl, and so on. And last, there are shared iconic images—these pictures that stay in the mind of the audience. So how many of these characteristics did I list? Six? O.K. Well, there are more, but let's leave it at that.

Um, before we get into the two historical periods for today, let me review from last time. I was talking about historical dramas, and one type of historical drama is the immigration story. You have something like *Far and Away*, which takes place around 1845 and shows the hardships of Irish immigrants. But these immigration stories aren't always dramas, and they don't always take place a long time ago. What's that movie with Tom Hanks—you know, the one in the airport from maybe 2004 or so? Yeah—*The Terminal*. Here we have not a drama but a romantic comedy about this guy from some Eastern European country who's stuck in a New York airport for *months*. The point is that immigration is a natural subject for American films because it has always been an important part of U.S. history.

Section 2

Lecturer: Last time, I spoke a little about the period that we call "The Wild West." I need to continue with that today because the iconic images are so much a part of American culture. Lemme give a quick definition. When we say "The Wild West," we're referring not only to a place but also to a time. The place was the huge area west of the Mississippi River, although in movies it's usually a more specific region: the areas that today are Texas, New Mexico, Colorado, Wyoming, places like that. The time was very short—from only about 1865, which was the end of the Civil War between the North and the South, to about 1900 or maybe 1910. Not long. A short period. But the images from that time are central to the American national identity.

O.K., that's where and when. Now, *what?* What was happening during this period? Well, after the Civil War, two railroad companies built train tracks across the country. It was hard, dangerous work. One company built from east to west. Many of the workers were immigrants—most of them Irish. The other company built from west to east. Many of those workers were also immigrants—most of them Chinese. Finally, in 1869, they joined up and finished the track,

and people could cross from one end of the country to the other in, oh, a week or so instead of *months*.

Because of the railroad, more and more people began to move to the west. They came for a lot of reasons. Any ideas on this? Well, many came for land. Back in Europe, where most of them came from, they were farmers but couldn't own their own land. Here, that dream seemed possible. And they came for other reasons—gold, silver, even *adventure*. The point is that there was this idea that life might be better over *there,* someplace further west, someplace new.

Because so many people were moving west, small towns began to appear everywhere—especially where people discovered gold or silver. Suddenly there was this really busy little town, for example, full of thousands of people, and then, when the gold or silver ran out, the people moved on to a different place, and the town disappeared. But with all these people moving around, most of them strangers to one another, the problem was lack of *law.* Most of these towns didn't have any police. So that's why we call it the "wild" west. It was exciting and full of opportunity, but it was also pretty dangerous.

O.K. So movies about this period are called westerns, right? Westerns, like any other genre, share certain elements. First, most westerns are simple morality stories—in other words, they're about the conflict between good and evil. Second, there's always a hero and a villain, or bad guy—sometimes *guys,* and there's almost always a heroine—a beautiful young woman. Third, all westerns are action stories. They have violence and chase scenes on horses. And fourth, the theme of most westerns is pretty much the same. It's either about the dangers of moving west or about the hero who saves a town from the villains, the bad guys.

Now, remember those iconic images? Well, I want you to bring to your mind any western that you've ever seen. Just imagine it in your head. What do you see? Are you picturing it? *Those* are the iconic images. You have the image of the cowboy, of course. He's alone. He's riding a horse. The only things he owns are his clothing and a gun. He's wearing boots and jeans and a cowboy hat. And he's always on the move, right? Never stays in one place. Part of this image is the symbol of the cowboy hat. If the guy is wearing a white hat, what do you know about him? Right. He's our hero. He's the good guy. And a black hat? He's the bad guy. Of course, you know that this image is a complete stereotype, right? But that's not something we need to consider right now.

O.K. Two more iconic images. There's the shootout. And what's that? On the main street of the little town, you see two men, two cowboys, one in a black hat, one in a white hat. They stand facing each other, oh, about 40 feet apart. They're tense. They're each wearing two guns— one on each hip. In just a minute, they're going to pull out their guns and shoot at each other. Only one will survive. Have you all seen this? Great. Now, I think you can figure out the symbolic meaning of this image, so I don't need to tell you.

One more iconic image from westerns: the land itself. It's huge. It's vast. It goes on forever and ever. Even our hero, the cowboy, is seen as very small against this enormous background. And this image is important. Why? It's symbolic of endless possibilities.

Section 3

Lecturer: Today I'm going to jump ahead to cover one more historical period that actually led to *several* film genres. That period is the Great Depression, from the year 1929 to about 1940. Lemme start with a quick history of the time. Well, just before this time, the 1920s were a time of great prosperity. People had money. Life was good. Then came 1929. The stock market crashed, and suddenly everyone lost their money. Well, almost everyone. Anyway, the 1930s were years when many, many people were very poor and hungry. The Great Depression was also the time of Prohibition. Prohibition was a law from Congress that made alcohol illegal, so people couldn't drink whiskey, wine, beer, anything alcoholic. But many people still *did* drink because there was a huge amount of organized crime. The criminals, called gangsters, secretly brought alcohol in from other countries or made it themselves. Clearly, Prohibition was not a success, and in 1933, Congress changed its mind and made alcohol legal again.

I need to mention one significant government action during the Depression. The U.S. government wanted to help the poor people and improve the economy, so they started a program called the W.P.A. This stands for the Works Progress Administration. It gave jobs to thousands of homeless, jobless people. Two good things happened. One: people had jobs. Two: they improved the country. For example, they built post offices and built bridges. They also built roads all across the country.

O.K. How do movies reflect this time? There are three important film genres that come from this period, and these genres still exist in many movies today.

First, there were musicals. Musicals were an important form of escape for a country in the middle of an economic depression. These were big, expensive, happy Hollywood productions with singing and dancing and amazing costumes. A typical plot, or story, in these musicals involves a poor young woman who has a little job as a singer or dancer in some production. The star of the production, who is not a nice person, gets sick or has some accident, and the young woman takes her place. She becomes an immediate success—and rich and famous. Examples of such films are *42nd Street* (from 1933) and *Top Hat* (from 1935). Perhaps the most famous iconic image of this genre is the elegant dancing couple of Fred Astaire and Ginger Rogers. Long after the Depression ended, musicals remained as an important part of American culture. Think of such films as *Singing in the Rain* (from 1952), *A Chorus Line* (1985), or *Chicago* (2002).

The second genre is the crime drama. As you can imagine, all those gangsters during Prohibition were common characters in movies. One of the iconic images of this genre is the gangster wearing an expensive suit with a hat pulled over one eye and holding a gun. One of the famous crime dramas from this time was *Public Enemy,* from 1931. This type of movie has been popular ever since then. Think of *Bonnie and Clyde,* from 1967 or *The Godfather,* from 1972.

The third genre is an especially American form: the road trip. Remember those W.P.A. projects I mentioned, when people got jobs building roads all over the country? Well, all those roads made it possible to move around the country easily, by car, and Hollywood began to make movies about people on grand journeys—sometimes funny, sometimes tragic. All of these films, like musicals, provided something that people needed in the Depression: escape from their problems. The first famous road trip movie was *It Happened One Night,* a wonderful, funny story about a rich young woman who runs away from home and the jobless newspaper writer who joins her. Like many Depression movies, the idea is that love wins over class differences. At the end of the Depression came the famous 1940 film *The Grapes of Wrath,* which told the story of poor homeless farmers moving from Oklahoma to California to try to find work. Road trip films, like musicals and crime dramas, are still popular today. Think of *Rain Man,* from 1988, or *Thelma and Louise,* from 1991. The point is that they all share the iconic image of people in a car on an endless road through the desert—and this sounds very similar to what? Right. That image of the *land* from westerns—land that goes on forever and ever.

And this brings me to my last point. Many, many movies fall into more than one genre. They're both westerns and road trips. They're both road trips and crime dramas. O.K. So for homework, after you read Chapter 7, 1 want you to think of five movies that fall into more than one genre. See you next week, when we're on to *Italian* history through film. Have a good weekend.

VOCABULARY INDEX

Getting Started
campus
college
community college
definition
degree
doctor of philosophy
freshman
graduate school
junior
lecture
major
master's degree
phrases
reply
senior
small talk
sophomore
synonym
tag question
undergraduates
university

UNIT 1
Chapter 1
academic
advantages
advice
appeals to you
apply yourself
career
contrast
disadvantages
don't get sucked in by social
    pressures
dropping out
experimenting
figurative
formal outline
goal
graphic organizer
guess the meaning from context
higher education
highlighter
income

inference
informal outline
joy
key
literal
majority
outline (formal, informal)
percent
process of
quarters
roughly
seek out
self-assessment
set
signposts
silly
skills
statistics
support
transition
tutor
values
workshop

Chapter 2
acquaintances
advertisement (ad)
American
bad
beverage
British
bucks
cheap
cool
copy
curious
diversity
dominate
effective
flourish
fruit pulp
global economy
highly desirable trait
industry
infrastructure
keep track of

labels
little
local
manufacture
market
marketer
marketing
marketplace
nope
nutritious
odd
old
overseas
perfect
postmodern
route
seed
stuff
target audience
textile
thirst quenching
whoa
wild
workforce
yeah

Vocabulary Workshop: Unit 1
High Frequency Words
college
continue
degree
first
four
highest
receive
second
students
studies
university
years

UNIT 2
Chapter 3
acquire

adopted
aggressive
animals
beach
border
branch
capacity
colleagues
crawl
details
do
dolphins
embarrassed
example
familiar
fetch
galah
grasp
hates
humans
inferences
insulted
laughs
linguistic
macaque
make inferences
monkey
nonverbal communication
novel
O.K.
on command
point of view
potential
predators
prey
prodigies
prompt
protecting
push
remarkable
sea otter
sensitive
skeptic
skeptical
slide
smart
species
stupid
survived
swept
syntax

trouble
unconscious
wag
workaholic
you're kidding
zillion

Chapter 4
50 percent
after all
altered
anecdotes
antioxidants
associated with
burns
carbohydrate (simple, com-
    pound)
chronic illness
collaborate
complex carbohydrates
concentrated
consume
cover
critical
cuisine
decreasing
diet
endorsed
energy
essential
ethnic food
fifth
five or more
ginkgo
gram
herbs
in abundance
incidence
intrigue
kimchi
life expectancy
linked
maintain
milligrams
moderation
myths
nutrients
nutrition
phytochemicals
profound
promotes

safeguarding
sedentary
simple carbohydrate
sound
statistics
stores
such as
supplements
theories
third
to tell you the truth
two or less
vitamins
well-balanced diet

Vocabulary Workshop: Unit 2
High Frequency Words
asleep
baby
curled
female
hit
hungry
hunt
male
ocean
park
swept
terrible

UNIT 3
Chapter 5
affirming
analyze
arrested
bump into
captions
chronological (order)
code songs
colony
come into existence
conductors
crops
denounced
depended
dimension
drop by
drop in (on)
economy

SKILLS INDEX

Academic Focus
Academic Life, 1–15
Biology, 81–142
    Animal Behavior, 83–109
    Nutrition, 111–140
Business, 17–80
    Career Planning, 19–50
    Global Economy, 51–78
U.S. History, 143–200
    Slavery, 145–173
    U.S. History Through Film, 175–198

Academic Skills
Charts, 7, 20–22, 25, 26, 32, 35, 41, 54, 56, 58, 71, 76, 87, 91, 93, 98, 102, 105, 109, 115, 124, 125, 127, 138, 140, 158, 169, 171, 179, 181, 184, 195, 198
    graphic organizers, 38, 50, 69, 100, 194
    timelines, 149, 170
Critical thinking, SEE Critical Thinking heading
Research (using books or websites),
    animals, 101–102
    colleges or universities, 49–50
    film, 197–198
    Mediterranean diet, 137
    movements (for social or political change), 171–173
    nonverbal communication, 108–109
    nutrition information, 139–140
Taking notes,
    checking your notes, 48, 75, 106 (for details), 136, 170, 195
    lecture notes, 193–195
    organizing your notes, 46
    timelines, 149, 170
    using a chart, 102, 105–106

using a graphic organizer, 38, 50
using an outline, 43–45, 46–48, 73–74, 132–135, 172
using your notes, 48, 76, 106–107, 136, 170, 196
Test-taking skills,
    bubbles, 15, 42, 79, 90, 112, 125, 162, 166–167
    checks (for answers that apply), 127, 186
    circling (best choice), 11, 12, 33, 37, 60, 94, 120, 157, 188
    fill in the blank, 10, 36, 37, 38, 39, 56–57, 60, 61, 62–63, 66–67, 71, 72, 80, 89–90, 96, 99, 107, 117, 119, 122, 126, 128, 131, 142, 155, 156, 165, 190, 200
    matching, 31, 48, 55, 79, 92, 116, 117, 141, 152, 161, 166, 186, 199
    multiple choice, 42, 162, 166–167
    true/false, 15, 112, 125
Test-taking strategies,
    brainstorming possible vocabulary, 160
    guessing the meaning from context, 27
    listening for stressed words, 89–90, 183–184
    making predictions, 67
    previewing by brainstorming possible vocabulary, 160
    taking lecture notes, 193

Critical Thinking
Applying information, 164
Brainstorming, 54, 88, 124–125, 171
Comparing, 23, 25, 179
    sources of information, 137

Contrasting, 179
Evaluating the source of information, 137
Inferences, 23, 101, 196
Interpreting information on tables, 22, 23
Making comparisons, 23, 25, 179
    sources of information, 137
Making connections, 49, 70, 108, 137, 171, 196
Making inferences, 23, 101, 196
Making predictions, 25, 67
Meanings (literal, figurative), 41
Organizing general and specific points, 44–45
Point of view, 108
Predicting, 25, 67
Ranking, 23
Recognizing literal and figurative meanings, 41
Reviewing, 136
Synthesizing, 196
Tables, 22, 23
Thinking ahead, 20, 25, 35, 42, 52, 66, 71, 84, 87, 98, 112, 115, 125, 130, 147, 151–152, 165, 176, 182–183, 189–190, 192
Timelines, 149, 170
Understanding a speaker's point of view, 108
Using a timeline, 149, 170

Discussion, 9, 15, 30, 54, 86, 113, 150, 180
Chapter introduction discussions, 1, 19, 51, 83, 111, 145, 175
Post-listening, 28, 40, 101, 118, 129, 136, 154, 163, 185, 191
Results (survey/interview), 41, 58, 76, 88, 197–198

CREDITS

Photo Credits

Cover: (top right.): © Universal/Everett Collection; (middle lft): Comstock Images/ JupiterImages; (bottom right): © The McGraw-Hill Companies, Inc. **Getting Started:** P. 1: © Erik Dreyer/Getty Images; 2: © Bob Rowan; Progressive Image/CORBIS; p. 3: © Tony Savino/The Image Works; 5: © Royalty-Free/CORBIS; p. 6 (all), 7, 11: © The McGraw-Hill Companies, Inc; 15: © Jack Hollingsworth/Getty Images. **Unit 1:** P. 17: © Smith Collection/Getty Images; 19: © Digital Vision/Getty Iages; 20 (left): © Ray Krantz/CORBIS; 20 (right): © Getty Images; 26, 30: © The McGraw-Hill Companies, Inc.; 35: © BananaStock/JupiterImages; 40: © Scott T. Baxter/Getty Images; 42: © The McGraw-Hill Companies, Inc.; 46: © BananaStock/JupiterImages; 51: © Jan Caudron/Getty Images; 52 (top left): AP/Wide World Photos; 52 (top right): © Monika Graff/The Image Works; 52 (bottom left): © Hoang Dinh Nam/AFP/Getty Images; 52 (bottom right): © Jeff Morgan/Alamy; 53: Image courtesy of The Advertising Archives; 56: © The McGraw-Hill Companies, Inc.; 60: © Digital Vision; 65: © Ryan McVay/Getty Images; 66: © Royalty-Free/ CORBIS; 70 (left): © Toru Yamanaka/AFP/Getty Images.; 73: © The McGraw-Hill Companies, Inc.

Unit 2: P. 81: © PhotoDisc/Getty Images; 83: © Jim & Jamie Dutcher/Getty Images; 84 (top left): © Kirk Yarnell/SuperStock; 84 (top right): © Art Wolfe/Getty Images; 84 (bottom left): © Comstock/PunchStock; 84 (bottom right): © Peter Greste/Reuters/ CORBIS; 87 (both): © Royalty-Free/CORBIS; 88: © Creatas/ PunchStock; 89: © The McGraw-Hill Companies, Inc.; 92 (top all, middle all): © SuperStock; 92 (bottom left): © Richard Pasley/Stock Boston; 92 (bottom middle): © Henry Horenstein/Stock Boston; 92 (bottom right): © Index Stock/Getty Images; 94: © Ryan McVay/Getty Images; 98 (left): © Manuela Hartling/Reuters/CORBIS; 98 (right): AP/Wide World Photos; 103 (left): © Royalty-Free/CORBIS; 103 (right): © PhotoDisc/Getty Images; 105: © The McGraw-Hill Companies, Inc.; 111: © Blend Images/Getty Images; 112 (top left): Linda S. O'Roke; 112 (top right): ©Comstock/PunchStock; 112 (bottom left): © Nathan Benn/CORBIS; 112 (bottom right): © Banana Stock/Jupiter Images; 124 (top left): © Stockdisc/PunchStock; 124 (top right & bottom left): © C Squared Studios/Getty Images; 124 (bottom right & left): © Stockdisc/PunchStock; 125 (right): © C Squared Studios/Getty Images; 130: © BananaStock/PunchStock; 133 (left): © Royalty-Free/CORBIS; 133 (right): © Brian Hagiwara/FoodPix/Jupiter Images; 134: © SuperStock, Inc./SuperStock.

Unit 3: P. 143: © TriStar Pictures/Everett Collection; 145: © Smithsonian American Art Museum, Washington, DC/Art Resource, NY; 146 (left): The Granger Collection/New York; 146 (right): © Stock Montage/Alamy; 147: Collection of the New York Historical Society (Negative#50473); 149: © Hulton Archive/Getty Images; 153, 154: © The McGraw-Hill Companies, Inc.; 160: The McGraw-Hill Companies, Inc./Andrew Resek, photographer; 163: Library of Congress; 166: © The McGraw-Hill Companies, Inc.; 168: The Granger Collection/New York; 175: © Orion Pictures/Everett Collection; 176 (top left): © Sygma/CORBIS; 176 (middle right): © Topham/The Image works; 176 (bottom left): Everett Collection; 178: © Universal/Everett Collection; 182 (top left): © Bettmann/CORBIS; 182 (top right): © Hulton Archive/Getty Images; 182 (bottom): © 20th Century Fox/The Kobal Collection; 183: © The McGraw-Hill Companies, Inc.; 189 (top left): Everett Collection; 189 (top right): © Walt Disney Co./Everett Collection; 189 (bottom): Art Resource, NY; 192 (top left): © Royalty-Free/CORBIS; 192 (middle right): Everett Collection; 192 (bottom left): © United Artists/The Kobal Collection.

Radio Credits

Getting Started and Chapter 1: "Advice on Beginning College" on *Talk of the Nation*, August 18, 1997, National Public Radio. **Chapter 2:** "Behind Shanghai's Boom Is A Simple T-Shirt", *All Things Considered*, National Public Radio, April 27, 2005 **Chapter 3:** "Dog Prodigy Gives New Meaning to Language" on *All Things Considered*, June 10, 2004, National Public Radio. © 2005, National Public Radio, Inc. Used with permission. **Chapter 4:** "The Vegetable Chronicles: Mediterranean Diet" by David Freudberg, *KCRW*, Santa Clara, August 30, 1997. Used by permission of Human Media, Belmont Massachusetts, www.humanmedia.org. **Chapter 5:** "Steel Away (American History: Underground Railroad)" from *Weekend Edition*, February 22, 1998, National Public Radio. © 2005, National Public Radio, Inc. Used with permission. **Chapter 6:** "Analysis: Hollywood Westerns Making Comeback" from, *All Things Considered*, August 21, 2003, National Public Radio. © 2005, National Public Radio, Inc. Used with permission.

Text Credits

Unit 2: p. 113 Adapted from "Nutrition Myths 101" on University of California website, www.dining.ucla.edu. Copyright © 2006 The Regents of the University of California. Used with permission. **Unit 3**: p. 147 Adapted from *The American Journey* by Joyce Oldham Appleby, Alan Brinkley, James M. McPherson, 2005. Copyright © 1998 by The McGraw-Hill Companies, Inc. Reprint permission of the McGraw-Hill Companies; p. 151 Adapted from "Northern Attitudes toward Slavery" and "Southern Attitudes toward Slavery" adapted form Henry N. Drewry and Thomas H. O'Connor, *America Is*. Copyright © 1995 by Glencoe Publishing Company. Reprinted with the permission of Glencoe/McGraw-Hill, Inc.

 **NOTES**

 **NOTES**

NOTES

NOTES